Information Technology: An Introduction

Information Technology: An Introduction

Monica Hoskin

LANRYE
INTERNATIONAL
www.clanryeinternational.com

Clanrye International,
750 Third Avenue, 9th Floor,
New York, NY 10017, USA

ISBN: 978-1-63240-912-6

Cataloging-in-Publication Data

Information technology : an introduction / Monica Hoskin.
p. cm.
Includes bibliographical references and index.
ISBN 978-1-63240-912-6
1. Information technology. 2. Information storage and retrieval systems. 3. Computer science. I. Hoskin, Monica.
T58.5 .I54 2019
004--dc23

For information on all Clanrye International publications
visit our website at www.clanryeinternational.com

Contents

Permissions

Index

Preface

The use of computers for the storage, retrieval, transmission and manipulation of data or information for directing operations in a business or an enterprise is under the domain of information technology (IT). It is a sub-field of information and communications technology. The value of IT in businesses is in the automation of business operations, supplication of information to aid decision-making, provision of productivity tools for improved efficiency and for relationship building with customers. It also enables its integration with organizational needs and infrastructure, customization, maintenance and installation of IT applications for users, etc. This book aims to shed light on some of the unexplored aspects of information technology. Most of the topics introduced herein cover new techniques and applications of this field. Those in search of information to further their knowledge will be greatly assisted by this textbook.

To facilitate a deeper understanding of the contents of this book a short introduction of every chapter is written below:

Chapter 1- Information technology (IT) is the utilization of computer for the storage, transmission, retrieval and manipulation of data or information for application in businesses or enterprises. This chapter will provide an introduction to information technology. It includes topics such as information technology infrastructure, converged infrastructure, hyper-converged infrastructure, dynamic infrastructure, etc.

Chapter 2- Computer hardware refers to the physical components and parts of a computer such as the CPU, keyboard, monitor, mouse, etc. This chapter has been carefully written to provide an understanding of computer hardware with the inclusion of topics like central processing unit, motherboard, power supply unit, hard disk drive, motherboard, etc.

Chapter 3- A computer network is a telecommunications network that allows nodes to share resources. The topics elucidated in this chapter cover some of the important concepts relating to networking in computers, such as wireless network, network packet, networking hardware and Internet protocol address.

Chapter 4- An operating system (OS) is the software, which manages the software and hardware resources and also provides services for computer programs. This aim of this chapter is to provide a comprehensive understanding of operating systems. It discusses the fundamental types of OS such as distributed operating system, embedded operating system and real-time operating system as well as the major operating systems used across the world.

Chapter 5- A computer file records data in a computer storage device. All complete files are organized in a file system. It allows the easy access and manipulation of files. A file system cataloging structure that contains references to computer files and directories is called a directory. This chapter closely examines the different types of computer files, file systems and directories such as data files, binary and text files, sparse files, etc.

I owe the completion of this book to the never-ending support of my family, who supported me throughout the project.

Monica Hoskin

Introduction to Information Technology

Information technology (IT) is the utilization of computer for the storage, transmission, retrieval and manipulation of data or information for application in businesses or enterprises. This chapter will provide an introduction to information technology. It includes topics such as information technology infrastructure, converged infrastructure, hyper-converged infrastructure, dynamic infrastructure, etc.

Information technology (IT) is the use of any computers, storage, networking and other physical devices, infrastructure and processes to create, process, store, secure and exchange all forms of electronic data.

Typically, IT is used in the context of enterprise operations as opposed to personal or entertainment technologies. The commercial use of IT encompasses both computer technology and telephony.

The term information technology was coined by the Harvard Business Review, in order to make a distinction between purpose-built machines designed to perform a limited scope of functions and general-purpose computing machines that could be programmed for various tasks. As the IT industry evolved from the mid-20th century, it encompassed transistors and integrated circuits - computing capability advanced while device cost and energy consumption fell lower, a cycle that continues today when new technologies emerge.

Uses of Information Technology

Use of Information Technology in Business

Either small or big business, they will need to scale out a plan to utilize opportunities brought by "Information Technology". Businesses use IT in four ways to support (1) information-processing tasks, (2) decision making, (3) shared information through decentralized computing and (4) innovation. Below are detailed points on how business can use Information technology to succeed.

- Supports Information Process Tasks: Businesses are using IT to help basic information-processing tasks. These tasks range from computing and printing payroll checks to creating presentations, to setting up Web sites from which customers can make orders for products or services. During this stage, a business can use IT to create company database applications which can allow employees access information at any given moment. They can also use IT tools to set up networks that enable departments to share information without any hassle or wastage of time.

- Supports Decision Making Tasks: Businesses also use information technology to support decision-making tasks, and this is achieved through (OLAP) online analytical processing.

"OLAP" is the manipulation of information to support decision making. OLAP can range from performing simple queries on a database to determine which customers have overdue accounts to employing sophisticated artificial intelligence tools such as neural networks and genetic algorithms to solve a complex problem or take advantage of an opportunity. In case, let's say the "OLAP" supports effective decision making. You can also perform OLAP by using databases and data warehouses.

- Supports Shared Information through Decentralized Computing: Decentralize computing is an environment in which an organization splits computing power and locates it in functional business areas as well as on the desktop of knowledge workers. Shared information is an environment in which an organization's information is organized in one central location, allowing anyone to access and use it as they need to. Today, most businesses have created a decentralized computing structure which brings together the entire spectrum of the business's information in an orderly fashion so that it can be accessed and used by anyone who needs it. This structure of information is most often a database, which is designed to support the concept of shared information directly.

- Supports Innovation: Information technology tools not only help information-processing tasks, decision-making tasks, and shared information through decentralized computing, but they also enable innovation. Tools like the internet, present us with the opportunity to make research on any subject, the information acquired during the process can be used in the creative design of services or products.

Use of Information Technology to Society

Society has embraced information technology "IT" in various ways.

- Social Networks and mobile phones: Society has used information technology to create technologies which can simplify communication and relationships. Mobile phones have made communication more convenient and social networks like "Facebook.com" have played a significant role in helping people discover their old friends and create new ones as well. Also, people use online dating platforms to find longtime lovers, sites like Match.com are known for connecting people and these relationships always result in marriage, which is a good deed for the society.

- Job Creation: Today, there are so many companies which have been created using information technology and this has solved the problem of job scarcity to a certain degree. Many of these big IT corporations were started from homes and bedrooms, but now they employe lots of people hence adding value to our society. An excellent example of these companies includes Google, Facebook, Amazon, Dell, Microsoft, Linkedin, and Twitter just to mention but a few.

- Modernized Agriculture: Information technology has also played a prominent role in advancing the agricultural sector. Nowadays a farmer can sell his/her products right from the farm using the internet. All they have to do is set up a website for their products, orders are placed directly via the online site and the farmer will deliver to the client fresh products; this cuts out the middlemen who tend to increase the price of agricultural products with the aim of making profits. In this case, both the farmer and the consumer benefit. The consumer gets the product at a low price when it is still fresh, and the farmer makes more money.

- **Modernized Entertainment:** The invention of technologies like iPads, video games, home entertainment system, enhances user life. Music and movies can be accessed online for a small subscription fee. Companies like Netflix and Hulu, have played a significant role in making home entertainment better.

Use of Information Technology in Education

Access to Learning the Material

The internet is full of a lot of learning material that the learner can access and use to supplement whatever is provided for in the classroom. There are e-books, revision guides and past examination papers that are available on the World Wide Web and students can take advantage of these to improve their knowledge base.

Continuous Learning

In the modern world, you don't have to be in the classroom to learn. Using information technology in education has made it possible for students to keep on learning, irrespective of where they are. Teachers and professors can send assignments to students and they can complete and submit them even without physically stepping into the classrooms and so learning never has to stop. Students can keep on learning even when they are at home. This has greatly enhanced efficiency in the education sector.

Sharing of Knowledge

Through online discussion forums, students can share knowledge, engage in intellectual debates and generally learn from one another. Using information technology in education has basically made it possible for students from all over the world to come together and share experiences, the geographical distances notwithstanding. Information technology in education has also made students develop an appreciation for cultural diversity and in turn, create a more tolerant and unified world.

Using Audio and Visual Material as Learning Aids

The use of information technology in education has made it possible for tutors to teach students much more easily. By using audio and visual materials, students can develop a better understanding of the topics being taught. It is now much easier to perform demonstrations and put some practical aspect to the theory taught in class. Slow learners, therefore, have an opportunity to catch up with those who had grasped whatever was initially taught in class.

Distance Learning

To adapt to a changing population with unique demands, learning institutions have employed the use of information technology in education to cater to this new demographic. Online courses have enabled most of the employed and young population to go back to class and get second degrees or additional certifications. It is possible to attend a college overseas without even getting out of your home country and at your own convenience.

Proper Record Keeping

It is possible to keep student records in a more systematic and secure manner using technology. Unlike in the past when records used to be kept manually and there were many cases of lost files, the incorporation of information technology in education has made it possible for safe and proper record keeping. Retrieving of information has, therefore, become much easier.

Information Technology Infrastructure

IT infrastructure refers to the sum composite of hardware, software, network resources and services that an IT-based organization needs for its operation and management. It allows an organization to deliver quality IT solutions and services to its customers. The infrastructure is generally housed within an organization and deployed within owned facilities.

IT infrastructure consists of components that combine together in a synergic manner to play an important role in IT-related operations. It can be used for internal business operations or for developing customer IT or business solutions.

Software part of IT infrastructure includes productivity applications, ERP or enterprise resource planning, and CRM or customer relationship management.

Major IT Infrastructure Components

Network Switch

A network switch is pivotal to the rest of your IT infrastructure components. They create the network on which your entire business runs. It's what connects computers, printers, phones, and servers in a building.

The network switch is the control panel for your entire IT ecosystem. It allows different devices to communicate with each other. This increases employee productivity and saves your business money.

Firewall

Your firewall is another important component of your IT's infrastructure. This is the basis of your network security system, monitoring all of the online traffic. It controls incoming and out coming network data. This is all regulated by previously set rules for security. If your network switch is the king of the castle, the firewall is the royal guard. Therefore, it's just as important. Your firewall must be bulletproof. Choose security software that offers tremendous firewall protection.

Router

Your router is the main hookup for different networks. This is the actual hardware that connects your local network to either other local networks or the Internet. It's how you get Wi-Fi, communicates securely to somebody on another network, and is essentially your key to the outside world.

Without a router, your network can do just fine being by itself, connecting to all of the devices within the building or house. But, if you want to have online access or be tethered to someone else's network, then you'll need a router.

Server

This is a computer program that provides functionality for other devices on the network. It's the center of connectivity for all of your IT infrastructure components.

Depending on the scale of your business and building, the server could be in-house or it could be at a completely separate location. Your connection to your customers and website is crucial to the wellbeing of your business; your server keeps you in contact.

Because this can be either software or hardware, there are multiple ways of keeping your server safe. Of course, there is your firewall as previously mentioned. However, if the server is large enough, there could be physical security to keep it from being hacked.

Data Center/Plant

A data center is a physical storage facility that houses computer systems and other IT infrastructure components, like servers, telecommunications, and storage. Your business' entire history, communications, connectivity, and network data are stored at this location.

This is a critical element of your IT infrastructure. Usually, your data center is where a ton of other company's data centers are. There are rows and rows of data servers and various hardware stored within a warehouse building.

For everything related to your network, data centers are there to house it. Find out where your data center is and make sure the security of the building is second to none.

Infrastructure Software

This is a program or software specifically designed to help business organizations perform basic tasks. These tasks range from workforce support to business transactions online to any internal process.

Considering this is how your day-to-day business is probably run, infrastructure software is another big IT infrastructure component.

IT software is one of the last components that create a full IT ecosystem. As you can see, with all of this software, hardware, programs, and facilities, having IT support of some sort is extremely helpful.

Converged Infrastructure

Converged infrastructure, sometimes known as converged architecture, is an approach to data center management that packages computer, networking, servers, storage and virtualization tools on a prequalified turnkey appliance. Converged systems include a toolkit of management software.

Converged infrastructure is gaining momentum as IT organizations shift away from owning and managing hardware to a flexible self-service model in which resources are consumed on demand. Rather than multiple IT assets existing in independent silos, converged infrastructure bundles hardware components with management software to orchestrate and provision the resources as a single integrated system.

The goal of converged infrastructure is to reduce complexity in data center management. The principle design factor is to eliminate issues of hardware incompatibility. Ease of deployment of converged infrastructure is appealing to enterprises that write cloud-native applications or host an internal hybrid or private cloud.

Gartner classifies converged infrastructure, along with hyper-converged infrastructure (HCI), within the category of integrated infrastructure systems or integrated stack systems.

Comparing Converged Infrastructure to Traditional Data Center Design

Traditional data center design requires that application servers, backup appliances, hypervisors, network cards and file storage systems be individually configured and linked together. Typically, each component is managed separately by a dedicated IT team. This arrangement serves organizations that have petabytes of data across thousands of applications, but management challenges can arise when trying to rationalize the costs or undertake a refresh cycle.

For example, the storage you buy comes from a different vendor than the one who supplies your servers and network cards, with each hardware device having different warranty periods and service-level agreements.

By contrast, converged infrastructure vendors offer branded and supported products in which all the components, servers, software, storage and switches, reside natively on a qualified hardware appliance. Owing to its smaller physical footprint in the data center, converged infrastructure helps to reduce the costs associated with cabling, cooling and power.

Key features of converged infrastructure products		
FEATURE	WHAT CHOICES	WHAT TO EVALUATE
Data protection	RAID (dedicated storage) Replication Erasure coding	Rebuild time Performance during rebuild Erasure coding
Solid-state storage	Flash in server Flash in shared array	Data locality Tiering Quality of service
Flexibility	Turnkey (no choice) Software only	Install on bare-metal system Ability to add only capacity or performance nodes
Data efficiency	Deduplication Compression Thin provisioning Writeable snapshots (clones)	Level or rate of optimization Performance impact of optimization Scalability of optimization

Converged Infrastructure Cloud use Cases: Benefits and Drawbacks

Converged architecture is based on a modular design that presents resources as pooled capacity. Each preconfigured module added to the system provides a predictable unit of compute, memory or storage. This visibility into resource consumption enables organizations to rapidly scale private cloud infrastructure to support cloud computing, virtualization and IT management at remote branch offices.

One advantage to buying a converged system is the peace of mind that comes with purchasing a vendor's validated platform. A typical converged infrastructure stack is preconfigured to address the needs of a specific workload, such as virtual desktop infrastructure or database applications.

Converged infrastructure products enable users to independently tune the individual components that comprise the architecture. This flexibility offers improved management flexibility over other IT architectures. The vendor supplying the converged system provides a single point of contact for maintenance and service issues.

However, there are limitations as to what you can do with converged technology. A user has little latitude to alter the basic converged infrastructure configuration. Separately adding components following the initial installation increases cost and complexity, negating the advantages that make converged infrastructure attractive in the first place.

How to Deploy a Converged Infrastructure

There are various ways to implement converged infrastructure. You could use vendor-tested hardware reference architecture, install a cluster of stand-alone appliances or take a software-driven, hyper-converged approach.

A converged infrastructure reference architecture refers to a set of preconfigured and validated hardware recommendations that pinpoint specific data center workloads. A vendor's reference architecture helps guide enterprises on the optimal deployment and use of the converged infrastructure components.

Users may opt to purchase a dedicated appliance as the platform on which to run a converged infrastructure. Using this approach, a vendor will provide a single hardware appliance that consolidates compute, storage, networking and virtualization resources, either sourced directly from the vendor or its partners. Customers can expand the converged cluster by purchasing additional appliances to achieve horizontal scalability.

Leading Converged Infrastructure Vendors and Products

Nutanix Inc. is credited with pioneering hyper-converged infrastructure as an alternative to complex NAS and SAN systems. Nutanix's hardware platforms include the NX-1000, NX-3000, NX-6000 and NX-8000. Nutanix does not sell servers, but packages its Virtual Computing Platform HCI software on OEM partners' hardware.

Dell EMC XC Series is a Nutanix-powered hyper-converged platform based on Dell Power Edge servers. Server vendor Lenovo markets the Lenovo Converged HX Series arrays, which packages the Nutanix hyper-converged software, including the Nutanix Acropolis hypervisor.

Virtually all legacy storage vendors offer branded converged infrastructure platforms, either directly or through channel partners. The list of products includes:

- Atlantis Computing Hyper Scale all-flash nodes;
- Cisco Hyper Flex integrates Spring path file system software on Cisco Unified Computing System (UCS) servers;
- Dell EMC VxRack SDDC Systems and VxRail (HCI) products are part of the Dell EMC Converged Infrastructure Division, the Dell EMC VxBlock line replaced the VCE Vblock products;
- Hewlett Packard Enterprise (HPE) Converged System;
- HPE SimpliVity HCI is based on HPE ProLiant servers;
- Hitachi Unified Compute Platform;
- IBM Versa Stack reference architecture includes Cisco UCS, Cisco switching and IBM Storwize V7000 arrays;
- Net App Flex Pod also incorporates Cisco UCS servers and Cisco switching;
- Oracle Cloud Converged Storage software installed on Oracle ZFS arrays; and
- VMware vSAN hyper-converged software that runs on commodity hardware.

Startup storage vendors with converged and HCI products include:

- Hyper Grid Hyper Converged Infrastructure;
- Pivot3 Acuity and vSTAC HCI;
- Scale Computing HC3 Hyper Core;
- Stratoscale Symphony;
- Tegile Intelli Stack; and
- Tintri VMstack.

Red Hat Hyper converged Infrastructure is an open source reference architecture for deploying Red Hat software on recommended servers.

Hyper-converged Infrastructure

Data center infrastructure is constantly improving, but every so often a whole new way of thinking emerges. These new infrastructure paradigms are almost always birthed as a solution to pressing business needs which the existing technology is incapable of meeting. Hyper convergence is one of these new ways of doing IT.

Fundamentally, hyper convergence is a way of constructing private data centers that seeks to emulate public cloud consumption in terms of its operational simplicity, economic model, and scaling granularity. And it provides all of this, of course, without sacrificing the performance, reliability, and workload availability that businesses today rely on.

Advantages of Hyper-converged Infrastructure

The most exciting benefits for adopters of hyper converged infrastructure are the following:

- Focus on the Workload: For too long, infrastructure policy and management have focused on the wrong constructs. Managing LUNs and hosts and clusters is old school. In the post-cloud era, the workload should be the focus. In the hyper converged model, the application is the focus.

- Data Efficiency: The nature of hyper converged infrastructure lends itself well to a high degree of data reduction by way of de duplication and compression, which leads to more approachable requirements for storage capacity, network bandwidth, and IOPS requirements.

- Elasticity: The beauty of the cloud is that if you need to scale out or in, you just click a few times and it's done. Hyper convergence focuses heavily on scaling easily, in bite-sized units; this model stands in stark contrast to the 3- or 5-year purchasing model of traditional IT.

- Data Protection: Hyper convergence is about simplifying and unifying infrastructure features. Rather than manage a separate backup and replication product, hyper converged systems typically have this critical technology built right in.

Difference between Converged and Hyper-converged Infrastructure

Converged systems are products where consumable resources such as compute, memory, storage, and networking are made available in an engineered solution. One element not represented in hyper-converged systems is that a general converged system usually has scale-up model for expanding various consumable elements.

Some would argue there is no true "convergence" in what are billed as converged infrastructure. Converged infrastructure solutions are simply pre-configured (or pre-validated as a configuration) combinations of servers, storage and sometimes networking switches, orchestration software, etc., but have none of the type of redundancy eliminations you would expect from a converged solution such as hardware or management tiers.

One big difference between the two is in expansion. In a converged infrastructure, compute and memory is expanded by additional servers. Storage capacity and performance are increased by adding additional shelves of disks. These can be expanded independently, but still fit in an engineered solution.

Hyper-converged is a type of converged system intended to be a scale out architecture where all resources are in nodes in a small form factor, 1U-2U racks, and growth is done by adding nodes. This adds compute, memory, network, and storage all at once, even if those resources are not necessarily needed. You might only need more storage, for example, but you have to add more compute and networking along with it. So there tends to be more control over the hardware resources in a converged infrastructure.

Hyper converged solutions move all of the intelligence out of the proprietary hardware and put it into software. For example, an HCI solution aggregates the local storage (disk/flash) among many servers or nodes and presents it as one local volume.

In a converged architecture, the storage is attached directly to the physical servers, usually a mix of flash and traditional hard disk-based storage. The HCI system has the storage controller function running as a service on each node in the cluster to improve scalability and resilience. If a storage node goes down, simply point to another node to keeps it running while you repair the downed node.

Because HCI turns the infrastructure stack into an elastic pool of x86 resources, everything is run by software, to the point that some people refer to the HCI system as a software-defined data center (SDDC). Because it's a single shared resource pool, many more software services are available. They include:

- Data protection like backup, replication, snapshots, and disaster recovery.

- De duplication applications.

- SSD and SSD cache arrays.

- Replication appliances or software.

- System management, provisioning, monitoring, and reporting.

Finally, another difference between the two is the vendor(s). While virtually every major server vendor offers a unified/converged system, you do still have the option to mix and match an Oracle server with EMC storage, for example. It's all about the hardware. In HCI, much of the work is defined in software and integration is a must, so they tend to come from a single vendor. You certainly have a choice of HCI providers, but it will be a single provider nonetheless.

Uses of Converged and Hyper Converged Infrastructure

The main difference between converged and hyper-converged systems is how they scale. With converged infrastructure, you scale up by adding more drives, memory or CPUs. With a HCI system, you scale out.

Supporters of converged infrastructure promote the concept in green field, remote centers and data center renovation projects, especially in a highly virtualized data centers building a private cloud. Dell EMC says that typically a converged infrastructure is used in major Platform 2.0 applications such as Enterprise Resource Planning (ERP), Customer Relationship Management (CRM), database grids, SAP workloads and enterprise messaging.

These are platforms where you get the most out of blade servers, modular storage arrays, virtualized networks and a hypervisor, since they all compliment each other for maximum efficacy. As said before, converged infrastructure is primarily a hardware play and gets the most out of the hardware, and the above-listed apps are very hardware-intensive.

HCI then, is used in a different way. Dell EMC says it is a good fit for cloud-oriented Platform 3.0 applications such as application development environments, Big Data analytics, life cycle and cloud applications, all of which need agility and the ability to scale up and down quickly at the lowest cost per unit.

So HCI are not in competition with each other. They are used in very different circumstances and applications. So your choice is not either/or, it's both. Most IT operations would be best served to have a mix of these two options to serve each workload.

Another stark difference is their cloud usage. A CI offering is best suited for a company's internal cloud, where they need the benefits of a cloud system but don't have to expose it to the outside world. A HCI system is better suited for a public or hybrid environment because it can better integrate with the hypervisors of public cloud providers, and thanks to all the software controls, the company can better manage orchestration and automation between their data center and the cloud provider.

So the bottom line is a company needs to decide its IT needs and applications, and then decide on CI or HCI from there.

Dynamic Infrastructure

Dynamic infrastructure refers to a collection of data center resources, such as computer, networking and storage that can automatically provision and adjust itself as workload demands change. IT administrators can also choose to manage these resources manually.

Dynamic infrastructure relies primarily on software to identify, virtualize, classify and track data center resources. These resources are grouped into pools, regardless of their physical location within one or multiple data centers. By classifying data center resources, IT teams can establish and monitor multiple service tiers to ensure more demanding workloads receive more compute and storage resources.

In most cases, the software used in dynamic infrastructures can automatically allocate resources from the appropriate pools to meet workload demands. The software adds resources when workload demands increase, and then returns resources to the pool when demands decrease – a process known as workload balancing.

Dynamic infrastructure helps align IT use with business policies. For example, a critical workload can retain more resources longer to ensure top performance, while less-important business applications can use fewer resources or release unneeded resources sooner. Such behaviors help maximize resource use and reduce the need for new IT purchases.

Although dynamic infrastructure can work with any data center hardware, it is often deployed with highly integrated and expandable hardware systems, known as a hyper-converged infrastructure (HCI). These are typically appliances that include compute, storage and network capabilities.

Dynamic infrastructure is an evolution of traditional network and application network solutions to be more adaptable, support integration with its environment and other foundational technologies, and to be aware of context (connectivity intelligence).

Adaptable

It is able to understand its environment and react to conditions in that environment in order to provide scale, security, and optimal performance for applications. This adaptability comes in many forms, from the ability to make management and configuration changes on the fly as necessary to providing the means by which administrators and developers can manually or automatically make changes to the way in which applications are being delivered. The configuration and policies applied by dynamic infrastructure are not static; they are able to change based on predefined criteria or events that occur in the environment such that the security, scalability, or performance of an application and its environs are preserved.

Some solutions implement this capability through event-driven architectures, such as "IP_AD-DRESS_ASSIGNED" or "HTTP_REQUEST_MADE". Some provide network-side scripting capabilities to extend the ability to react and adapt to situations requiring flexibility while others provide the means by which third-party solutions can be deployed on the solution to address the need for application and user specific capabilities at specific touch-points in the architecture.

Context Aware

Dynamic infrastructure is able to understand the context that surrounds an application, its deployment environment, and its users and apply relevant policies based on that information. Being context aware means being able to recognize that a user accessing Application X from a coffee shop has different needs than the same user accessing Application X from home or from the corporate office. It is able to recognize that a user accessing an application over a WAN or high-latency connection requires different policies than one accessing that application via a LAN or from close physical proximity over the Internet. Being context aware means being able to recognize the current conditions of the network and the application, and then leveraging its adaptable nature to choose the right policies at the time the request is made such that the application is delivered most efficiently and quickly.

Collaborative

Dynamic infrastructure is capable of integrating with other application network and network infrastructure, as well as the management and control solutions required to manage both the infrastructure and the applications it is tasked with delivering. The integration capabilities of dynamic infrastructure requires that the solution be able to direct and take direction from other solutions such that changes in the infrastructure at all layers of the stack can be recognized and acted upon. This integration allows network and application network solutions to leverage its awareness of context in a way that ensures it is adaptable and can support the delivery of applications in an elastic, flexible manner.

Most solutions use a standards-based control plane through which they can be integrated with other systems to provide the connectivity intelligence necessary to implement IaaS, virtualized architectures, and other cloud computing models in such a way that the perceived benefits of reduced operating expenses and increased productivity through automation can actually be realized.

These three properties of dynamic infrastructure work together, in concert, to provide the connectivity intelligence and ability to act on information gathered through that intelligence. All three together forms the basis for a fluid, adaptable, dynamic application infrastructure foundation on which emerging compute models such as cloud computing and virtualized architectures can be implemented.

But dynamic infrastructure is not exclusively tied to emerging compute models and next-generation application architectures. Dynamic infrastructure can be leveraged to provide benefit to traditional architectures, as well. The connectivity intelligence and adaptable nature of dynamic infrastructure improves the security, availability, and performance of applications in so-called legacy architectures as well.

Dynamic infrastructure is a set of capabilities implemented by network and application network solutions that provide the means by which an organization can improve the efficiency of their application delivery and network architecture.

Benefits

Global organizations already have the foundation for a dynamic infrastructure that will bring together the business and IT infrastructure to create new possibilities. For example:

- Transportation companies can optimize their vehicles' routes leveraging GPS and traffic information.

- Facilities organizations can secure access to locations and track the movement of assets by leveraging RFID technology.

- Production environments can monitor and manage presses, valves and assembly equipment through embedded electronics.

- Technology systems can be optimized for energy efficiency, managing spikes in demand, and ensuring disaster recovery readiness.

- Communications companies can better monitor usage by location, user or function, and optimize routing to enhance user experience.

- Utility companies can reduce energy usage with a "smart grid."

Software-defined Infrastructure

Software-Defined Infrastructure (SDI) has emerged as a promising approach to address the extensive demands on maximizing the value potential of infrastructure deployments. SDI refers to the operation and control of IT infrastructure entirely using software technologies and without involvement of the human element. Processes including infrastructure control, management, provisioning, configuration and other architectural operations are performed automatically via software as per application requirements and the defined operational policies. Since the changes are not dependent or limited to the human involvement, SDI enables intelligent infrastructure processes based on the changing IT operation requirements in real-time. The IT infrastructure therefore becomes intelligent, taking smart decisions on its own in order to meet the defined goals on SLAs, performance, security and other considerations. SDI allows the infrastructure to operate as a self-aware, self-healing, self-scaling and self-optimizing IT environment to enable truly agile business processes.

The Software-Defined Infrastructure stack typically comprises of the following components:

- Physical Infrastructure: At the machine level, SDI comprises of the hardware resources such as servers and networking devices, as well as firmware, hypervisors and other endpoint terminals. The infrastructure components may be scaled on an ongoing basis to address changing IT needs, while the SDI functionality can encompass the expanding infrastructure.

- Virtualization Layers: Virtualization is applied to the infrastructure resources such as storage and network components. A heterogeneous architecture of computing resources is maintained. This component sits directly above the physical infrastructure level within an SDI architecture.

- Software-Defined Capabilities: Capabilities such as Software-Defined Networking (SDN), Software-Defined Compute and Software Defined Storage are applied to the virtualized layer of computing resources. Intelligent monitoring and control systems are deployed to automatically transform the network, compute and storage resources as per the architecture policies. End-users may define their requirements pertaining to resource provisioning and server deployment, while the intelligent control systems will take on the responsibility of configuring the underlying infrastructure and managing the virtualized resources.

- Management Services: At the infrastructure management level, SDI may involve the user-interface to define parameters such as SLA performance, availability, scalability and elasticity. IT admins or internal IT users may also request provisioning of resources. The management services layer will take care of all infrastructure operations necessary to ensure that desired standards of SLA and performance are maintained.

The SDI approach goes beyond the deployment of core SDI components and should be designed to realize the key attributes of a successful SDI strategy. These attributes may vary based on organizational requirements regarding the infrastructure scalability, agility, security, performance, reliability and compliance. Common attributes may include the following:

Intelligent Virtualization: SDI should aim to enhance the portability of IT workloads and remove dependencies from the underlying infrastructure. While virtualization and layers of abstraction are necessary, an effective SDI infrastructure comprises of strong intelligence capabilities to orchestrate the infrastructure resources and architecture for maximum performance and reliability.

Software-Driven Innovation: Software-centric SDI strategy focuses on using commercial off the shelf hardware instead of investing in proprietary and customized hardware solutions. Software is used to fill the gap in transforming commercial hardware platforms into a flexible and scalable infrastructure backend. Open source hardware designs can further help remove the barriers in scaling the infrastructure to meet the desired standards of an SDI architecture.

Modular Design: Adaptability is a key attribute of an effective SDI strategy and enabled by introducing modularity in the design of the software architecture. The roles of different infrastructure resources are distributed across different technical functionality as defined by the software. Techniques such as Software Orient Architecture (SOA) design or micro services may be used for modularity.

Context Awareness: Legacy infrastructure architecture may not be designed to collect information on context such as incidents, triggers, warning, events or other parameters from related infrastructure components. An effective SDI strategy should involve selective identification, access and analysis of relevant metrics to accurately determine and manage performance, security and compliance of the IT infrastructure.

Performance Focused: Organizations may assess the performance in terms of availability, security and compliance posture of the wider infrastructure. The SDI approach should be designed to achieve high standards of performance by introducing capabilities such as strong encryption and access controls, redundancy in architecture, monitoring, visibility and control over the infrastructure.

Policy Based Systems: The SDI should be designed to meet the purpose and goals of the organization's infrastructure operations. A policy-driven approach should be established to continuously monitor infrastructure performance and enforce the changes necessary to comply with the IT, operational and business policies. Instead of introducing manual automation scripts every time a change is needed, SDI can automatically identify the requirements and issues appropriate commands to infrastructure components.

Open Source Driven: Open source technologies remove the barriers that prevent elastic and flexible operations of the infrastructure. An SDI architecture requires multiple interfaces and components to operate as integrated, interoperable, elastic and flexible pool of infrastructure resources. By following the open standards, organizations can build an open and agile IT environment that allows the software to manage, configure, provision and operate the infrastructure autonomously while meeting intended SLA performance standards.

Software Defined Infrastructure allows organizations to control how IT workloads are distributed and optimized to maximize the value potential of infrastructure deployments. Early movers in the SDI journey can take advantage of the technology and deliver optimum levels of service delivery for customers in terms of low latency and high performance of apps as their key competitive differentiation. The ability to realize the true potential of infrastructure deployments and operate agile software-driven architecture empowers organizations to test new business models and offer improved customer experiences in response to changing market trends. For progressive organizations, SDI continues to prevail as a key business enabler with its expanding scope of automation, intelligence and virtualization applied to cloud-based data center technologies.

References

- Information-technology: useoftechnology.com, Retrieved 29 July 2018
- The-uses-of-information-technology-in-education: fedena.com, Retrieved 16 May 2018
- What-are-the-7-major-it-infrastructure-components-1763: sitereportcard.com, Retrieved 18 June 2018
- Hyperconverged-infrastructure-basics-2: hyperconverged.org, Retrieved 11 June 2018
- Converged-vs.-hyperconverged-whats-best-for-you: datamation.com, Retrieved 21 April 2018
- Software-defined-infrastructure: bmc.com, Retrieved 31 March 2018

Computer Hardware

Computer hardware refers to the physical components and parts of a computer such as the CPU, keyboard, monitor, mouse, etc. This chapter has been carefully written to provide an understanding of computer hardware with the inclusion of topics like central processing unit, motherboard, power supply unit, hard disk drive, motherboard, etc.

Computer hardware refers to the physical devices that make up a computer. Examples include the keyboard, monitor and disk drive.

Hardware devices can be classified into four distinct categories:

- Input devices: For raw data input.

- Processing devices: To process raw data instructions into information.

- Output devices: To disseminate data and information.

- Storage devices: For data and information retention.

Input Devices

Components which are used to input raw data are categorized under input devices. They aid in feeding data such as text, images, and audiovisual recordings. They even aid in file transfers between computers.

The keyboard is probably the most commonly used input device. Below are just some other types of input devices.

Input Type	Examples
Pointing Device	Mouse, touchpad, touchscreen, multi-touch screen, pen input, motion sensor, graphics tablet, interactive smart board, and fingerprint scanner.
Game Controller	Joystick, gamepad, and steering wheel.
Audio Input Device	Microphone and midi keyboard.
Bluetooth Peripheral	Keyboard, mouse, headset, gamepad, printer.
Visual and Imaging Device	Webcam, digital camera, digital camcorder, TV capture card, biometric scanner, and barcode reader.
Network Device	Ethernet hardware and Bluetooth/wireless hardware.

Processing Devices

Processing is the core function of a computer. It is the stage where raw data is transformed into information. Once data has been processed, it can be used for useful purposes.

Components that manipulate data into information are categorized under processing.

The microprocessor is the major device in this category. It works closely with primary memory during its operations. Data is stored temporarily in processor cache and primary memory during the processing period.

The microprocessor is subdivided into three important units, which work together in order to accomplish its function. The units are:

- The control unit: It manages and supervises the operations of the processor and other components that are crucial in data manipulation.

- Arithmetic and logic unit: The ALU is responsible for all arithmetic and logic operations like addition, multiplication, subtraction, division, and comparison logic operations.

- Register and cache: These are storage locations inside the processor that respond to the instructions of the control unit by moving relevant data around during processing.

Output Devices

Hardware components that disseminate and display both data and information are classified under the output category.

Output is the culmination of a cycle which starts with the input of raw data and processing.

These components are sub-categorized under softcopy and hardcopy output.

Softcopy output includes the intangible experience. The user derives visual satisfaction by reading a message through display components or listens to audio files through speakers.

On the other hand, hardcopy output devices are tangible, like printouts of paper and 3D models.

Popular Softcopy Devices

Visual display devices include:

- Monitor
- Projection display
- Interactive (electronic) smart board
- Touchscreen

Sound devices include:

- Speakers
- Headphones and earphones

Network input/output includes:

- Ethernet cables
- Wireless and Bluetooth transmissions

USB input/output includes:

- Flash drives
- External drives
- Optical drives

Popular Hardcopy Devices

Impact printers include:

- Dot matrix printer
- 3D printer

Non-impact printers include:

- Inkjet printer
- Laser jet printer
- Thermal printer

Memory/Storage Devices

Components that retain/store data are classified under memory/storage devices.

Storage is sub-divided under primary and secondary memory and is either volatile or nonvolatile.

Primary memory usually refers to random-access memory (RAM) but can also refer to all memory that works in tandem with the processor. RAM is volatile, meaning that it retains data only when the computer is powered up.

The central processing unit (CPU) or accelerated processing unit (APU) reads instructions stored in this memory and executes them as required.

Secondary memory is labeled as such because data stored within secondary storage media (usually disk drives) do not communicate directly with the microprocessor. Any data stored in such media is first transferred to a RAM device for processing to take place.

This type of memory is also non-volatile since it permits long time storage as opposed to volatile memory.

To give some examples of these devices, primary memory includes:

- DRAM
- SRAM
- ROM

Secondary memory is subdivided into two categories:

- Internal devices are designed to be placed inside the computer at all times. Examples include hard disk and solid state disk drives.

- External devices are plug and play media used to transfer files between computers. Examples include optical disks, flash disks, and external disk drives.

Computer Case

The computer case serves mainly as a way to physically mount and contain all of the actual components inside of a computer, like the motherboard, hard drive, optical drive, floppy disk drive, etc. They typically come bundled with a power supply.

The housing of a laptop, netbook, or tablet is also considered a case but since they aren't purchased separately or very replaceable, the computer case tends to refer to the one that's part of a traditional desktop PC.

Some popular computer case manufacturers include Xoxide, NZXT, and Antec.

The computer case is also known as a tower, box, system unit, base unit, enclosure, housing, chassis, and cabinet.

Importance of Computer Case

There are several reasons why we use computer cases. One is for protection, which is easy to assume because it's the most obvious. Dust, animals, toys, liquids, etc. can all damage the internal parts of a computer if the hard shell of a computer case doesn't enclose them and keep them away from the outside environment.

A computer case also doubles as a way to hide all those parts of the computer that nobody really wants to see each time they look in that direction.

Another good reason to use a computer case is to keep the area cool. Proper airflow over the computer components is one more benefit to using a computer case. While the case has special vents to allow some of the fan air to escape, the rest of it can be used to cool down the hardware, which would otherwise get pretty hot and possibly overheat to the point of malfunction.

Keeping noisy computer parts, like the fans, in a closed space within the computer case is one way to reduce the noise that they make.

The structure of the computer case is also important. The different parts can fit together and become easily accessible to the user by being compacted in a case to hold it all together. For example, USB ports and the power button are easily accessible and the disc drive can be opened at any time.

Computer Case Description

The computer case itself can be constructed from any material that still allows the internal devices to be supported. This is usually steel, plastic, or aluminum but might instead be wood, glass, or Styrofoam.

Most computer cases are rectangular and black. Case modding is the term used to describe the styling of a case to personalize it with things like custom internal lighting, paint, or a liquid cooling system.

The front of the computer case contains a power button and sometimes a reset button. Small LED lights are also typical, representing the current power status, hard drive activity, and sometimes other internal processes. These buttons and lights connect directly to the motherboard which is secured to the inside of the case.

Cases usually contain multiple 5.25 inch and 3.5 inch expansion bays for optical drives, floppy disk drives, hard drives, and other media drives. These expansion bays are located at the front of the case so that, for example, the DVD drive can be easily reached by the user when in use.

At least one side of the case, perhaps both, slide or swing open to allow access to the internal components.

The rear of the computer case contains small openings to fit the connectors contained on the motherboard which is mounted inside. The power supply is also mounted just inside the back of the case and a large opening allows for the connection of the power cord and use of the built-in fan. Fans or other cooling devices may be attached to any and all sides of the case.

Central Processing Unit

CPU or Central processing unit is the brain of the computer system. A function of CPU varies from data processing to controlling input-output devices. Each and every instruction no matter how complex or simple, it has to go through the CPU.

So, let us say we press a key on the keyboard and it instantly appears on our computer monitor so the CPU of the computer is what makes this possible. The central processing unit is also responsible for storing data or information, intermediate results and instructions in the memory system. It also controls the operations of all other parts of the computer system.

Functions of a CPU:

CPU generally performs the arithmetical and logical operations, controlling of different input-output devices. These operations are performed based on some predefined algorithms and instructions normally referred as computer programs.

A computer program is a set of instructions written by a human to perform a specific operation by the CPU. A computer program is normally stored in the memory unit of the Central Processing Unit.

A CPU mainly consists of ALU (Arithmetic & Logic Unit), Control Unit and Memory Unit. These 3 units are the primary components of a CPU. Various functions of CPU and operations are generally performed by these 3 units are described below.

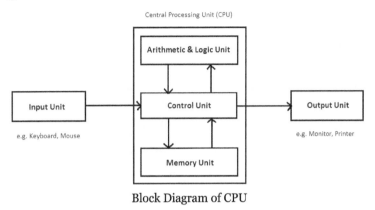

Block Diagram of CPU

Components of CPU and their Functions

Memory Unit

The primary job of the memory unit is to store data or instructions and intermediate results. Memory unit supplies data to the other units of a CPU. In Computer Organization, memory can be divided into two major parts primary memory and secondary memory. Speed and power and performance of a memory depend on the size and type of the memory.

When an instruction is processed by the central processing unit, the main memory or the RAM (Random Access Memory) stores the final result before it is sent to the output device. All inputs and outputs are intermediate and are transmitted through the main memory.

Control Unit

It is the unit which controls all the operations of the different units but does not carry out any actual data processing operation. Control unit transfers data or instruction among different units of a computer system. It receives the instructions from the memory, interprets them and sends the operation to various units as instructed.

Control unit is also responsible for communicating with all input and output devices for transferring or receiving the instruction from the storage units. So, the control unit is the main coordinator since it sends signals and find the sequence of instructions to be executed.

Arithmetic and Logic Unit

ALU can also be subdivided into 2 sections namely, arithmetic unit and logic unit. It is a complex digital circuit which consists of registers and which performs arithmetic and logical operations. Arithmetic sections perform arithmetic operations like addition, subtraction, multiplication, division etc. All other Complex operations can also be performed by repetition of these above basic operations.

The logic unit is responsible for performing logical operations such as comparing, selecting, matching and merging of different data or information.

So basically ALU is the major part of the computer system which handles different calculations. Depending on the design of ALU it makes the CPU more powerful and efficient.

Power Supply Unit

The computer's power supply unit (PSU) converts the domestic alternating current (ac) mains supply voltage (220-240 volts in Europe) into various regulated, low voltage direct current (dc) outputs required by the components that make up the computer system.

The PSU usually takes the form of a metal box 150mm wide x 86mm high x (typically) 140mm deep. It is mounted inside the system case using four screws in a standard location such that the on/off switch and power cord socket mounted on the back of the PSU are accessible via an aperture in the rear of the case. The same aperture also allows air to flow into the PSU's cooling fan.

In some cases, there may be a voltage selector switch to allow the user to select a voltage according to their geographical location (the United States, for example, has a domestic power supply operating at a nominal 120 volts). Inside the case, a bundle of cables emerges from the front of the PSU. The cables are often grouped and colour-coded according to the type of device they will be connected to.

Although in the past several form factors have been used for the power supply unit, some of them quite heavy and bulky, most desktop personal computers now use power supplies that conform to the standard ATX format, the most recent version of which is 2.3.1. The illustration below shows a typical ATX PSU.

A typical ATX power supply unit

ATX PSUs are designed to work specifically with the ATX family of motherboards and fit into an ATX system case, and can be turned on or off (or placed into standby mode) using signals generated by the motherboard. The maximum rated power output of a PSU can range from around 250 watts up to as high as 2 kilowatts, depending on the type of system they are intended for.

Small form factor computer systems tend to have low power supply requirements in the order of 300 watts or less. Systems used for gaming have much higher power requirements (typically

450 to 800 watts), mainly because they employ high-end graphics adapters which consume large amounts of power. The highest power consumption is found in commercial network servers or high-performance personal computers featuring multiple processors, a number of disk drives, and multiple graphics cards.

The amount of power required by a particular computer system will depend on the power requirements of the motherboard, processor and RAM, and on the number of add-on cards and peripheral devices drawing power from the PSU. In reality, few personal computers currently need more than about 350 watts.

Even so, care should be taken when selecting a power supply unit, since the rated maximum power output claimed by some manufacturers does not always reflect the actual power output that can be achieved under various load conditions. As a result, manufacturers and vendors of PC systems and system components (especially high-end graphics cards) have a tendency to over-specify the minimum power requirements when it comes to recommending a power supply rating for PSUs to be used with their products.

Whilst it is true that an inadequate power supply can fail if it becomes overloaded, it is not a good idea to use a high-output power supply regardless of the actual power requirements. On the contrary, you should select a PSU with a power output that reflects the power requirements of the system. Energy efficiency is at its highest when the load on the power supply is between 50% and 75% of the maximum output. This means that the PSU dissipates less power as heat.

If the PSU fan speed is being regulated by the motherboard, as is often the case, the system will run more quietly because less airflow is required to cool the PSU. At low loads (less than 20% of capacity), energy efficiency drops significantly and more power will be dissipated as heat than would be the case in a more appropriately rated PSU. Even worse, if the load drops below 15% of capacity the PSU may not function properly, and there is a good chance that it will shut down altogether.

The information supplied on the label or plate attached to the power supply provides technical information about the power supply which will include the ac mains supply voltages, currents and frequencies that the unit can be used with, the maximum total power output in watts, and the various dc voltage and current outputs available. It will also display hazard warnings and the required safety certification information (in Europe, this is the CE mark). A typical PSU label is shown below.

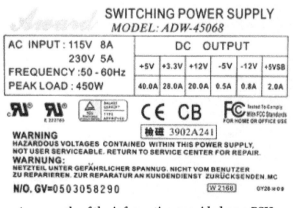

An example of the information provided on a PSU

The connectors provided can vary from one model to another, but those typically included are summarised in the table below.

Common PSU Connectors		
Type	Description	Illustration
P1	A 20-pin or 24-pin connector that provides Power to the motherboard. On some PSUs, the P1 is split into one 20-pin connector and one 4- pin connector which can be combined if required (see illustration) to form a 24-pin connector.	
ATX12V (or P4)	A 4-pin power connector that goes to the motherboard in addition to a 20-pin P1 to supply power to the processor	
Molex	A 4-pin peripheral power connector that supplies power to IDE disk drives and CD- ROM/DVD drives.	
Berg (or Mini-Molex)	A 4-pin power connector that supplies power to the floppy disk drive (it can also be used as an auxiliary connector for AGP video cards).	
Serial ATA	This is a 15-pin power connector mainly used for SATA hard drives.	

PCI Express	A 6-pin or (more recently) 8-pin power connector used for PCI Express graphics cards. Some 8-pin connections allow for either a 6-pin or an 8-pin card to be connected by using two separate connectors on the same cable (one with 6 pins and another with 2 pins).	

Working of Power Supply Unit

The type of power supply unit found in a modern PC is referred to as a switched mode power supply unit (SMPSU). What this means in essence us that the ac mains voltage coming into the PSU is rectified to produce a dc voltage without using a mains transformer (these are usually rather heavy due to the need for a coil with a ferrite core). The voltage thus obtained is then switched on and off at very high speeds using electronic switching circuitry, effectively producing a high-frequency square wave voltage (effectively, a series of dc pulses). A light and relatively inexpensive high-frequency transformer can then be used to produce the required dc output.

The dc output voltage and current are regulated (kept constant) using a feedback controller that increases or decreases power output in accordance with variations in load current. It does this by increasing or decreasing the duty cycle (essentially, this means increasing or decreasing the number of voltage pulses produced by the switching circuitry in a given time frame).

Note that most PSUs can shut themselves down if load current exceeds a certain threshold, reducing the possibility of damage to the computer system (or its user) in the event of an electrical fault such as a short circuit. The same principle applies to the absence of a load current (or a very low load current), since the PSU cannot operate correctly below a certain power output level and will shut down if insufficient load current is detected.

When first turned on, it can take half a second or so for the power supply to stabilise and start generating the correct dc voltages required by the computer. The power supply therefore sends a signal to the motherboard called the Power Good signal, once it has carried out its internal tests and is satisfied that the power outputs are all as they should be. The motherboard must wait for this signal before powering up the system.

A power surge or momentary power failure will sometimes cause a short interruption in the Power Good signal, which will cause the system to reboot when it is resumed. Note also that for practical reasons the different voltages produced by a power supply unit are actually produced by several different switched-mode supplies that are linked together within the PSU, each of which varies its output according to component power requirements.

One recent trend in PSU design has been the concept of a modular power supply, in which cables can be attached to the PSU via connectors at the power supply end, allowing the user to install only the cables they actually need. The idea is that the omission of cables that are not required will reduce clutter inside the case and improve airflow. It also provides more choice in the type of power cable the user can install (e.g. Serial ATA or Molex for hard drives).

Critics of this development have pointed out that electrical resistance will be increased due to the greater number of electrical connections. Proponents point out that the increase in resistance is very small. In practical terms however, problems are only likely to occur if the connectors are old and worn (in which case the connection may be a loose one) or the connection has not been made correctly during installation. The obvious answer is to replace old cables and check all connections prior to first use. The main PSU connectors and their pin outputs are illustrated in the figure below.

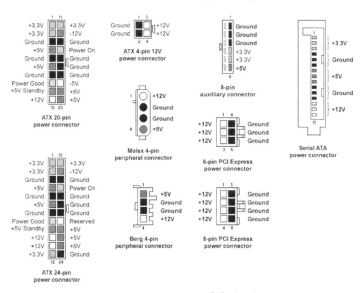

Common PSU connectors and their pin outputs

Power supply failure will invariably require the replacement of the PSU, since the computer will obviously not function without it. Such failures often result from overheating due to the breakdown of the cooling fan. The system subsequently powers itself off and cannot be rebooted or, as sometimes happens, repeatedly reboots itself at apparently random intervals.

In critical computer systems such as network servers, it is not uncommon to find redundant power supplies acting as a backup for the main power supply. The backup unit takes over in the event of a failure in the primary power supply, which can then be replaced during a scheduled maintenance period.

At the other end of the scale, portable computers such as laptops and netbooks require far less power (200 watts or less) enabling them to be powered by a removable rechargeable battery which can easily be replaced if necessary. An external power supply is used to charge the battery, and can supply power to the system while it is connected. This external power supply unit typically supplies 19.5V direct current.

The facility to power the computer's power supply on or off by grounding the +5V standby voltage means that the system can be powered on or off by a signal generated by the motherboard in response to a software interrupt (or system call - a signal generated by the operating system) or a hardware interrupt (a signal generated by a hardware component on the system).

The ability to control power using a system call means that the user can power down the system by clicking on an icon or menu item rather than having to physically switch off the system using the power switch. It also means that power management software can be configured to power down the computer in the absence of user input for a given period of time. The system can be set to power on again in the event of some predetermined occurrence, such as the user pressing a key on the keyboard or the activation of a network connection.

Motherboard

The main printed circuit board in a computer is known as the motherboard. Other names for this central computer unit are system board, mainboard, or printed wired board (PWB).

Numerous major components, crucial for the functioning of the computer, are attached to the motherboard. These include the processor, memory, and expansion slots. The motherboard connects directly or indirectly to every part of the PC.

The type of motherboard installed in a PC has a great effect on a computer's system speed and expansion capabilities.

Computer's Microprocessor

Also known as the microprocessor or the processor, the CPU is the computer's brain. It is responsible for fetching, decoding, and executing program instructions as well as performing mathematical and logical calculations.

The processor chip is identified by the processor type and the manufacturer. This information is usually inscribed on the chip itself. For example, Intel 386, Advanced Micro Devices (AMD) 386, Cyrix 486, Pentium MMX, Intel Core 2Duo, or iCore7.

If the processor chip is not on the motherboard, you can identify the processor socket as socket 1 to Socket 8, LGA 775 among others. This can help you identify the processor that fits in the socket. For example, a 486DX processor fits into Socket 3.

Computer Memory

Random Access Memory, or RAM, usually refers to computer chips that temporarily store dynamic data to enhance computer performance while you are working.

In other words, it is the working place of your computer, where active programs and data are loaded so that any time the processor requires them, it doesn't have to fetch them from the hard disk.

Random access memory is volatile, meaning it loses its contents once power is turned off. This is different from non-volatile memory, such as hard disks and flash memory, which do not require a power source to retain data.

When a computer shuts down properly, all data located in RAM is returned back to permanent storage on the hard drive or flash drive. At the next boot-up, RAM begins to fill with programs automatically loaded at startup, a process called booting. Later on, the user opens other files and programs that are still loaded in the memory.

BIOS

BIOS stands for Basic Input/Output System. BIOS is a "read-only" memory, which consists of low-level software that controls the system hardware and acts as an interface between the operating system and the hardware. Most people know the term BIOS by another name—device drivers, or just drivers. BIOS is essentially the link between the computer hardware and software in a system.

All motherboards include a small block of Read Only Memory (ROM) which is separate from the main system memory used for loading and running software. On PCs, the BIOS contains all the code required to control the keyboard, display screen, disk drives, serial communications, and a number of miscellaneous functions.

The system BIOS is a ROM chip on the motherboard used during the startup routine (boot process) to check out the system and prepare to run the hardware. The BIOS is stored on a ROM chip because ROM retains information even when no power is being supplied to the computer.

CMOS Battery

Motherboards also include a small separate block of memory made from CMOS RAM chips which are kept alive by a battery (known as a CMOS battery) even when the PC's power is off. This prevents reconfiguration when the PC is powered on.

CMOS devices require very little power to operate.

The CMOS RAM is used to store basic Information about the PC's configuration for instance:-

- Floppy disk and hard disk drive types
- Information about CPU
- RAM size
- Date and time
- Serial and parallel port information
- Plug and Play information
- Power Saving settings

Other Important data kept in CMOS memory is the time and date, which is updated by a Real Time Clock (RTC).

Computer Cache Memory

Cache memory is a small block of high-speed memory (RAM) that enhances PC performance by pre-loading information from the (relatively slow) main memory and passing it to the processor on demand.

Most CPUs have an internal cache memory (built into the processor) which is referred to as Level 1 or primary cache memory. This can be supplemented by external cache memory fitted on the motherboard. This is the Level 2 or secondary cache.

In modern computers, Levels 1 and 2 cache memory are built into the processor die. If a third cache is implemented outside the die, it is referred to as the Level 3 (L3) cache.

Expansion Buses

An expansion bus is an input/output pathway from the CPU to peripheral devices and it is typically made up of a series of slots on the motherboard. Expansion boards (cards) plug into the bus. PCI is the most common expansion bus in a PC and other hardware platforms. Buses carry signals such as data, memory addresses, power, and control signals from component to component. Other types of buses include ISA and EISA.

Expansion buses enhance the PCs capabilities by allowing users to add missing features in their computers by slotting adapter cards into expansion slots.

Computer Chip-sets

A chipset is a group of small circuits that coordinate the flow of data to and from a PC's key components. These key components include the CPU itself, the main memory, the secondary cache, and any devices situated on the buses. A chipset also controls data flow to and from hard disks and other devices connected to the IDE channels.

A computer has got two main chipsets:

- The North Bridge (also called the memory controller) is in charge of controlling transfers between the processor and the RAM, which is why it is located physically near the processor. It is sometimes called the GMCH, for Graphic and Memory Controller Hub.

- The South Bridge (also called the input/output controller or expansion controller) handles communications between slower peripheral devices. It is also called the ICH (I/O Controller Hub). The term "bridge" is generally used to designate a component which connects two buses.

CPU Clock

The CPU clock synchronizes the operation of all parts of the PC and provides the basic timing signal for the CPU. Using a quartz crystal, the CPU clock breathes life into the microprocessor by feeding it a constant flow of pulses.

For example, a 200 MHz CPU receives 200 million pulses per second from the clock. A 2 GHz CPU gets two billion pulses per second. Similarly, in any communications device, a clock may be used to synchronize the data pulses between sender and receiver.

A "real-time clock," also called the "system clock," keeps track of the time of day and makes this data available to the software. A "time-sharing clock" interrupts the CPU at regular intervals and allows the operating system to divide its time between active users and/or applications.

Switches and Jumpers

- DIP (Dual In-line Package) switches are small electronic switches found on the circuit board that can be turned on or off just like a normal switch. They are very small and so are usually flipped with a pointed object, such as the tip of a screwdriver, a bent paper clip, or a pen top. Take care when cleaning near DIP switches, as some solvents may destroy them. Dip switches are obsolete and you will not find them in modern systems.

- Jumper pins are small protruding pins on the motherboard. A jumper cap or bridge is used to connect or short a pair of jumper pins. When the bridge is connected to any two pins, via a shorting link, it completes the circuit and a certain configuration has been achieved.

- Jumper caps are metal bridges that close an electrical circuit. Typically, a jumper consists of a plastic plug that fits over a pair of protruding pins. Jumpers are sometimes used to configure expansion boards. By placing a jumper plug over a different set of pins, you can change a board's parameters.

Expansion Card

An expansion card is a printed circuit board that can be installed in a computer to add functionality to it. For example, a user may add a new graphics card to his computer to give it more 3D graphics processing power. An audio engineer may add a professional sound card to his machine to increase the computer's audio input and output connections. Users that need more Fire wire or USB ports can add Fire wire or USB expansion cards, which provide additional connections.

Most expansion cards are installed in PCI slots. This includes variations of PCI, such as PCI-X and PCI Express. Graphics cards may also be installed in an AGP slot, which is designed specifically for video cards. Since expansion cards require open slots, they can only be installed in computers that have available expansion slots. Therefore, computers like the Apple iMac and other all-in-one machines cannot accept expansion cards. Computer towers, however, often have two or three open expansion slots, and can accept multiple cards.

Some Popular Cards used in a Computer

Sound Card

Also known as an audio card, this type of expansion card deals with everything to do with sounds and audio signals within the computer that are under the control of programs on the computer. This can include allowing applications on the computer to play music, programs which edit videos or audio, presentation software, games equipment and any other type of program which plays audio.

The ability to play sound is often integrated into the motherboard of the computer, however this is not necessarily the best way to achieve high-quality sound. Sound expansion cards convert digital sound data into analog format, which is then relayed to an external device capable of playing sound such as headphones or a speaker. Sound cards also need to be capable of processing multiple sounds at the same time, splitting them up into audio channels. This allows different sound configurations to be produced, such as surround sound and stereo sound. Modern sound cards providing advanced sound mixing such as this are sometimes referred to as Hardware Audio Accelerators and can provide features such as positional audio and 3D sound.

Video Card

A video card is more often called a graphics card or display card, and is responsible for generating images to a visual display such as a computer monitor or laptop screen. Although all motherboards have some degree of integrated graphics, a dedicated video card allows for higher quality graphics and better speeds. Video cards can offer such functions as the rendering of high-quality 3D and 2D graphics, the ability to connect to a TV and the ability to display graphics across multiple display screens.

A dedicated video card comes with its own RAM and cooling system, decreasing the reliance on the motherboard and allowing more processing power to be sectioned off solely for the display and processing of graphics. This can also help the computer as a whole to run faster and more efficiently as less system RAM power is being taken up by high demand graphics programs.

Network Card

Often called a Network Interface Card or LAN Adapter, a network card is an expansion card which allows a computer to connect to a computer network such as a Local Area Network or Wide Area Network. This type of expansion card was most popular in early models of computers, in more modern machines almost all computers have a network interface built directly into the motherboard.

This is because it is cheaper and more convenient to use the Ethernet standard connection, which is easy to install as a chip straight from the motherboard and does not necessarily require a separate expansion card any more. For this reason, separate network cards are all but obsolete in newer computers other than in exceptional circumstances where a different type of network connection is required.

Serial and Parallel Cards

Serial and Parallel expansion cards are used to provide additional connection ports to a computer, specifically to provide either parallel or serial port connections. A parallel port is only able to transmit data one way to a secondary device, commonly a printer or similar, using a dual data transmission system.

This type of one-way transmission was also used for older external storage devices. Serial ports are able to process data in a two-way direction, and are often slightly slower than parallel ports due to the more accurate transmission of data they send. Both serial ports and parallel ports have been mostly superseded by the faster and more efficient USB port in modern computers.

USB Card

A USB expansion card is used to provide additional connection ports to a computer by connecting the card to the motherboard. USB is short for Universal Serial Bus, and is the most common type of port found in modern computers. Peripherals such as printers, keyboards, printers, removable flash drives and mice can be attached to the computer.

USB cards are necessary if a computer does not already have this capability, or to add additional ports for more use of external devices at once. USB connections are faster at transmitting data and quickly became a general industry standard for cross-platform communication.

Firewire Card

A firewire card is used to provide computers with an IEEE 1394 interface connection, also known as a firewire. The term was coined by Apple in the early 1990s, and the ports themselves have been included on most apple computers since the year 2000. Recently Apple has begun replacing this port with the Thunderbolt interface on all modern Mac computers. The port itself is very similar to a USB connection, although USB is much more popular across a range of cross-platform devices and the two are not interchangeable.

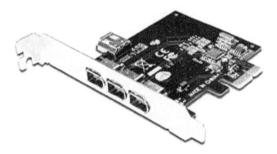

Storage Card

A storage card, often also called a flash memory card or simply a memory card that is connected to a computer in order to provide users with extra space to store their data on. This can include data such as music, pictures, text or video and is transferable to other devices such as digital cameras and mobile phones. These cards vary in both physical size and data capacity, and are constantly being developed and upgraded. Some of the most common on the market today include the Secure Digital (SD) Card, the Mini/Micro SD Card, and the MultiMediaCard (MMC).

Data secured on storage cards is very stable and not in much danger of being lost or damaged outside of any actual physical damage to the card itself. Cards are much smaller physically than they were even as recently as 10 years ago, and some such as the Compact Flash card have been made almost obsolete by the introduction of more stable non-volatile memory devices. Storage cards also have an advantage over hard disk drives as they are very portable, allow immediate access when booted up and do not require cooling. There is a huge market among users for small, lightweight and low power storage devices with increasingly large amounts of data storage capacities.

Modem Card

A modem card allows a computer to send an analog carrier signal carrying digital information, and decodes the reverse of this signal in return to reproduce the original digital data. The most common way of doing this in the past was by using electrical signals transmitted over telephone lines, although more modern systems such as satellite, WiFi, mobile phones and mobile broadband modems also use this type of communication. Wireless modems can be embedded inside of a device or be external to it, and can be locked to only receive certain types of frequency signals, for example only those from one particular network provider.

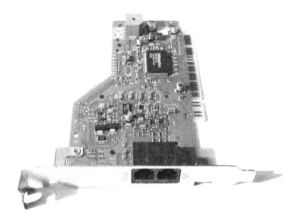

Modern broadband modems are not limited to using telephone line, with newer types using satellite, television cables and power lines to transmit data signals. These are much more advanced than the older 'dial-up' style of modem, with much faster transmission of data and a hugely expanded range of channels available for use simultaneously. Modems are usually classified by how much data they are able to transfer in a set amount of time, generally bits per second (bps) or bytes per second (B/s), and this data can be used to compare modems when buying or choosing between them.

Wireless/cellular Card

A wireless card is used to provide a computer with the capability of connecting to a radio-based computer network rather that one which is connected using wires. These can come preinstalled inside of a computer or laptop or be external, come separately, although almost all modern devices come with this already included inside of the computer. The most common use of this card is to allow a device to connect to WiFi, using a wireless router or access point. The WiFi point receives data through wires and transmits it using radio waves, for a wireless card inside of a device to pick up and decode, as well as receiving the signals in the opposite direction.

The signals transmitted are on a different frequency to other radio wave transmissions, such as those used by radios and mobile phones, and are able to handle much more data than these other types. Wireless cards can also move around onto different frequency channels if one becomes too full with users, helping to make sure the transmission of data is always fast and efficient. Wireless cards can come in several different types, including PCI, mini PCI and PCIe, different ones of which are more suitable for different devices. Some USB devices also exist which are capable of acting as a wireless card and allowing a device to connect to WiFi or Bluetooth networks.

TV Tuner Card

A Television Tuner card is a card which is inserted into a computer to allow a device to receive television signals that would not otherwise be suited to picking them up. Cards are usually either PCI, mini PCI or PCIe, or sometimes as an external USB device. Most cards have an inbuilt processor to free up space from the system's CPU and ease the pressure on the computer. Cards can be either analog or digital depending on which type of television the user wishes to view, and many hybrid tuners exist which are able to switch between the two types. High-end tuner cards often include a special chip to encode and decode the data being transmitted, however smaller and cheaper cards are less likely to have this capability due to the high power it takes to run them.

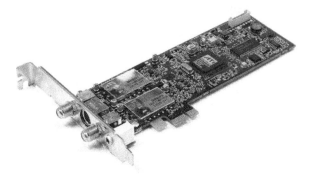

Many TV tuner cards also include a form of flash memory which allows them to store several different types of decoding software, meaning the tuner card can be used in many different countries and with different video formats without reformatting the system to recognize the new data.

Video Capture Card

A video capture card is used to allow a computer to convert an analog video signal into a digital video data form. Many TV tuner cards double up as video capture cards, allowing the user to record TV transmissions as they are being broadcast and viewed.

The inclusion of a dedicated video card is important in a system as the circuitry required to convert analog video to digital video is quite specialised and high-performance. Data must be digitised and modified to account for colour differences and encoded to a completely different format, as well as separating the different aspects of composite video if this is captured.

System Memory

The system memory is the place where the computer holds current programs and data that are in use. The term "memory" is somewhat ambiguous; it can refer to many different parts of the PC because there are so many different kinds of memory that a PC uses. However, when used by itself, "memory" usually refers to the main system memory, which holds the instructions that the processor executes and the data that those instructions work with. Your system memory is an important part of the main processing subsystem of the PC, tied in with the processor, cache, motherboard and chipset.

Memory plays a significant role in the following important aspects of your computer system:

- Performance: The amount and type of system memory you have is an important contributing factor to overall performance. In many ways, it is more important than the processor, because insufficient memory can cause a processor to work at 50% or even more below its performance potential. This is an important point that is often overlooked.

- Software Support: Newer programs require more memory than old ones. More memory will give you access to programs that you cannot use with a lesser amount.

- Reliability and Stability: Bad memory is a leading cause of mysterious system problems. Ensuring you have high-quality memory will result in a PC that runs smoothly and exhibits fewer problems. Also, even high-quality memory will not work well if you use the wrong kind.

- Upgradability: There are many different types of memory available, and some are more universal than others. Making a wise choice can allow you to migrate your memory to a future system or continue to use it after you upgrade your motherboard.

Hard Disk Drive

Hard disk drives have been the dominant type of storage since the early days of computers. A hard disk drive consists of a rigid disc made with non-magnetic material, which is coated with a thin layer of magnetic material. Data is stored by magnetizing this thin film. The disk spins at a high speed and a magnetic head mounted on a moving arm is used to read and write data. A typical hard disk drive operates at a speed of 7,200 rpm (rotations per minute), so you will often see this number as part of the technical specifications of a computer. The spinning of the disk is also the source of the humming noise of a computer, although most modern hard disk drives are fairly quiet.

In general, hard disk drives are very robust and can be used for many years without problems. However, hard disk drives can fail and one of the most common reasons is a head crash. This occurs when the magnetic head scratches the magnetic film. This typically happens as a result of a physical shock, like dropping a computer while it's on. When your hard drives experience mechanical failure you can often hear a grinding or scratching sound. Such a crash results in data loss since the magnetic film gets damaged. It is, therefore, always a good idea to have a backup copy of the important files on your hard drive.

Solid State Drive

An SSD (solid-state drive) is a type of nonvolatile storage media that stores persistent data on solid-state flash memory. Two key components make up an SSD: a flash controller and NAND flash memory chips. The architectural configuration of the SSD controller is optimized to deliver high read and write performance for both sequential and random data requests. SSDs are sometimes referred to as flash drives or solid-state disks.

Unlike a hard disk drive (HDD), an SSD has no moving parts to break or spin up or down. A traditional HDD consists of a spinning disk with a read/write head on a mechanical arm called an actuator. The HDD mechanism and hard disk are packaged as an integrated unit. Businesses and computer manufacturers have used spinning disk historically, owing to their lower unit cost and higher average durability, although SSDs are now common in desktop and laptop PCs.

A spinning HDD reads and writes data magnetically, which is one of the oldest storage media in continuous use. The magnetic properties, however, can lead to mechanical breakdowns. An SSD, conversely, reads and writes the data to a substrate of interconnected flash memory chips, which are fabricated out of silicon. Manufacturers build SSDs by stacking chips in a grid to achieve varying densities.

To prevent volatility, SSD manufacturers design the devices with floating gate transistors (FGRs) to hold the electrical charge. This allows an SSD to retain stored data even when it is not connected to a power source. Each FGR contains a single bit of data, designated either as a 1 for a charged cell or a 0 if the cell has no electrical charge.

Uses of SSD

SSDs provide faster storage and other performance benefits than fixed disk. Businesses with a rapidly expanding need for higher input/output (I/O) have fueled the development and adoption of SSDs. Because SSDs offer lower latency than HDDs, they can efficiently handle both heavy read and random workloads. That lower latency stems from the ability of a flash SSD to read data directly and immediately from a specific flash SSD cell location.

An all-flash array takes only SSDs as storage. A hybrid flash array combines disk storage and SSDs with the flash used to cache hot data that is later written to disk or tape. In server-side flash configurations, SSDs are installed in x86 computers to support targeted workloads, sometimes in conjunction with networked storage.

High-performance servers, laptops, desktops or any application that needs to deliver information in real time or near real time can benefit from solid-state drive technology. Those characteristics make enterprise SSDs suitable to offload reads from transaction-heavy databases, to alleviate boot storms with virtual desktop infrastructure (VDI), or inside a storage array to stage hot data locally for off-site storage in a hybrid cloud scenario.

SSDs are used in a range of consumer devices, including computer games, digital cameras, digital music players, laptops, PCs, smartphones, tablets and thumb drives. These devices are not engineered to provide the same level of performance or durability as an enterprise SSD.

Features of a SSD

Several features characterize the design of an SSD. Because it uses no moving parts, an SSD is not subject to the mechanical failure that occurs with HDDs. It is also quieter and consumes less power than its disk counterpart. And because SSDs weigh less than hard drives, they are good fits for laptop and mobile computing devices.

In addition, the SSD controller software includes predictive analytics that alert a user in advance of a potential drive failure. Because flash memory is malleable, all-flash array vendors can manipulate the usable storage capacity with data reduction techniques.

SSDs usually are built with single-level cell (SLC) or MLC flash memory. SLC drives store 1 bit of data per cell of flash media. MLC-based SSDs double the drive capacity by writing data in two segments. Newer SSDs, known as TLC, are being marketed that store 3 bits of data per flash cell. TLC is less expensive than SLC or MLC, which makes it an attractive option for manufacturers of consumer-based flash devices. TLC-based SSDs deliver more flash capacity and are cheaper than MLC or SLC, albeit with a higher likelihood for bit rot due to having eight states within the cell.

Input Device

The Input devices of computer systems are electromagnetic devices which acknowledge information and accept data or set of instruction from outside the world and translate this data into machine meaningful and readable form. Computer Input devices acts as a medium of communication and correspondence between computer and the outside world.

With the help and assistance of these devices user can enter the data, and later the data can be store in computer memory for further additional processing and preparing. After the processing and handling are finished the desired and converted outcome can be obtained with the help and assistance of output devices of computers. Keyboard and mouse are the general examples of input devices of computer system, there are several more devices which are used for input, with the use of these devices user are able to enter text, images, audio etc.

Following are some of the important input devices which are used in a computer –

Keyboard	Graphic Tablet
Mouse	Microphone
Joy Stick	Magnetic Ink Card Reader(MICR)
Light pen	Optical Character Reader(OCR)
Track Ball	Bar Code Reader
Scanner	Optical Mark Reader(OMR)

Keyboard

Keyboard is the most common and very popular input device which helps to input data to the computer. The layout of the keyboard is like that of traditional typewriter, although there are some additional keys provided for performing additional functions.

Keyboards are of two sizes 84 keys or 101/102 keys, but now keyboards with 104 keys or 108 keys are also available for Windows and Internet.

The keys on the keyboard are as follows –

S.No	Keys & Description
1	**Typing Keys** These keys include the letter keys (A-Z) and digit keys (09) which generally give the same layout as that of typewriters.
2	**Numeric Keypad** It is used to enter the numeric data or cursor movement. Generally, it consists of a set of 17 keys that are laid out in the same configuration used by most adding machines and calculators.

3	**Function Keys**	
	The twelve function keys are present on the keyboard which are arranged in a row at the top of the keyboard. Each function key has a unique meaning and is used for some specific purpose.	
4	**Control keys**	
	These keys provide cursor and screen control. It includes four directional arrow keys. Control keys also include Home, End, Insert, Delete, Page Up, Page Down, Control(Ctrl), Alternate(Alt), Escape(Esc).	
5	**Special Purpose Keys**	
	Keyboard also contains some special purpose keys such as Enter, Shift, Caps Lock, Num Lock, Space bar, Tab, and Print Screen.	

Mouse

Mouse is the most popular pointing device. It is a very famous cursor-control device having a small palm size box with a round ball at its base, which senses the movement of the mouse and sends corresponding signals to the CPU when the mouse buttons are pressed.

Generally, it has two buttons called the left and the right button and a wheel is present between the buttons. A mouse can be used to control the position of the cursor on the screen, but it cannot be used to enter text into the computer.

Advantages

- Easy to use
- Not very expensive
- Moves the cursor faster than the arrow keys of the keyboard

Joystick

Joystick is also a pointing device, which is used to move the cursor position on a monitor screen. It is a stick having a spherical ball at its both lower and upper ends. The lower spherical ball moves in a socket. The joystick can be moved in all four directions.

The function of the joystick is similar to that of a mouse. It is mainly used in Computer Aided Designing (CAD) and playing computer games.

Light Pen

Light pen is a pointing device similar to a pen. It is used to select a displayed menu item or draw pictures on the monitor screen. It consists of a photocell and an optical system placed in a small tube.

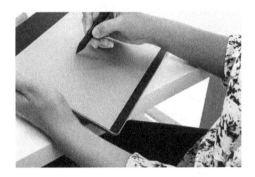

When the tip of a light pen is moved over the monitor screen and the pen button is pressed, its photocell sensing element detects the screen location and sends the corresponding signal to the CPU.

Track Ball

Track ball is an input device that is mostly used in notebook or laptop computer, instead of a mouse. This is a ball which is half inserted and by moving fingers on the ball, the pointer can be moved.

Since the whole device is not moved, a track ball requires less space than a mouse. A track ball comes in various shapes like a ball, a button, or a square.

Scanner

Scanner is an input device, which works more like a photocopy machine. It is used when some information is available on paper and it is to be transferred to the hard disk of the computer for further manipulation.

Scanner captures images from the source which are then converted into a digital form that can be stored on the disk. These images can be edited before they are printed.

Digitizer

Digitizer is an input device which converts analog information into digital form. Digitizer can convert a signal from the television or camera into a series of numbers that could be stored in a computer. They can be used by the computer to create a picture of whatever the camera had been pointed at.

Digitizer is also known as Tablet or Graphics Tablet as it converts graphics and pictorial data into binary inputs. A graphic tablet as digitizer is used for fine works of drawing and image manipulation applications.

Microphone

Microphone is an input device to input sound that is then stored in a digital form.

The microphone is used for various applications such as adding sound to a multimedia presentation or for mixing music.

Magnetic Ink Card Reader (MICR)

MICR input device is generally used in banks as there are large number of cheques to be processed every day. The bank's code number and cheque number are printed on the cheques with a special type of ink that contains particles of magnetic material that are machine readable.

This reading process is called Magnetic Ink Character Recognition (MICR). The main advantage of MICR is that it is fast and less error prone.

Optical Character Reader (OCR)

OCR is an input device used to read a printed text.

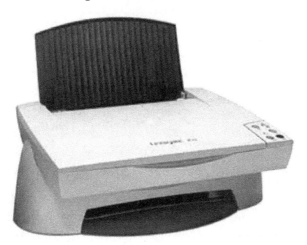

OCR scans the text optically, character by character, converts them into a machine readable code, and stores the text on the system memory.

Bar Code Readers

Bar Code Reader is a device used for reading bar coded data (data in the form of light and dark lines). Bar coded data is generally used in labelling goods, numbering the books, etc. It may be a handheld scanner or may be embedded in a stationary scanner.

Bar Code Reader scans a bar code image, converts it into an alphanumeric value, which is then fed to the computer that the bar code reader is connected to.

Optical Mark Reader (OMR)

OMR is a special type of optical scanner used to recognize the type of mark made by pen or pencil. It is used where one out of a few alternatives is to be selected and marked.

It is specially used for checking the answer sheets of examinations having multiple choice questions.

Output Device

An output device is any peripheral that receives data from a computer, usually for display, projection, or physical reproduction. For example, the image shows an inkjet printer, an output device that can make a hard copy of any information shown on your monitor, which is another example of an output device. Monitors and printers are two of the most common output devices used with a computer.

A computer can still work without an output device. However, without an output device, you'd have no way of determining what the computer is doing, if there are errors, or if it needs additional input. For example, you can disconnect your monitor from your computer, and it will still function, but it's not going to be very useful.

Following are some of the important output devices used in a computer.

- Monitors
- Graphic plotter
- Printer

Monitors

Monitors, commonly called as Visual Display Unit (VDU), are the main output device of a computer. It forms images from tiny dots, called pixels that are arranged in a rectangular form. The sharpness of the image depends upon the number of pixels.

There are two kinds of viewing screen used for monitors.

- Cathode-ray tube (CRT)
- Flat-panel display

Cathode-ray Tube (CRT) Monitor

The CRT display is made up of small picture elements called pixels. The smaller the pixels, the better the image clarity or resolution. It takes more than one illuminated pixel to form a whole character, such as the letter 'e' in the word help.

A finite number of characters can be displayed on a screen at once. The screen can be divided into a series of character boxes - fixed location on the screen where a standard character can be placed. Most screens are capable of displaying 80 characters of data horizontally and 25 lines vertically.

There are some disadvantages of CRT –

- Large in size
- High power consumption

Flat-panel Display Monitor

The flat-panel display refers to a class of video devices that have reduced volume, weight and power requirement in comparison to the CRT. You can hang them on walls or wear them on your wrists. Current uses of flat-panel displays include calculators, video games, monitors, laptop computer, and graphics display.

The flat-panel display is divided into two categories:

- Emissive Displays – Emissive displays are devices that convert electrical energy into light. For example, plasma panel and LED (Light-Emitting Diodes).

- Non-Emissive Displays – Non-emissive displays use optical effects to convert sunlight or light from some other source into graphics patterns. For example, LCD (Liquid-Crystal Device).

Printers

Printer is an output device, which is used to print information on paper.

There are two types of printers:

- Impact Printers
- Non-Impact Printers

Impact Printers

Impact printers print the characters by striking them on the ribbon, which is then pressed on the paper.

Characteristics of Impact Printers are the following:

- Very low consumable costs
- Very noisy
- Useful for bulk printing due to low cost
- There is physical contact with the paper to produce an image

These printers are of two types:

- Character printers
- Line printers

Character Printers

Character printers are the printers which print one character at a time.

These are further divided into two types:

- Dot Matrix Printer (DMP)
- Daisy Wheel

Dot Matrix Printer

In the market, one of the most popular printers is Dot Matrix Printer. These printers are popular because of their ease of printing and economical price. Each character printed is in the form of pattern of dots and head consists of a Matrix of Pins of size (5*7, 7*9, 9*7 or 9*9) which come out to form a character which is why it is called Dot Matrix Printer.

Advantages

- Inexpensive
- Widely used
- Other language characters can be printed

Disadvantages

- Slow speed
- Poor quality

Daisy Wheel

Head is lying on a wheel and pins corresponding to characters are like petals of Daisy (flower) which is why it is called Daisy Wheel Printer. These printers are generally used for word-processing in offices that require a few letters to be sent here and there with very nice quality.

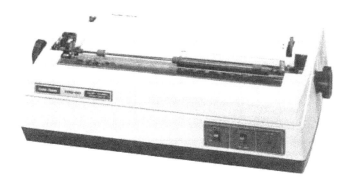

Advantages

- More reliable than DMP
- Better quality
- Fonts of character can be easily changed

Disadvantages

- Slower than DMP
- Noisy
- More expensive than DMP

Line Printers

Line printers are the printers which print one line at a time.

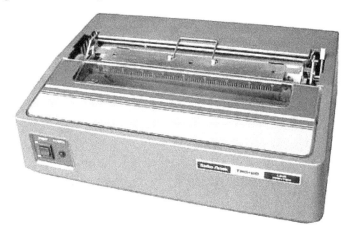

These are of two types:

- Drum Printer
- Chain Printer

Drum Printer

This printer is like a drum in shape hence it is called drum printer. The surface of the drum is divided into a number of tracks. Total tracks are equal to the size of the paper, i.e. for a paper width of 132 characters, drum will have 132 tracks. A character set is embossed on the track. Different character sets available in the market are 48 character set, 64 and 96 characters set. One rotation of drum prints one line. Drum printers are fast in speed and can print 300 to 2000 lines per minute.

Advantages

- Very high speed

Disadvantages

- Very expensive
- Characters fonts cannot be changed

Chain Printer

In this printer, a chain of character sets is used, hence it is called Chain Printer. A standard character set may have 48, 64, or 96 characters.

Advantages

- Character fonts can easily be changed.
- Different languages can be used with the same printer.

Disadvantages

- Noisy

Non-impact Printers

Non-impact printers print the characters without using the ribbon. These printers print a complete page at a time, thus they are also called as Page Printers.

These printers are of two types:

- Laser Printers
- Inkjet Printers

Characteristics of Non-impact Printers

- Faster than impact printers
- They are not noisy
- High quality
- Supports many fonts and different character size

Laser Printers

These are non-impact page printers. They use laser lights to produce the dots needed to form the characters to be printed on a page.

Advantages

- Very high speed
- Very high quality output
- Good graphics quality
- Supports many fonts and different character size

Disadvantages

- Expensive
- Cannot be used to produce multiple copies of a document in a single printing

Inkjet Printers

Inkjet printers are non-impact character printers based on a relatively new technology. They print characters by spraying small drops of ink onto paper. Inkjet printers produce high quality output with presentable features.

They make less noise because no hammering is done and these have many styles of printing modes available. Color printing is also possible. Some models of Inkjet printers can produce multiple copies of printing also.

Advantages

- High quality printing
- More reliable

Disadvantages

- Expensive as the cost per page is high
- Slow as compared to laser printer

References

- The-Four-Main-Categories-Of-Computer-Hardware-Parts: turbofuture.com, Retrieved 21 July 2018
- What-is-a-computer-case-2618149: lifewire.com, Retrieved 26 May 2018
- Components-of-cpu-and-their-functions: csetutor.com, Retrieved 16 March 2018
- The-motherboard-components, computers: turbofuture.com, Retrieved 15 June 2018
- Expansion-cards, free-comptia-aplus-study-guide, comptia-certification: Retrieved 14 May 2018
- Input-devices-of-computer-system, computer-fundamentals: chtips.com, Retrieved 19 July 2018

Networking in Computer

A computer network is a telecommunications network that allows nodes to share resources. The topics elucidated in this chapter cover some of the important concepts relating to networking in computers, such as wireless network, network packet, networking hardware and Internet protocol address.

Computer Network

A computer network can be defined as a collection of interconnected computers in such a way that they share resources. A computer system only referred to a group of the computers and hardware components interconnected by communicating channels that allow sharing of resources and information. Technically, If at least one process in one computer can send or receive data to/from at least one process residing on a remote computer, then two machines are said to be a network.

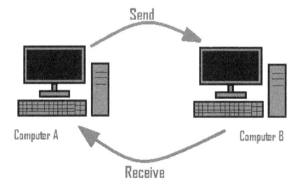

Any computer that engages with another computer by Sending/Receiving messages is supposed to be in a network. A system classifies according to a wide variety of characteristics such as, "Medium used to transport data," "Communication protocols used," "Scale,"Topology" and "Organizational scope."

Protocol

Protocols are the Rules and data format for exchange of information between computers. And all the computers agree to follow these rules. These rules are:

- OSI which stands for Open System Interconnection.

- TCP/IP is another important protocol that computers use to exchange information between computers.

Components of a Computer Network:

Server: Server or Domain Controller is a powerful computer used in Domain network to manage and control all hardware and software, resources of a network. The server uses the server OS (Operating System), e.g., Win Server 2012. There are two types of Domain Controllers (Servers):

- PDC (Primary Domain Controller): A type of server that manages and controls the resources of a whole network. One domain network can have only one PDC.

- BDC (Backup Domain Controller): BDC is a server that keeps a complete backup of PDC. In the case of failure of PDC the BDC act as PDC. A network can have more than one BDC's according to requirement.

Client: A type of computer in a network that can request for resources to the server. There are two types of clients.

Intelligent Client

This kind of client can only process data; they don't have the ability to store the data.

Smart Client:

These types of consumer benefit from both, they can process as well as store the data.

- Peer: Peer is a type of computer in a workgroup network that can act as a server as well as a client at the same time. Meaning, a peer can request and process a request simultaneously. Hence, it can act as both client and server.

- Media: Network Media or medium is the path through which data travels on a network.

Two Types of Media

Guided Media

The media that has physical existence is called guided media or bounded media. Guided media consists of the following types of cables: Coaxial cable, twisted pair cable, and Fiber Optic cable.

Non Guided Media

A type of media which has no physical existence (Wireless) as a guided media. Some of the examples of Non-guided media are Radio Waves, Microwaves, and Infrared waves.

Connecting Devices

These devices are used to connect a network media together. They act as a middleware between two computers or networks. The network contains the following connecting devices:

- Connectors
- Hub
- Switch

- Router

- B-Router

- Bridge

- Gateways

Types of Computer Network:

Personal Area Network (PAN): A personal area network (PAN), is a computer network used for communication among computer and different technological devices close to one or two people, usually at home. For example Computer, Printer, Scanner, Gaming Consoles, Cell phone, PDA.

Local Area Network (LAN): A local area network is a network in which two or more devices are connected locally. LAN covers short distance such as a building, Campus, a hotel, etc. Devices are connected either wirelessly or through a high-speed cable called Ethernet. This ethernet cable is a very high-speed cable with the speed of 100 MB/Sec. LAN has a slight chance of errors. LAN is highly reliable. The only drawback is it covers a small geographical area.

Home Network: A Home network is a very similar to LAN, but this LAN has a primary use for residentially. A Home network is used to connect devices in a home, such as a wireless printer that is attached to a computer and mobile device to print or scan wirelessly anywhere in the home. The source of sharing is through DSL (Digital Subscriber Line) provider. Usually, a smaller number of devices can be connected to this type of network.

Storage Area Network: Storage Area Network (SAN), Unlike other networks, this network allows a user to access and store data. SAN's are primarily used to make storage devices such as Disk arrays, and they are connected to the server giving an impression as if they are connected.

Campus Area Network: A Campus area network also known as corporate area network is just an interconnection of multiple Local Area Network (LAN). A CAN or campus area network spans over a shorter distance than Wide Area Network (WAN) and Metropolitan Area Network (MAN).

Metropolitan Area Network (MAN): A metropolitan area network spans over even larger area, usually covers city, large campus, even states. Metropolitan Area Network (MAN) comparatively spans over a larger area than Local Area Network (LAN). On the other hand, this spanned area is but shorter when compared with Wide area network.

Wide Area Network (WAN): A wide area network (WAN) is spread over greater regions. WAN can be span over a city as big as Toronto; WAN can also span over a whole Country, as big as, Australia, It can span over even an intercontinental distance. Wide Area Network, as the name suggests, is the most extensive network available.

Enterprise Area Network: Enterprise area network is used to interconnect various enterprise websites, for example, Head offices, remote offices, shops, etc. in order to share resources. Enterprise area network act as a backbone for business communication.

Virtual Private Network: A Virtual private network act as a private network, It allows users to send/Receive information publicly as if they were directly connected to each other. VPN provide security over network to its users.

Internetwork: Internetwork uses gateways to connect computer networks having a common method of routing information between networks. The internet is an aggregation of many connected internetworks, spanning the earth.

- Intranet: Intranet is a set of networks, which is only available to organization's staff. It is a private network.

- Extranet: Extranet is a system that provides limited access to an authorized person, without giving much of the organization's detail.

Internet: Internet is an agreement between millions of people using the network. They agree to connect to other network and share resources. It is successor of the ARPANET. Internet is also referred to connection of connection.

Network Media:

A network media acts like a path through which data flows on a network. Web media has two main types:

- Guided Media: A network media that has physical existence guided media consists many types of cables. Following are the types of cables:

  ○ Co-axial copper wire.

  ○ Twisted Pair cable.

  ○ Fiber Optic cable.

  ○ Transatlantic cable.

- Non Guided Media: Non guided media contains the following wireless media:

  ○ Radio Waves.

  ○ Microwaves such as Satellite waves, terrestrial waves.

  ○ Infrared waves.

Network Topologies

Physical layout of a network is called a network topology. A network topology refers to how computers are connected.

Network Topology

Network topology is the arrangement of the different networking elements like network links, computers, switches, nodes, Wi-Fi access points, laptops and other network devices in a computer network.

There are two types of Network Topologies:

- Physical Network topology and,

- Logical Network topology

Physical Topology

A Physical topology defines how all the network devices are connected physically in a computer network. It mostly defines the physical connections among the devices.

Logical Topology

A logical topology defines the logical connectivity of network devices on a computer network. So, it might happen that the devices connected in one type of physical topology might have different underlying logical topology.

If we elaborate more on the physical topology, it is essentially the placement of the various network components in a computer like the placement of the devices, the connection among the devices, installation of the cables etc. On the other hand, logical connection defines how data flows among the devices.

For example, let say there are five devices (A, B, C, D, and E) that are connected in a row. This configuration of network devices might look more like a Bus topology. But let's say device A can directly transmit the data to the device E. That means it looks more like a Circle which a Ring topology logically but a bus topology physically.

Bus Network

A bus network topology relies on a common foundation (which may take the form of a main cable or backbone for the system) to connect all devices on the network. This main cable or bus forms a common medium of communication which any device may tap into or attach itself to via an interface connector. If only two endpoints form a network by connecting to a single cable, this is known as a linear bus topology.

All devices on the network are effectively connected to each other, so any communication sent onto the bus by a device is visible to all the other devices – but only the specific device for which the message is intended should access and process it. Data is typically transmitted in only one direction.

Bus network topologies based on Ethernet cabling are relatively easy and economical to install, though runs are limited by the maximum available length of cable. Expansion may be achieved by joining two bus cables together, but this topology works best with a limited number of devices (typically 12 devices or less, on a single bus). The system relies on its main cable for stability – and if this goes down, so does the entire network.

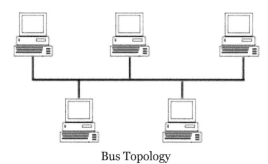

Bus Topology

Advantages of Bus Topology

1. It is easy to connect a device to the network

If the computer or peripheral has the appropriate connection mechanism, then it can be easily added to the network. The new device connects to the linear bus topology and becomes part of the network immediately. For those who need a temporary network that can be setup quickly, there isn't a better option that is available right now. If several users need mutual access to a printer, adding the printer to the network meets that need immediately.

2. It is cheaper than other network options:

Compared to ring, star, or hybrid networks, bus topology is the cheapest to implement. That is because it requires less cable length than the other network options. Although terminators are required at both ends of the backbone to ensure the network can function properly, it is still easy and affordable to install when a small network is required.

3. The failure of one station does not affect the rest of the network:

If one computer or peripheral should fail when using bus topology, the rest of the network is not affected by this change in performance. The linear nature of the network means that each unit transmits to the backbone and that data is then available to the other units that remain connected. This makes it an effective way to share uninterrupted communication.

4. No hubs or switches are required:

With bus topology, the linear nature of the network allows data to flow freely throughout the network. Although this limits outside connections, it does create a localized network that can effectively work with each terminal that has been connected. A central file server is used instead of hubs and switches, which means there are fewer points of potential failure that must be managed with this setup compared to others.

5. Extensions can be made to the network:

The size and scope of bus topology is naturally limited. It can, however, be extended quite easily. Joining cable with a repeater or connector allows for additional peripherals or computers to be added to the network. Although this can increase the number of packet collisions that may occur, it is a simplified solution that can get people up and working quickly and for a minimal overall cost.

6. Multiple nodes can be installed without difficulty:

For a small network, another option that is often considered is point-to-point topology. Bus topology has an advantage here because it supports multiple nodes instead of just 2 nodes. That is how the original form of an Ethernet network came about. 10BASE2, which is popularly known as "thinnet," utilizes bus topology to create a local area network that can be used to form departments or working groups.

7. Multiple peripherals can be supported through bus topology:

Routers, printers, and other data devices can be connected to this network in addition to computers or terminals. This can increase the speed of productivity because instead of sending commands to a centralized network, a command can be sent directly to the needed peripheral. A print command from a computer, for example, can stay local and improve production speed, which keeps workers more productive over time.

8. Wiring terminators take no power requirements:

The terminators that are used for most bus topology systems are passive devices. They're made of resistors and capacitors, which means there isn't a power requirement that must be met. This makes it easy to install a simple LAN at virtually any location where networking would be beneficial to a department or working group.

Disadvantages of Bus Topology

1. Additional devices slow the network down:

Because bus topology links every computer and peripheral through a backbone, additional devices will slow down the entire network since only one cable is being used. That also places the entire network at-risk should something happen to that cable. If the backbone is damaged for some reason, it can either cause the entire network to fail or have it split into two networks instead of one.

2. Size limitations are always present:

A backbone has limited length, which means there is a maximum number of computers and peripherals that can be added to the network. That size limitation also increases the risk that collisions will occur within the bus topology because communication spacing is at such a premium.

3. Security options are limited with bus topology:

Any computer that is connected to the backbone of a bus topology network will be able to see all the data transmissions that occur on all the other computers. Each terminal has full access to every other terminal. That means security options are difficult to install on such a setup because everyone can see what everyone else is doing.

4. Maintenance costs are higher:

Although bus topology is cheaper to setup, the costs of maintaining this network are higher in the long run. It may be a good network for those with small, short-term needs. Because it is not scalable and the costs increase over time, however, it may not be the best choice for those who anticipate growth occurring within their network.

5. A break in the backbone can cause an entire network to collapse:

Because the size of bus topology is limited, a break in the backbone causes the entire network to collapse in some way. Full communication cannot be restored until the issue is repaired or the backbone is completely replaced. That means it cannot be used as a stand-alone solution. A breakage event will cause any computer or peripheral to lose its communication with devices on the other side of the network. Without a second terminator in place, the likely result is network collapse.

6. The quality of the data is placed at-risk on large bus topology setups:

In addition to the speed issues that occur with a larger network using bus topology, there are data quality issues that must be considered. When data packets collide with one another, the outcome is data loss. Increasing the number of nodes that are present on the network has a direct impact on the quality of communication that occurs. That is why the size of these networks is naturally limited.

7. Bus termination issues can lead to network issues:

Communication problems in bus topology can occur when there is improper termination. Terminators are required by ISO 11898 to be at the two extreme ends of the network, which tends to be the controller node and the node which is furthest away from the controller. Even if termination is not appropriately used, certain baud rates can still be successful in their port-to-port communication, which can lead to a lengthy identification process of the network issue.

8. The computers may share data, but they don't communicate:

Bus topology would be much more efficient if the computers on the network could coordinate with one another regarding transmission times. They do not coordinate, however, which means multiple transmissions can occur simultaneously and this creates heavy network traffic with a high potential of data loss. Even if the backbone is extended with repeaters to boost the signal, there is too much simplicity in this network setup to make it an effective system for a large setup.

9. A T-connection failure immediately limits access:

Because each node is independently connected to the backbone, bus topology doesn't provide a secondary connection resource. If there is a T-connection failure for the connection, then there is no way for data to be shared along the network or to the computer or peripheral that has been separated from the backbone.

Star Network

A star topology is a network topology in which all the network nodes are individually connected to a central switch, hub or computer which acts as a central point of communication to pass on the messages.

In a star topology, there are different nodes called hosts and there is a central point of communication called server or hub. Each host or computer is individually connected to the central hub. We can also term the server as the root and peripheral hosts as the leaves.

In this topology, if nodes want to communicate with a central node, then they pass on the message to the central server and the central server forwards their messages to the different nodes. Thus, they form a topology like the representation of a star.

Communication in a Start Network

Let's say all the computers of a floor are connected to a common hub or switch. The switch maintains a CAM table in this case. The CAM table is Content Addressable Memory where hardware addresses of the all the connected devices are stored inside a memory in the switch.

For example, if computer A wants to send a data packet to computer B then computer A will forward the message to the switch. The switch will check the address of the destination computer and forward the message to the same.

In the case of a hub, a hub has no memory of its own. So when computer A sends a message to computer B, then hub announces "Hello all the ports connected to me, I have got a packet for this address. Who of you has this address?" This procedure is called ARP (Address Resolution Protocol) and using this network protocol the hub is able to find the address of the intended machine and hence, it transfers the packet to the destination machine.

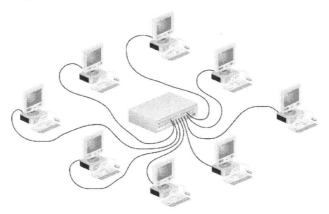

Advantages of Star Network

Isolation of devices: each device is isolated by the link that connects it to the hub. By so doing it makes the isolation of the individual devices simple. This isolation nature also prevents any non-centralized failure from affecting the network. In a star network, a cable failure will isolate the workstation that it links to the central computer, but only that workstation will be isolated. All the other workstations will continue to function normally, except that they will not be able to communicate with the isolated workstation.

Simplicity: The topology is easy to understand, establish, and navigate. The simple topology obviates the need for complex routing or message passing protocols. As noted earlier, the isolation and centralization simplifies fault detection, as each link or device can be probed individually. Due to its centralized nature, the topology offers simplicity of operation.

If any cable is not working then the whole network will not be affected: in a star topology, each network device has a home run of cabling back to a network hub, giving each device a separate connection to the network. If there is a problem with a cable, it will generally not affect the rest of the network. The most common cable media in use for star topologies is unshielded twisted pair copper cabling. If small numbers of devices are utilized in this topology the data rate will be high. It is best for short distance.

You can easily add new computers or devices to the network without interrupting other nodes: The star network topology works well when computers are at scattered points. It is easy to add or remove computers. New devices or nodes can easily be added to the Star Network by just extending a cable from the hub. If the hub adds a device for example a printer or a fax machine, all the other computers on the network can access the new device by simply accessing the hub. The device need not be installed on all the computers in the network. The central function is cost effective and easier to maintain. If the computers are reasonably close to the vertices of a convex polygon and the system requirements are modest. And also when one computer falls short then it won't affect the whole communication.

Centralization: the star topologies ease the chance of a network failure by linking all of the computers to a central node. All computers may therefore communicate with all others by transmitting to and receiving from the central node only. Benefits from centralization: As the central hub is the bottleneck, increasing capacity of the central hub or adding additional devices to the star, can help scale the network very easily. The central nature also allows the check up of traffic through the network. This helps evaluate all the traffic in the network and establish apprehensive behavior.

Easy to troubleshoot: in a star network the whole network is reliant on the hub so if the entire network is not working then there could be a problem with the hub. This feature makes it easy to troubleshoot by offering a single point for error connection ad at the same time the dependency is also very high on that single point

Better performance: star network prevents unnecessary passing of the data packet through nodes. At most 3 devices and 2 links are involved in any communication between any two devices which are part of this topology. This topology encourage a huge overhead on the central hub, however if the central hub has plenty of capacity, then very high network used by one device in the network does not affect the other devices in the network. Data Packets are sent quickly as they do not have to travel through any unnecessary. The big advantage of the star network is that it is fast. This is because each computer terminal is attached directly to the central computer.

Easy installation: Installation is simple, inexpensive, and fast because of the flexible cable and the modular connector.

Disadvantages of Star Network

If the hub or concentrator fails, nodes attached are disabled: The primary disadvantage of a star topology is the high dependence of the system on the functioning of the central hub. While the failure of an individual link only results in the isolation of a single node, the failure of the central hub renders the network inoperable, immediately isolating all nodes.

The performance and scalability of the network also depend on the capabilities of the hub: Network size is limited by the number of connections that can be made to the hub, and performance for the whole network is limited by its throughput. While in theory traffic between the hub and a node is isolated from other nodes on the network, other nodes may see a performance drop if traffic to another node occupies a significant portion of the central node's processing capability or throughput. Furthermore, wiring up of the system can be very complex.

The primary disadvantage of the star topology is the hub is a single point of failure: If the hub were to fall short the whole network would fail as a result of the hub being connected to every computer on the network. There will be communication break down between the computers when the hub fails.

Star topology requires more cable length: When the network is being extended then there will be the need of more cables and this result in intricate installation.

More Expensive than other topologies: it is expensive due to cost of the hub. Star topology uses a lot of cables thus making it the most costly network to set up as you also have to trunk to keep the cables out of harm way. Every computer requires a separate cable to form the network. . A common cable that is used in Star Network is the UTP or the unshielded twisted pair cable. Another common cable that is used in star networks is the RJ45 or the Ethernet cables.

Usages of Star Network

Star topology is a networking setup used with 10BASE-T cabling (also called UTP or twisted-pair) and a hub. Each item on the network is connected to the hub like points of a star. The protocols used with star configurations are usually Ethernet or local-talk. Token Ring uses a similar topology, called the star-wired ring.

Star Topology is the most common type of network topology that is used in homes and offices. In the Star Topology there is a central connection point called the hub which is a computer hub or sometimes just a switch. In a Star Network the best advantage is when there is a failure in cable then only one computer might get affected and not the entire network.

Star topology is used to ease the probabilities of network failure by connecting all of the systems to a central node. This central hub rebroadcasts all transmissions received from any peripheral node to all peripheral nodes on the network, sometimes including the originating node. All peripheral nodes may thus communicate with all others by transmitting to, and receiving from, the central node only.

Star network is used to transmit data across the central hub between the network nodes. When a packet comes to the hub it transfers that packet to all nodes connected through a hub but only one node at a time successfully transmits it.

In local area networks where the star topology is used, each machine is connected to a central hub. In contrast to the bus topology, the star topology allows each machine on the network to have a point to point connection to the central hub and there is no single point of failure. All of the traffic which transverses the network passes through the central hub. The hub acts as a signal booster or repeater which in turn allows the signal to travel greater distances.

When it is important that your network have increased stability and speed, the star topology should be considered. When you use a hub, you get centralized administration and security control, low configuration costs and easy troubleshooting. When one node or workstation goes down, the rest of your network will still be functional.

Ring Network

A ring network is a local area network (LAN) in which the nodes (workstations or other devices) are connected in a closed loop configuration. Adjacent pairs of nodes are directly connected. Other pairs of nodes are indirectly connected, the data passing through one or more intermediate nodes.

The illustration shows a ring network with five nodes. Each node is shown as a sphere, and connections are shown as straight lines. The connections can consist of wired or wireless links.

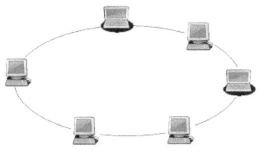

Ring Network

The ring topology may prove optimum when system requirements are modest and workstations are at scattered points. If the workstations are reasonably close to the vertices of a convex polygon (such as the pentagon shown in the illustration), the cost can be lower than that of any other topology when cable routes are chosen to minimize the total length of cable needed.

A break in the cable of a ring network may result in degraded data speed between pairs of workstations for which the data path is increased as a result of the break. If two breaks occur and they are not both in the same section of cable, some workstations will be cut off from some of the others. When system reliability is a critical concern, a bus network or star network may prove superior to a ring network. If redundancy is required, the mesh network topology may be preferable.

A token ring is a widely-implemented kind of ring network.

Token contains a piece of information which along with data is sent by the source computer. This token then passes to next node, which checks if the signal is intended to it. If yes, it receives it and passes the empty to into the network, otherwise passes token along with the data to next node. This process continues until the signal reaches its intended destination.

The nodes with token are the ones only allowed to send data. Other nodes have to wait for an empty token to reach them. This network is usually found in offices, schools and small buildings.

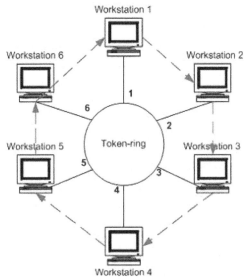

Ring Topology & token

Advantages of Ring Topology

1) This type of network topology is very organized. Each node gets to send the data when it receives an empty token. This helps to reduces chances of collision. Also in ring topology all the traffic flows in only one direction at very high speed.

2) Even when the load on the network increases, its performance is better than that of bus topology.

3) There is no need for network server to control the connectivity between workstations.

4) Additional components do not affect the performance of network.

5) Each computer has equal access to resources.

Disadvantages of Ring Topology

1) Each packet of data must pass through all the computers between source and destination. This makes it slower than star topology.

2) If one workstation or port goes down, the entire network gets affected.

3) Network is highly dependent on the wire which connects different components.

4) MAU's and network cards are expensive as compared to ethernet cards and hubs.

Mesh Networking

Mesh networking is a type of network topology in which a device (node) transmits its own data as well as serves as a relay for other nodes. Routers are used to provide the best and most efficient data path for effective communication. In the event of a hardware failure, many routes are available to continue the network communication process.

There are two types of mesh networking topologies:

- Total Mesh Topology: This kind of topology is in effect when every node in the network is connected to all the other nodes with direct links. This provides greater redundancy, because if any node fails, the network traffic can be directed using other nodes. Each node accesses the working nodes in close proximity and finds the best route for efficient and reliable communication.

- Partial Mesh Topology: This kind of topology is in effect when some nodes are connected with all the other nodes using direct links, while some are just connected to one or two nodes only. This is less expensive to implement compared to total mesh topology, but has less redundancy.

A mesh networking layout is not commonly used because of high costs related to cabling, devices and its complex infrastructure. However, wireless mesh networks are very popular among wireless networks and their users. This is because, by definition, a wireless network does not need cabling or any other physical infrastructure other than an access point.

Advantages of a Mesh Topology

Scalability

One of the advantages of a mesh topology is that (in theory) you don't need to add routers to the network, as each node can act as a router. If you're working on a mesh network for the lighting in your office building, and you want to add a light in a particular room, you should be able to add the light and have it automatically connect to the network. There isn't a lot of extra management that needs to happen, which makes the network scalable.

Robustness

Another benefit of a mesh network topology is that if one of the nodes goes down, it doesn't necessarily bring the entire network down. The network can heal itself around a bad node if other nodes can complete the mesh. Additionally, if you need to get more range out of a mesh system, you can add another node and the messages can hop through the mesh back to the gateway—which is why some believe mesh networks are more robust.

Because all nodes in a mesh are receiving and translating information, there is some redundancy in a mesh topology; however, you can also gain speed with the excess bandwidth. If one route happens to be slow, a mesh network could potentially find a better route and optimize itself.

Disadvantages of a Mesh Topology

Complexity

Each node needs to both send messages as well as act as a router, which causes the complexity of each node to go up pretty significantly. Let's say you're making a small, low-power device—like a room occupancy sensor—and you are looking to get better range out of your system. The nodes have to now keep track of messages from five or 10 of their neighbors, which exponentially increases the amount of data that node has to deal with in order to pass along a message. Thus, if you add additional sensors to the mesh just to benefit the range, you're naturally making the system more complex.

Network Planning

As we mentioned previously, mesh networks are often considered highly scalable, and adding a node to the network typically isn't very involved. But planning the network as a whole is a different story. Let's say you have poor latency in one area of your building and you need a particular light to turn on faster than it currently turns on. With a mesh network, you'd need to add a dedicated node that only forwards messages. But this complicates your network planning, because you now have to deploy a piece of equipment just to get your messages properly routed in a reasonable amount of time.

Latency

As mentioned, latency—the time it takes a message to get from a node to the gateway—can impact your mesh network planning. Interestingly, you may improve some latency by using a mesh network with a larger scale system with more bandwidth, memory, and power. But latency becomes an issue in smaller low power, wide-area networks (LPWANs) because it doesn't have the processing capability to handle the messaging. Thus, if you have a WiFi mesh, messages will likely be translated much quicker than a ZigBee mesh. This is something to consider based on the protocol you'll be using and the latency your application requires.

Power Consumption

Because each node in a mesh has to act as an endpoint and a router, it has to draw more power to operate. Thus, if you have battery-powered, low-power nodes, a mesh may be difficult to deploy without a lot of network planning.

Let's say you have battery-powered nodes in windows and doors for your smart security system. The customer keeps the control panel in the basement, but all of the sensors are on the first and second floor. So while a second-floor window may be low power, because it only transmits messages, the sensors on the first floor will have to handle messages from the second floor windows and doors. In other words, you're compounding the amount of data each node has to handle in a mesh, and so batteries on some nodes are likely to die faster.

Tree Network

In telecommunication networks, a tree network is a combination of two or more star networks connected together. Each star network is a local area network (LAN) in which there is a central computer or server to which all the workstation nodes are directly linked. The central computers of the star networks are connected to a main cable called the bus. Thus, a tree network is a bus network of star networks.

The illustration shows a tree network with five star networks connected to a common bus. The workstations are shown as small spheres, the central computers of the star networks are shown as larger spheres, connections within star networks are shown as short lines, and the bus is shown as a long, heavy line. The connections can consist of wire cables, optical fiber cables, or wireless links.

Tree Network

The tree network topology is ideal when the workstations are located in groups, with each group occupying a relatively small physical region. An example is a university campus in which each building has its own star network, and all the central computers are linked in a campus-wide system. It is easy to add or remove workstations from each star network. Entire star networks can be added to, or removed from, the bus. If the bus has low loss and/or is equipped with repeaters, this topology can be used in a wide area network (WAN) configuration.

In a tree network, a cable failure in one of the star networks will isolate the workstation that it links to the central computer of that star network, but only that workstation will be isolated. All the other workstations will continue to function normally, except that they will not be able to communicate with the isolated workstation. If any workstation goes down, none of the other workstations will be affected. If a central computer goes down, the entire portion of the network served by it will suffer degraded performance or complete failure, but rest of the network will continue to function normally. If the bus is broken, serious network disruption may occur. If redundancy is needed, the central computers of the star networks can be interconnected in a mesh network topology.

Advantages of Tree Network

- It is the best topology for a large computer network, for which a star or ring topology are unsuitable due to the sheer scale of the entire network. Tree topology divides the whole network into parts that are easily manageable.

- The topology makes it possible to have a point-to-point network.

- All computers have access to their immediate neighbors in the network and also the central hub. This kind of network makes it possible for multiple network devices to be connected with the central hub.

- It overcomes the limitation of star network topology, which has a limitation of hub connection points and the broadcast traffic induced limitation of a bus network topology.

- A tree network provides enough room for future expansion.

Disadvantages of Tree Network

- Dependence of the entire network on one central hub is a point of vulnerability for this topology. A failure of the central hub or failure of the main data trunk cable can cripple the whole network.

- With increase in size beyond a point, the management becomes difficult.

Hybrid Network

Hybrid, as the name suggests, is mixture of two different things. Similarly in this type of topology we integrate two or more different topologies to form a resultant topology which has good points (as well as weaknesses) of all the constituent basic topologies rather than having characteristics of one specific topology. This combination of topologies is done according to the requirements of the organization.

Types of Hybrid Network Topologies

There are different types of hybrid network topologies depending on the basic topologies that make up the hybrid and the adjoining topology that interconnects the basic topologies.

The following are some of the hybrid network topologies.

Star-wired Ring Network Topology

In a Star-Wired Ring hybrid topology, a set of Star topologies are connected by a Ring topology as the adjoining topology. Joining each star topology to the ring topology is a wired connection.

In below figure, individual nodes of a given Star topology like Star Topology 1 are interconnected by a central switch which in turn provides an external connection to other star topologies through a node A in the main ring topology.

Information from a given star topology reaching a connecting node in the main ring topology like flows either in a bidirectional or unidirectional manner.

A bidirectional flow will ensure that a failure in one node of the main ring topology does not lead to the complete breakdown of information flow in the main ring topology.

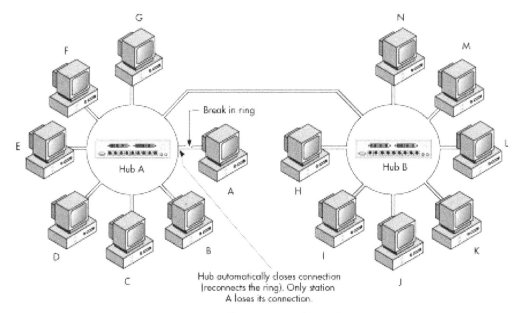

A Star-Wired Ring Network Topology

Star-wired bus Network Topology

A Star-Wired Bus topology is made up of a set of Star topologies interconnected by a central Bus topology. Joining each Star topology to the Bus topology is a wired connection.

In this setup, the main Bus topology provides a backbone connection that interconnects the individual Star topologies.

The backbone in this case is a wired connection.

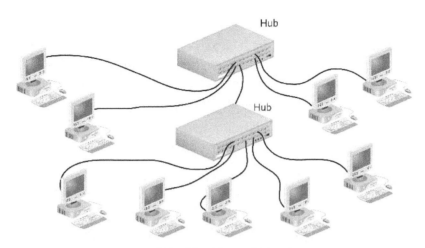

A Star-Wired Bus Network Topology

Hierarchical Network Topology

Hierarchical Network topology is structured in different levels as a hierarchical tree. It is also referred to as Tree network topology.

Connection of the lower levels like level 2 to higher levels like level 1 is done through wired connection.

The top most level, level 0, contains the parent (root) node. The second level, level 1 contains the child nodes which in turn have child nodes in level 3. All the nodes in a given level have a higher parent node except for the node(s) at the top most level.

The nodes at the bottom most level are called leaf nodes as they are peripheral and are parent to no other node. At the basic level, a tree network topology is a collection of star network topologies arranged in different levels.

Each level including the top most can contain one or more nodes.

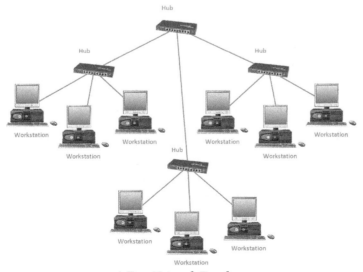

A Tree Network Topology

Advantages of Hybrid Network Topology

1) Reliable: Unlike other networks, fault detection and troubleshooting is easy in this type of topology. The part in which fault is detected can be isolated from the rest of network and required corrective measures can be taken, without affecting the functioning of rest of the network.

2) Scalable: Its easy to increase the size of network by adding new components, without disturbing existing architecture.

3) Flexible: Hybrid Network can be designed according to the requirements of the organization and by optimizing the available resources. Special care can be given to nodes where traffic is high as well as where chances of fault are high.

4) Effective: Hybrid topology is the combination of two or more topologies, so we can design it in such a way that strengths of constituent topologies are maximized while there weaknesses are neutralized. For example we saw Ring Topology has good data reliability (achieved by use of tokens) and Star topology has high tolerance capability (as each node is not directly connected to other but through central device), so these two can be used effectively in hybrid star-ring topology.

Disadvantages of Hybrid Topology

1) Complexity of Design: One of the biggest drawback of hybrid topology is its design. Its not easy to design this type of architecture and its a tough job for designers. Configuration and installation process needs to be very efficient.

2) Costly Hub: The hubs used to connect two distinct networks, are very expensive. These hubs are different from usual hubs as they need to be intelligent enough to work with different architectures and should be function even if a part of network is down.

3) Costly Infrastructure: As hybrid architectures are usually larger in scale, they require a lot of cables; cooling systems, sophisticate network devices, etc.

Daisy Chain

Daisy chaining is a common way practiced by the network administrator to add extra or new hosts to a network topology. But it depends on the kind of topology we are using.

For example, if we are using a linear network topology, we need to add the new host at the end of the chain (sometimes in the middle as well). However, in the ring topology, there is no end point in the network topology; so, the extra node becomes a part of the topology.

Connecting one or more computer in a series next to each other in a computer network is called daisy chaining. Daisy chaining is used to pass a message down the line for a computer partway. Once the message is passed, it goes down the line until the message reaches the intended computer.

There are two types of daisy-chained networks:

- Liner daisy chain and,
- Ring daisy chain

Linear Daisy Chain

In a linear daisy chain, one computer is connected to the next using two-way link in between them.

To understand linear daisy chain, let's say, there are already five computers in a row and you want the sixth one to be a part of the bus topology. In that condition, you can add the sixth condition at the end of the fifth computer using a two-way link in between them.

Ring Daisy Chain

In a ring daisy chain, one computer becomes a part of the ring topology by being inserted in the middle of the ring chain.

Thus, ring daisy chain topology becomes advantageous over linear daisy chain because instead of a two-way link, only one-way link is needed to connect the new computer to the chain. Also, if the ring breaks, then the transmission happens in the reverse path thereby ensuring that the connectivity is not affected. So, a ring topology is considered mostly for the MAN (Metropolitan Area Network).

Wireless Network

A wireless network enables people to communicate and access applications and information without wires. This provides freedom of movement and the ability to extend applications to different parts of a building, city, or nearly anywhere in the world. Wireless networks allow people to interact with e-mail or browse the Internet from a location that they prefer.

Many types of wireless communication systems exist, but a distinguishing attribute of a wireless network is that communication takes place between computer devices. These devices include personal digital assistants (PDAs), laptops, personal computers (PCs), servers, and printers. Computer devices have processors, memory, and a means of interfacing with a particular type of network. Traditional cell phones don't fall within the definition of a computer device; however, newer phones and even audio headsets are beginning to incorporate computing power and network adapters. Eventually, most electronics will offer wireless network connections.

As with networks based on wire, or optical fiber, wireless networks convey information between computer devices. The information can take the form of e-mail messages, web pages, and database records, streaming video or voice. In most cases, wireless networks transfer data, such as e-mail messages and files, but advancements in the performance of wireless networks is enabling support for video and voice communications as well.

Types of Wireless Networks

WLANs: Wireless Local Area Networks

WLANs allow users in a local area, such as a university campus or library, to form a network or gain access to the internet. A temporary network can be formed by a small number of users without the need of an access point; given that they do not need access to network resources.

WPANs: Wireless Personal Area Networks

The two current technologies for wireless personal area networks are Infra Red (IR) and Bluetooth (IEEE 802.15). These will allow the connectivity of personal devices within an area of about 30 feet. However, IR requires a direct line of site and the range is less.

WMANs: Wireless Metropolitan Area Networks

This technology allows the connection of multiple networks in a metropolitan area such as different buildings in a city, which can be an alternative or backup to laying copper or fiber cabling.

WWANs: Wireless Wide Area Networks

These types of networks can be maintained over large areas, such as cities or countries, via multiple satellite systems or antenna sites looked after by an ISP. These types of systems are referred to as 2G (2nd Generation) systems.

Network Packet

A packet is the unit of data that is routed between an origin and a destination on the Internet or any other packet-switched network. When any file (e-mail message, HTML file, Graphics Interchange Format file, Uniform Resource Locator request, and so forth) is sent from one place to another on the Internet, the Transmission Control Protocol (TCP) layer of TCP/IP divides the file into "chunks" of an efficient size for routing. Each of these packets is separately numbered and includes the Internet address of the destination. The individual packets for a given file may travel different routes through the Internet. When they have all arrived, they are reassembled into the original file (by the TCP layer at the receiving end).

A packet-switching scheme is an efficient way to handle transmissions on a connectionless network such as the Internet. An alternative scheme, circuit-switched, is used for networks allocated for voice connections. In circuit-switching, lines in the network are shared among many users as with packet-switching, but each connection requires the dedication of a particular path for the duration of the connection.

Networking Hardware

Network Interface Card

NIC is short for network interface card. It's network adapter hardware in the form of an add-in card that fits in an expansion slot on a computer's motherboard. Most computers have them built-in (in which case they're just a part of the circuit board) but you can also add your own NIC to expand the functionality of the system.

The NIC is what provides the hardware interface between a computer and a network. This is true whether the network is wired or wirelesses since the NIC can be used for Ethernet networks as well as Wi-Fi ones, as well as whether it's a desktop or laptop.

"Network cards" that connect over USB are not actually cards but instead regular USB devices that enable network connections through the USB port. These are called network adapters.

NIC also stands for Network Information Center. For example, the organization InterNIC is a NIC that provides information to the general public on internet domain names.

Purpose of NIC

Put simply, a network interface card enables a device to network with other devices. This is true whether the devices are connected to a central network (like in infrastructure mode) or even if they're paired together, directly from one device to the other (i.e. ad-hoc mode).

However, a NIC isn't always the only component needed to interface with other devices. For example, if the device is part of a larger network and you want it to have access to the internet, like at home or in a business, a router is required too. The device, then, uses the network interface card to connect to the router, which is connected to the internet.

NIC Physical Description

Network cards come in many different forms but the two main ones are wired and wireless.

Wireless NICs need to use wireless technologies to access the network, so they have one or more antennas sticking out of the card.

Wired NICs just use an RJ45 port since they have an Ethernet cable attached to the end. This makes them much flatter than wireless network cards.

No matter which is used, the NIC protrudes from the back of the computer next to the other plugs, like for the monitor. If the NIC is plugged into a laptop, it's most likely attached to the side.

NIC: Speed

All NICs feature a speed rating, such as 11 Mbps, 54 Mbps or 100 Mbps, that suggest the general performance of the unit. You can find this information in Windows by right-clicking the network connection from the Network and Sharing Center > Change adapter settings section of Control Panel.

It's important to keep in mind that the speed of the NIC does not necessarily determine the speed of the internet connection. This is due to reasons like available bandwidth and the speed you're paying for.

For example, if you're only paying for 20 Mbps download speeds, using a 100 Mbps NIC will not increase your speeds to 100 Mbps, or even to anything over 20 Mbps. However, if you're paying for 20 Mbps but your NIC only supports 11 Mbps, you will suffer from slower download speeds since the installed hardware can only work as fast as it's rated to work.

In other words, the speed of the network, when just these two factors are considered, is determined by the slower of the two.

Another major player in network speeds is bandwidth. If you're supposed to be getting 100 Mbps and your card supports it, but you have three computers on the network that are downloading simultaneously, that 100 Mbps will be split in three, which will really only serve each client around 33 Mbps.

Network Switch

Switches occupy the same place in the network as hubs. Unlike hubs, switches examine each packet and process it accordingly rather than simply repeating the signal to all ports. Switches map the Ethernet addresses of the nodes residing on each network segment and then allow only the necessary traffic to pass through the switch. When a packet is received by the switch, the switch examines the destination and source hardware addresses and compares them to a table of network segments and addresses. If the segments are the same, the packet is dropped or "filtered"; if the segments are different, then the packet is "forwarded" to the proper segment. Additionally, switches prevent bad or misaligned packets from spreading by not forwarding them.

Filtering packets and regenerating forwarded packets enables switching technology to split a network into separate collision domains. The regeneration of packets allows for greater distances and more nodes to be used in the total network design, and dramatically lowers the overall collision rates. In switched networks, each segment is an independent collision domain. This also allows for parallelism, meaning up to one-half of the computers connected to a switch can send data at the same time. In shared networks all nodes reside in a single shared collision domain.

Easy to install, most switches are self learning. They determine the Ethernet addresses in use on each segment, building a table as packets are passed through the switch. This "plug and play" element makes switches an attractive alternative to hubs.

Switches can connect different network types (such as Ethernet and Fast Ethernet) or networks of the same type. Many switches today offer high-speed links, like Fast Ethernet, which can be used to link the switches together or to give added bandwidth to important servers that get a lot of traffic. A network composed of a number of switches linked together via these fast uplinks is called a "collapsed backbone" network.

Dedicating ports on switches to individual nodes is another way to speed access for critical computers. Servers and power users can take advantage of a full segment for one node, so some networks connect high traffic nodes to a dedicated switch port.

Full duplex is another method to increase bandwidth to dedicated workstations or servers. To use full duplex, both network interface cards used in the server or workstation and the switch must support full duplex operation. Full duplex doubles the potential bandwidth on that link.

Network Hub

A network hub is a node that broadcasts data to every computer or Ethernet-based device connected to it. A hub is less sophisticated than a switch, the latter of which can isolate data transmissions to specific devices.

Network hubs are best suited for small, simple local area network (LAN) environments. Hubs cannot provide routing capabilities or other advanced network services. Because they operate by forwarding packets across all ports indiscriminately, network hubs are sometimes referred to as "dumb switches."

With limited capabilities and poor scalability, network hubs had primarily one competitive advantage over switches: lower prices. As switch prices fell in the early to mid-2000s, hubs began getting phased out of use. Today, hubs are far less commonly deployed. But network hubs have some niche uses and continue to offer a simple means of networking.

How Network Hubs Work

Network hubs are categorized as Layer 1 devices in the Open Systems Interconnection (OSI) reference model. They connect multiple computers together, transmitting data received at one port to all of its other ports without restriction. Hubs operate in half-duplex.

This model raises security and privacy concerns, because traffic could not be safeguarded or quarantined. It also presents a practical issue in terms of traffic management. Devices on a hub function as a network segment and share a collision domain. Thus, when two devices connected to a network hub transmit data simultaneously, the packets will collide, causing network performance problems. This is mitigated in switches or routers, as each port represents a separate collision domain.

All devices connected to a network hub share all available bandwidth equally. This differs from a switch environment, where each port is allotted a dedicated amount of bandwidth.

Modem

Modem is abbreviation for Modulator – Demodulator. Modems are used for data transfer from one computer network to another computer network through telephone lines. The computer network works in digital mode, while analog technology is used for carrying massages across phone lines.

Modulator converts information from digital mode to analog mode at the transmitting end and demodulator converts the same from analog to digital at receiving end. The process of converting analog signals of one computer network into digital signals of another computer network so they can be processed by a receiving computer is referred to as digitizing.

When an analog facility is used for data communication between two digital devices called Data Terminal Equipment (DTE), modems are used at each end. DTE can be a terminal or a computer.

The modem at the transmitting end converts the digital signal generated by DTE into an analog signal by modulating a carrier. This modem at the receiving end demodulates the carrier and hand over the demodulated digital signal to the DTE.

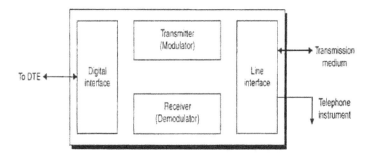

Building blocks of a modem

The transmission medium between the two modems can be dedicated circuit or a switched telephone circuit. If a switched telephone circuit is used, then the modems are connected to the local telephone exchanges. Whenever data transmission is required connection between the modems is established through telephone exchanges.

Types of Modems

- Modems can be of several types and they can be categorized in a number of ways.

- Categorization is usually based on the following basic modem features:

    1. Directional capacity: half duplex modem and full duplex modem.

    2. Connection to the line: 2-wire modem and 4-wire modem.

    3. Transmission mode: asynchronous modem and synchronous modem.

Half Duplex and Full Duplex Modems

Half Duplex

1. A half duplex modem permits transmission in one direction at a time.

2. If a carrier is detected on the line by the modem, I gives an indication of the incoming carrier to the DTE through a control signal of its digital interface.

3. As long as they camel' IS being received; the modem does not give permission to the DTE to transmit data.

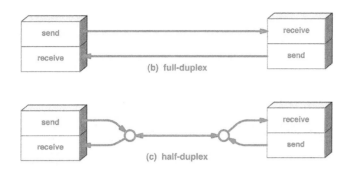

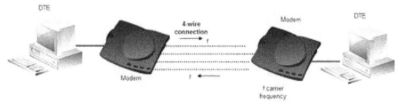

Full Duplex

- A full duplex modem allows simultaneous transmission in both directions.

- Therefore, there are two carriers on the line, one outgoing and the other incoming. Wire and 4-wire Modems

- The line interface of the modem can have a 2-wire or a 4-wire connection to transmission medium. 4-wire Modem

- In a 4-wire connection, one pair of wires is used for the outgoing carrier and the other pair is used for incoming carrier.

- Full duplex and half duplex modes of data transmission are possible on a 4- wire connection.

- As the physical transmission path for each direction is separate, the same carrier frequency can be used for both the directions.

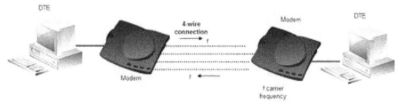

4wire-Modem

2-wire Modem

- 2-wire modems use the same pair of wires for outgoing and incoming carriers.

- A leased 2-wireconrlection is usually cheaper than a 4-wire connection as only one pair of wires is extended to the subscriber's premises.

- The data connection established through telephone exchange is also a 2-wire connection.

- In 2-wire modems, half duplex mode of transmission that uses the same frequency for the incoming and outgoing carriers can be easily implemented.

- For full duplex mode of operation, it is necessary to have two transmission channels, one for transmit direction and the other for receive direction.

- This is achieved by frequency division multiplexing of two different carrier frequencies. These carriers are placed within the bandwidth of the speech channel.

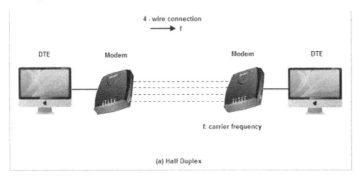

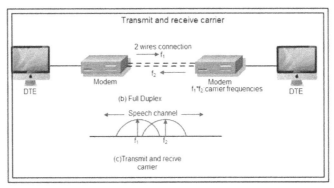

Asynchronous & Synchronous Modems

Asynchronous Modem

- Asynchronous modems can handle data bytes with start and stop bits.

- There is no separate timing signal or clock between the modem and the DTE.

- The internal timing pulses are synchronized repeatedly to the leading edge of the start pulse.

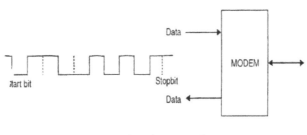

Asynchronous modem

Synchronous Modem

- Synchronous modems can handle a continuous stream of data bits but requires a clock signal.

- The data bits are always synchronized to the clock signal.

- There are separate clocks for the data bits being transmitted and received.

- For synchronous transmission of data bits, the DTE can use its internal clock and supply the same to the modem.

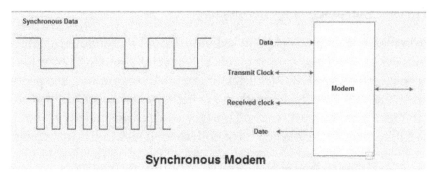

Synchronous Modem

Modulation Techniques used for Modem

The basic modulation techniques used by a modem to convert digital data to analog signals are:

- Amplitude shift keying (ASK).

- Frequency shift keying (FSK).

- Phase shift keying (PSK).

- Differential PSK (DPSK).

These techniques are known as the binary continuous wave (CW) modulation.

- Modems are always used in pairs. Any system whether simplex, half duplex or full duplex requires a modem at the transmitting as well as the receiving end.

- Thus a modem acts as the electronic bridge between two worlds - the world of purely digital signals and the established analog world.

Network and Communication Cables

Network and communication cables are network hardware used to connect one network device to other network devices. For example, connecting two or more computers to share printers and scanners; connecting several severs to an access switch. The range covers data and Ethernet cable assemblies, including twisted pair cable, coaxial cable, optical fiber cable, power line, etc. The twisted pair cable, coaxial cable and optical fiber cable are categories that are most often referred to.

Twisted Pair Cable

Twisted pair cabling is a type of wiring in which two conductors (usually copper) of a single circuit are twisted together. Because the two wires are carrying equal and opposite signals, one pair can induce crosstalk in another and the effect gets stronger along the length of the cable, which is bad for the transmission of signal. Twisting the pairs reduce the crosstalk between lines. Twisted pair cabling is often used in data networks for short and medium length connections because of its relatively lower costs compared to optical fiber and coaxial cable.

Shielded Twisted Pair vs. Unshielded Twisted Pair

Twisted pair cables are often shielded in an attempt to prevent electromagnetic interference. Twisted pair with shielding is known as shielded twisted pair (STP). In contrast to STP, unshielded twisted pair (UTP) is not surrounded by any shielding.

STP cable is also divided by overall shield and individual shield. Individual shielded twisted pair is with aluminum foil for each twisted pair or quad. This type of shielding protects cable from external electromagnetic interference (EMI) entering or exiting the cable and also protects neighboring pairs from crosstalk. Overall shielded twisted pair is with overall foil or braided shield across all of the pairs within the 100 Ω twisted pair cable. This type of shielding helps prevent EMI from entering or exiting the cable. One STP cable can have both overall and individual shielding.

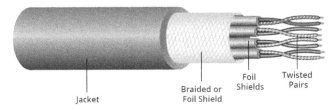

Shielded twisted pair construction

UTP cable without shielding is more prone to outside interference. For this reason, this cable type is more often found in indoor telephone applications. Outdoor telephone cables contain hundreds or thousands pairs. Pairs that have the same twisted rate within the cable can experience some degree of crosstalk, so wire pairs are usually selected carefully within a large cable to reduce the crosstalk.

Most UTP cable uses RJ45 connectors, which look like telephone connectors (RJ11) but have eight wires instead of four.

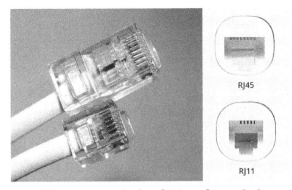

RJ45 connector (up) and RJ45 adaptor (up).

The Nearest Twisted Pair to Us: Ethernet Cable

Name	Typical Construction	Bandwidth	Applications
Cat 3	UTP	16 MHz	10BASE-T and 100BASE-T4 Ethernet
Cat 4	UTP	20 MHz	16Mbit/s Token Ring
Cat 5	UTP	100 MHz	100BASE-TX & 1000BASE-T Ethernet

Cat 5e	UTP	100 MHz	100BASE-TX & 1000BASE-T Ethernet
Cat 6	STP	250 MHz	10GBASE-T Ethernet
Cat 6a	STP	500 MHz	10GBASE-T Ethernet
Cat 7	STP	600 MHz	10GBASE-T Ethernet or POTS/CATV/1000BASE-T over single cable
Cat 7a	STP	1000 MHz	10GBASE-T Ethernet or POTS/CATV/1000BASE-T over single cable
Cat 8/8.1	STP	1600-2000 MHz	40GBASE-T Ethernet or POTS/CATV/1000BASE-T over single cable
Cat 8.2	STP	1600-2000 MHz	40GBASE-T Ethernet or POTS/CATV/1000BASE-T over single cable

Twisted Pair Cabling: T568A or T568B

Two wiring standards are commonly used with twisted pair cabling: T568A and T568B. These are telecommunications standards from TIA and EIA that specify the pin arrangements for the connectors (often RJ45) on UTP or STP cables. The number 568 refers to the order in which the wires within the twisted pair cable are terminated and attached to the connector. The signal is identical for both.

Pin numbers are read left to right, with the connector tab facing down. Notice that the pin-outs stay the same and the only difference is in the color coding of the wiring.

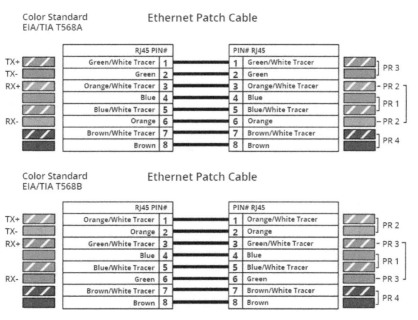

T568A and T568B wiring standards for twisted pair cabling.

Coaxial Cable

Coaxial cable is a type of cable that has an inner conductor surrounded by a tubular insulating layer, surrounded by a tubular conducting shield. The inner conductor and the outer shield share a geometric axis. Many coaxial cables have an insulating outer sheath or jacket.

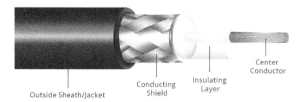

Coaxial cable construction.

Reasons why Coaxial Cable is Good for Radio Transmission

Coaxial cable is used as a transmission line for radio frequency (RF) signals. Its applications include feed lines connecting radio transmitters and receivers with their antennas, computer network connections, and digital audio and distributing cable television signals. Coaxial cable has an obvious advantage over other types of radio transmission line. In a good coaxial cable, the electromagnetic field carrying the signal exists only in the space between the inner conductor and the outer conducting shield. For this reason, coaxial cables are allowed to be installed next to metal objects without power losses that occur in other types of radio transmission line.

Widely used Coaxial Connector Types

Many coaxial connector types are available in the audio, digital, video, RF and microwave industries, each designed for a specific purpose and application. One consideration the number of connect-disconnect cycles that a connector pair could withstand while still performing as expected. Here are some common coaxial connector types.

Table: Coaxial connector types.

Connector Type	Other Name	Female	Male	Maximum Frequency, Application
Type F	Video			250 MHz to 1 GHz. The "F" series connectors are primarily utilized in television cable and antenna applications.
Type N	/			12 GHz or more. Type N connector was originally designed for military systems operating below 5 GHz, later improved to 12 GHz and higher. Type N connectors follow the military standard MIL-C-39012.
Phone plugs and jacks	TS, TRS			100 kHz or less. Same with the names, the phone plug is the male connector, a phone jack is the female connector.

RCA	Phono plugs and jacks			10 MHz. A round, press-on connector commonly used for consumer-grade audio and composite video connections.
7/16 DIN	/			.5 GHz. A relatively new connector used popularly as an interconnect in cellular and other so called "wireless" applications, especially on towers.
APC-7	7 mm		same	18 GHz. The genderless APC-7 (Amphenol Precision Connector - 7 mm) offers the lowest reflection coefficient and most repeatable measurement of all 18 GHz connectors, notably used for metrology and calibration.

Capable Optical Fiber Cable

Optical fiber cabling is an excellent transmission medium for its high data capacity and supported long distances. It is indispensable in any fiber optic network. It has a fiber/glass core within a rubber outer coating and uses beams of light rather than electrical signals to relay data. Because light doesn't diminish over distance the way electrical signals do, this cabling can run for distances measured in kilometers with transmission speeds from 10 Mbps up to 100 Gbps or higher.

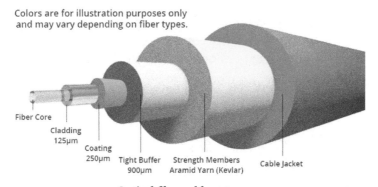

Optical fiber cable cutaway.

Fiber Core Size Matters: SMF and MMF

The inner fiber can be either single mode or multimode. Generally, a single mode fiber core is 9/125μm wide, whereas a multimode fiber core can be 62.5/125μm or 50/125μm wide. Only the early OM1 is 62.5/125μm fiber, the later generations OM2, OM3, OM4, OM5 50/125μm fiber. The letters "OM" stand for optical multimode. Both multimode fiber (MMF) and single mode fiber (SMF) can be used for high-speed transmission. MMF is often for short reach while SMF is for long reach.

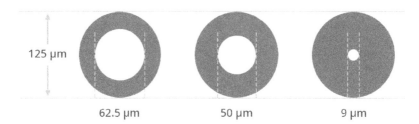

125 μm

62.5 μm   50 μm   9 μm

Multimode fiber and single mode fiber core diameters.

Multiple Fiber Optic Connectors

Optical fiber cables can be terminated with various types of fiber optic connectors that can be plugged into different ports of devices. The figure below shows some common fiber optic connector types, and the LC, SC and ST are most used three types.

LC Connector   SC Connector   ST Connector   FC Connector

MTRJ Connector   MU Connector   E2000 Connector

Common fiber optic connector types

In addition, there is a multi-fiber connector type called MTP/MPO (Multi-fiber Push On). It is designed for higher bandwidth applications such as 40GbE and 100GbE. 12- and 24-fiber versions are currently used to directly connect into 40G and 100G transceivers and also used in high density fiber distribution areas. Higher fiber versions are also available (48, 72 fibers) but their use and deployment is currently limited.

Internet Protocol Address

The Internet Protocol Address (or IP Address) is a unique address that computing devices such as personal computers, tablets, and smartphones use to identify itself and communicate with other devices in the IP network. Any device connected to the IP network must have a unique IP address within the network. An IP address is analogous to a street address or telephone number in that it is used to uniquely identify an entity.

Dotted Decimals

The traditional IP Address (known as IPv4) uses a 32-bit number to represent an IP address, and it defines both network and host address. A 32-bit number is capable of providing roughly 4 billion unique numbers, and hence IPv4 addresses running out as more devices are connected to the IP network. A new version of the IP protocol (IPv6) has been invented to offer virtually limitless number of unique addresses. An IP address is written in "dotted decimal" notation, which is 4 sets of numbers separated by period each set representing 8-bit number ranging from (0-255). An example of IPv4 address is 216.3.128.12, which is the IP address previously assigned to iplocation.net.

An IPv4 address is divided into two parts: network and host address. The network address determines how many of the 32 bits are used for the network address and the remaining bits are used for the host address. The host address can further divided into subnet work and host number.

Public and Private IP Addresses

In order to maintain uniqueness within global namespace, the IP addresses are publicly registered with the Network Information Center (NIC) to avoid address conflicts. The dDevices that need to be publicly identified, such as web or mail servers, must have a globally unique IP address; and they are assigned a public IP address. The devices that do not require public access may be assigned a private IP address and make it uniquely identifiable within one organization. For example, a network printer may be assigned a private IP address to prevent rest of the world from printing from it. To allow organizations to freely assign private IP addresses, the NIC has reserved certain address blocks for private use. A private network is a network that uses RFC 1918 IP address space. The following IP blocks are reserved for private IP addresses.

Class	Starting IP Address	Ending IP Address
A	10.0.0.0	10.255.255.255
B	172.16.0.0	172.31.255.255
C	192.168.0.0	192.168.255.255

In addition to above classful private addresses, 169.254.0.0 through 169.254.255.255 addresses are reserved for Zeroconf (or APIPA, Automatic Private IP Addressing) to automatically create the usable IP network without configuration.

References

- What-is-network-topology-and-types-of-network-topology: fossbytes.com, Retrieved 19 July 2018

- 17-advantages-and-disadvantages-of-bus-topology: vittana.org, Retrieved 15 May 2018

- Mesh-networking-24398: techopedia.com, Retrieved 22 March 2018

- Mesh-network-topology-advantages-disadvantages: link-labs.com, Retrieved 29 June 2018

- Hybrid-networking-topologies-types-uses-examples: study.com, Retrieved 24 April 2018

- Types-of-wireless-network-explained-with-standards, ccna-study-guide: computernetworkingnotes.com, Retrieved 20 April 2018

Operating Systems

An operating system (OS) is the software, which manages the software and hardware resources and also provides services for computer programs. This aim of this chapter is to provide a comprehensive understanding of operating systems. It discusses the fundamental types of OS such as distributed operating system, embedded operating system and real-time operating system as well as the major operating systems used across the world.

Operating System (OS) is one of the core software programs that runs on the hardware and makes it usable for the user to interact with the hardware so that they can send commands (input) and receive results (output). It provides a consistent environment for other software to execute commands. So we can say that the OS acts at the center through which the system hardware, other software's, and the user communicate. The following figure shows the basic working of the operating system and how it utilizes different hardware or resources.

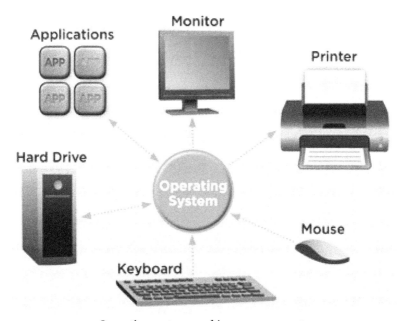

Operating system working as a core part

Basic Functions of the Operating System

The key five basic functions of any operating system are as following:

1. Interface between the user and the hardware: An OS provides an interface between user and machine. This interface can be a graphical user interface (GUI) in which users click onscreen elements to interact with the OS or a command-line interface (CLI) in which users type commands at the command-line interface (CLI) to tell the OS to do things.

GUI (Mac OSX)   v   CLI (DOS)

GUI vs CLI

2. Coordinate hardware components: An OS enables coordination of hardware components. Each hardware device speaks a different language, but the operating system can talk to them through the specific translational software's called device drivers. Every hardware component has different drivers for Operating systems. These drivers make the communication successful between the other software's and the hardware.

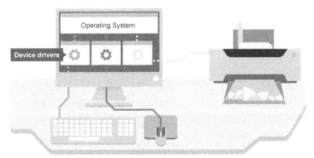

Device Drivers in between OS and Hardware devices

3. Provide environment for software to function: An OS provides an environment for software applications to function. Application software is specific software which is used to perform specific task. In GUI operating systems such as Windows and macOS, applications run within a consistent, graphical desktop environment.

4. Provide structure for data management: An OS displays structure/directories for data management. We can view file and folder listings and manipulate on those files and folders like (move, copy, rename, delete, and many others).

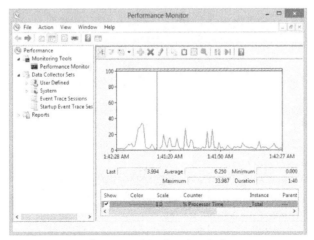

Performance Monitor in windows

5. Monitor system health and functionality: OS monitors the health of our system's hardware, giving us an idea of how well (or not) it's performing. We can see how busy our CPU is, or how quickly our hard drives retrieve data, or how much data our network card is sending etc. and it also monitors system activity for malware.

Operating System Characteristics

The Operating systems are different according to the three primary characteristics which are licensing, software compatibility, and complexity.

Licensing

There are basically three kinds of Operating systems. One is Open Source OS, another is Free OS and the third is Commercial OS.

Linux is an open source operating system which means that anyone can download and modify it for example Ubuntu etc.

A free OS doesn't have to be open source. They are free to download and use but cannot modify them. For example, Google owns Chrome OS and makes it free to use.

Commercial operating systems are privately owned by companies that charge money for them. Examples include Microsoft Windows and Apple macOS. These require to pay for the right (or license) to use their Operating systems.

Software Compatibility

The developers make the software's which may be compatible or incompatible in different versions within the same operating system's type but they can't be compatible with the other OS types. Every OS type has their own software compatibility.

Complexity

Operating systems come in basically two editions one is 32-bit and other is 64-bit editions. The 64-bit edition of an operating system best utilizes random access memory (RAM). A computer with a 64-bit CPU can run either a 32-bit or a 64-bit OS, but a computer with a 32-bit CPU can run only a 32-bit OS.

32-bit vs 64-bit Windows OS

Distributed Operating System

A distributed operating system is an operating system that runs on several machines whose purpose is to provide a useful set of services, generally to make the collection of machines behave more like a single machine. The distributed operating system plays the same role in making the collective resources of the machines more usable that a typical single-machine operating system plays in making that machine's resources more usable. Usually, the machines controlled by a distributed operating system are connected by a relatively high quality network, such as a high speed local area network. Most commonly, the participating nodes of the system are in a relatively small geographical area, something between an office and a campus.

Distributed operating systems typically run cooperatively on all machines whose resources they control. These machines might be capable of independent operation, or they might be usable merely as resources in the distributed system. In some architectures, each machine is an equally powerful peer as all the others. In other architectures, some machines are permanently designated as master or are given control of particular resources. In yet others, elections or other selection mechanisms are used to designate some machines as having special roles, often controlling roles.

Sometimes distinctions are made between parallel operating systems, distributed operating systems, and network operating systems, though the latter term is now a bit archaic. The distinctions are perhaps arbitrary, though they do point out differences in the design space for making operating systems control operations across multiple processing engines.

- A parallel operating system is usually defined as running on specially designed parallel processing hardware. It usually works on the assumption that elements of the hardware (such as the memory) are tightly coupled. Often, the machine is expected to be devoted to running a single task at very high speed.

- A distributed operating system is usually defined as running on more loosely coupled hardware. Unlike parallel operating systems, distributed operating systems are intended to make a collection of resources on multiple machines usable by a set of loosely cooperating users running independent tasks.

- Network operating systems are sometimes regarded as systems that attempt merely to make the network connecting the machines more usable, without regard for some of the larger problems of building effective distributed systems.

Although many interesting research distributed operating systems have been built since the 1970s, and some systems have been in use for many years, they have not displaced traditional operating systems designed primarily to support single machines; however, some of the components originally built for distributed operating systems have become commonplace in today's systems, notably services to access files stored on remote machines. The failure of distributed operating systems to capture a large share of the marketplace may be primarily due to our lack of understanding on how to build them, or perhaps their lack of popularity stems from users not really needing many distributed services not already provided.

Distributed operating systems are also an important field for study because they have helped drive general research in distributed systems. Replicated data systems, authentication services such as Kerberos, agreement protocols, methods of providing causal ordering in communications, voting and consensus protocols, and many other distributed services have been developed to support distributed operating systems, and have found varying degrees of success outside of that field. Popular distributed component services like CORBA owe some of their success to applying hard lessons learned by researchers in distributed operating systems. Increasingly, cooperative applications and services run across the Internet, and they face similar problems to those seen and frequently solved in the realm of distributed operating systems.

Distributed operating systems are hard to design because they face inherently hard problems, such as distributed consensus and synchronization. Further, they must properly trade off issues of performance, user interfaces, reliability, and simplicity. The relative scarcity of such systems, and the fact that most commercial operating systems' design still focuses on single-machine systems, suggests that no distributed operating system yet developed has found the proper trade-off among these issues.

Challenges in Building Distributed Operating Systems

One core problem for distributed operating system designers is concurrency and synchronization. These issues arise in single-machine operating systems, but they are easier to solve there. Typical single-machine systems run a single thread of control simultaneously, simplifying many synchronization problems. The advent of multicore machines is complicating this issue, but most multicore machines have relatively few cores, lessening the problem. Further, they typically have shared access to memory, registers, or other useful physical resources that are directly accessible by all processes that they must synchronize. These shared resources allow use of simple and fast synchronization primitives, such as semaphores. Even modern machines that have multiple processors typically include hardware that makes it easier to synchronize their operations.

Distributed operating systems lack these advantages. Typically, they must control a collection of processors connected by a network, most often a local area network (LAN), but occasionally a network with even more difficult characteristics. The access time across this network is orders of magnitude larger than the access time required to reach local main memory and even more orders of magnitude larger than that required to reach information in a local processor cache or register. Further, such networks are not as reliable as a typical bus, so messages are more likely to be lost or corrupted. At best, this unreliability increases the average access time.

This imbalance means that running blocking primitives across the network is often infeasible. The performance implications for the individual component systems and the system as a whole do not permit widespread use of such primitives. Designers must choose between looser synchronization (leading to odd user-visible behaviors and possibly fatal system inconsistencies) and sluggish performance. The increasing gap between processor and network speeds suggests that this effect will only get worse.

Theoretical results in distributed systems are discouraging. Research on various forms of the Byzantine General problem and other formulations of the problems of reaching decisions in distributed systems has provided surprising results with bad implications for the possibility of providing perfect synchronization of such systems. Briefly, these results suggest that reaching a distributed decision is not always possible in common circumstances. Even when it is possible, doing so in unfavorable conditions is very expensive and tricky. Although most distributed systems can be designed to operate in more favorable circumstances than these gloomy theoretical results describe (typically by assuming less drastic failure modes or less absolute need for complete consistency), experience has shown that even pragmatic algorithm design for this environment is difficult.

A further core problem is providing transparency. Transparency has various definitions and aspects, but at a high level it simply refers to the degree to which the operating system disguises the distributed nature of the system. Providing a high degree of transparency is good because it shields the user from the complexities of distribution. On the other hand, it sometimes hides more than it should, it can be expensive and tricky to provide, and ultimately it is not always possible. A key decision in designing a distributed operating system is how much transparency to provide, and where and when to provide it.

A related problem is that the hardware, which the distributed operating system must virtualize, is more varied. A distributed operating system must not only make a file on disk appear to be in the main memory, as a typical operating system does, but must make a file on a different machine appear to be on the local machine, even if it is simultaneously being accessed on yet a third machine. The system should not just make a multi-machine computation appear to run on a single machine, but should provide observers on all machines with the illusion that it is running only on their machine.

Distributed operating systems also face challenging problems because they are typically intended to continue correct operation despite failure of some of their components. Most single-machine operating systems provide very limited abilities to continue operation if key components fail. They are certainly not expected to provide useful service if their processor crashes. A single processor crash in a distributed operating system should allow the remainder of the system to continue operations largely unharmed. Achieving this ideal can be extremely challenging. If the topology of the network connecting the system's component nodes allows the network to split into disjoint pieces, the system might also need to continue operation in a partitioned mode and would be expected to rapidly reintegrate when the partitions merge.

The security problems of a distributed operating system are also harder. First, data typically moves over a network, sometimes over a network that the distributed operating system itself does not directly control. This network may be subject to eavesdropping or malicious insertion and alteration of messages. Even if protected by cryptography, denial of service attacks may cause disconnections or loss of critical messages. Second, access control and resource management mechanisms on single machines typically take advantage of hardware that helps keep processes separate, such as page tables. Distributed operating systems cannot rely on this advantage. Third, distributed operating systems are typically expected to provide some degree of local control to users on their individual machines, while still enforcing general access control mechanisms. When an individual user is legitimately able to access any bytes stored anywhere on his own machine, preventing him from accessing data that belongs to others is a much harder problem, particularly if the system strives to provide controlled high-performance access to that data.

Distributed operating systems must often address the issue of local autonomy. In many (but not all) architectures, the distributed system is composed of workstations whose primary job is to support one particular user. The distributed system must balance the needs of the entire collection of supported users against the natural expectation that one's machine should be under one's own control. The local autonomy question has clear security implications, but also relates to how resources are allocated, how scheduling is done, and other issues.

In many cases, distributed operating systems are expected to run on heterogeneous hardware. Although commercial convergence on a small set of popular processors has reduced this problem to some extent, the wide variety of peripheral devices and customizations of system settings provided by today's operating systems often makes supposedly identical hardware behave radically differently. If a distributed operating system cannot determine whether running the same operation on two different component nodes produces the same result, it will face difficulties in providing transparency and consistency.

All the previously mentioned problems are exacerbated if the system scale becomes sufficiently large. Many useful distributed algorithms scale poorly, because the number of messages they require faces combinatorial explosion, or because the delays required to include large numbers of nodes in computations become unreasonable, or because data structures grow in proportion to the number of participants. High scale ensures that partial failures will become more common, and that low probability events will begin to pop up every so often. High scale might also imply that the distributed operating system must operate away from the relatively friendly world of the LAN, leading to greater heterogeneity and uncertainty in communications.

An entirely different paradigm of building system software for distributed systems can avoid some of these difficulties. Sensor networks, rather than performing general purpose computing, are designed only to gather information from sensors and send it to places that need it. The nodes in a sensor network are typically very simple and have low power in many dimensions, from CPU speed to battery. As a result, while inherently distributed systems, sensor network nodes must run relatively simple code. Operating systems designed for sensor networks, like TinyOS, are thus themselves extremely simple. By proper design of the operating system and algorithms that perform the limited applications, a sensor network achieves a cooperative distributed goal without worrying about many of the classic issues of distributed operating systems, such as tight synchronization, data consistency, and partial failure. This approach does not seem to offer an alternative when one is designing a distributed operating system for typical desktop or server machines, but may prove to be a powerful tool for other circumstances in which the nodes in the distributed systems need only do very particular and limited tasks.

Other limited versions of distributed operating system also avoid many of the worst difficulties faced in the general case. In cloud computing, for example, the provider of the cloud does not himself have to worry about maintaining transparency or consistency among the vast number of nodes he supports. His distributed systems problems are more limited, relating to management of large numbers of nodes, providing strong security between the users of portions of his system, ensuring fair and fast use of the network, and, at most, providing some basic distributed system primitives to his users. By expecting the users or middleware to customize the basic node operations he provides to suit their individual distributed system needs, the cloud provider offloads many of the most troublesome problems in distributed operating systems. Since the majority of users of cloud computing don't need those problems solved, anyway, this approach suits both the requirements of the cloud provider and the desires of the typical customer. This is not to understate the challenges of providing a proper cloud environment, but to point out that there are interesting and useful distributed systems that need not solve all of the problems facing a general distributed operating system.

Embedded Operating System

An embedded operating system is essentially a stripped-down operating system with a limited number of features. It is typically designed for very specific functions for controlling an electronic device. For example, all cell phones use an operating system that boots up when the phone is turned on. It handles all the basic interface and features of the phone. Additional programs can be loaded onto the phones, but they are typically JAVA applications that run on top of the operating system.

Embedded operating systems can either be custom written operating systems specific to the device or one of the myriad of general-purpose operating systems that have been modified to run on top of the device. Common embedded operating systems include Symbian (cell phones), Windows Mobile/CE (handheld PDAs) and Linux. In the case of an embedded OS on a personal computer, this is an additional flash memory chip installed on a motherboard that is accessible on boot from the PC.

Use of Embedded OS

Since the PC doesn't require a separate operating system to use all of the features, what reason is there to put a separate hardware operating system? The main reason is to expand the capabilities of the system without the need to be running all of the hardware. After all, even in power save modes, running the full operating systems will use up more power than half of the components inside of the computer. If you are browsing the web but not saving data, do you need to use the optical drive or hard drive?

The other major benefit of an embedded operating system on a PC is to speed up the ability to use the system for specific functions. The average system takes anywhere from one to five minutes to fully boot up the Vista operating system from a cold start. An embedded operating system could be loaded up from a cold start in a matter of seconds. Sure, you will not be able to use all of the features of the PC, but do you really need to boot up the entire system if you are looking at flashing the BIOS or checking on a website?

Difference between Embedded OS and Media Features without the OS

One feature that has been prevalent on multimedia notebooks is the ability to launch either playback of an audio CD or a DVD movie on the PC without the need for booting up all of the system's functions and operating system from the OS. This actually is one example of an embedded operating system within a PC. The embedded operating system has been customized specifically to use the hardware features on the system for the playback of audio and video. This gives users media features in a faster time and without the need of using all the power required for the additional unused features when running the full OS.

Embedded OS on a PC

Having an embedded OS on a PC can be useful, but it really depends upon what applications and features are possible. It also depends upon the type of PC system that it is installed in. An embedded OS that is there solely for the purpose of being able to flash or restore a BIOS for a PC is useful on just about any PC. An embedded OS that will boot up into a web browser might be useful for a laptop PC but not for a desktop PC. One example of such a feature might be for a traveling business person to quickly check the status of a flight or rental car before departing for the airport. The same feature isn't as useful for a system that isn't mobile. You might as well take the time to boot up.

Real-time Operating System

The real-time operating system used for a real-time application means for those applications where data processing should be done in the fixed and small quantum of time. It is different from general purpose computer where time concept is not considered as much crucial as in Real-Time Operating System. RTOS is a time-sharing system based on clock interrupts. Interrupt Service Routine (ISR) serve the interrupt, raised by the system. RTOS used Priority to execute the process. When a high priority process enters in system low priority process preempted to serve higher priority process. Real-time operating system synchronized the process. So that they can communicate with each other. Resources can be used efficiently without wastage of time.

RTOS are controlling traffic signal; Nuclear reactors Control scientific experiments, medical imaging systems, industrial system, fuel injection system, home appliance are some application of Real Time operating system

Real time Operating Systems are very fast and quick respondent systems. These systems are used in an environment where a large number of events (generally external) must be accepted and processed in a short time. Real time processing requires quick transaction and characterized by supplying immediate response. For example, a measurement from a petroleum refinery indicating that temperature is getting too high and might demand for immediate attention to avoid an explosion.

In real time operating system there is a little swapping of programs between primary and secondary memory. Most of the time, processes remain in primary memory in order to provide quick response, therefore, memory management in real time system is less demanding compared to other systems.

Time Sharing Operating System is based on Event-driven and time-sharing the design.

The event Driven: In event-driven switching, higher priority task requires CPU service first than a lower priority task, known as priority scheduling.

Time Sharing: Switching takes place after fixed time quantum known as Round Robin Scheduling.

In these design, we mainly deal with three states of the process cycle

1) Running: when CPU is executing a process, then it is in running state.

2) Ready: When a process has all the resources require performing a process, but still it is not in running state because of the absence of CPU is known as the Ready state.

3) Blocked: when a process has not all required resources for execution, then it is blocked state.

Interrupt Latency: Interrupt latency is time between an interrupt is generated by a device and till it serviced. In RTOS, Interrupt maintained in a fixed amount of time, i.e., latency time bounded.

Memory Allocation: RTOS support static as well as dynamic memory allocation. Both allocations used for different purpose. Like Static Memory, the allocation is used for compile and design time using stacks data structure. Dynamic memory allocation used for runtime used heap data structure.

The primary functions of the real time operating system are to:

1. Manage the processor and other system resources to meet the requirements of an application.

2. Synchronize with and respond to the system events.

3. Move the data efficiently among processes and to perform coordination among these processes.

The Real Time systems are used in the environments where a large number of events (generally external to the computer system) is required to be accepted and is to be processed in the form of quick response. Such systems have to be the multitasking. So the primary function of the real time operating system is to manage certain system resources, such as the CPU, memory, and time. Each resource must be shared among the competing processes to accomplish the overall function of the system Apart from these primary functions of the real time operating system there are certain secondary functions that are not mandatory but are included to enhance the performance:

1. To provide an efficient management of RAM.

2. To provide an exclusive access to the computer resources.

The term real time refers to the technique of updating files with the transaction data immediately just after the event that it relates with.

Few more examples of real time processing are:

1. Airlines reservation system.

2. Air traffic control system.

3. Systems that provide immediate updating.

4. Systems that provide up to the minute information on stock prices.

5. Defense application systems like as RADAR.

Real time operating systems mostly use the preemptive priority scheduling. These support more than one scheduling policy and often allow the user to set parameters associated with such policies, such as the time-slice in Round Robin scheduling where each task in the task queue is scheduled up to a maximum time, set by the time-slice parameter, in a round robin manner. Hundred of the priority levels are commonly available for scheduling. Some specific tasks can also be indicated to be non-preemptive.

Types of Real-time Operating System

1) Soft Real-Time Operating System: A process might not be executed in given deadline. It can be crossed it then executed next, without harming the system. Example are a digital camera, mobile phones, etc.

2) Hard Real-Time Operating System: A process should be executed in given deadline. The deadline should not be crossed. Preemption time for Hard Real-Time Operating System is almost less than few microseconds.

Examples are Airbag control in cars, anti-lock brake, engine control system, etc.

Advantages of Real Time Operating System

There are some of the features of using RTOS that is described below

Maximum Consumption: – RTOS give maximum consumption of the system and gives us more output while using all the resources and keeping all devices active. There is little or no down time in these systems. So it can be also using by the servers that are hosted to give maximum output of hosting companies.

Task Shifting: – There is very little time assigned to shifting tasks in these systems. For example in older systems it takes about 10 micro seconds in shifting one task to another and in latest systems it takes 3 micro seconds.

Focus on Application: – These type of operating system focus on applications which are running and usually give less importance to other application residing in waiting stage of life cycle. So less applications or tasks are managed and give exact result on current execution work.

Real time operating system in embedded system: – Due to small size of programs RTOS can also be used in embedded systems like in transport and others.

Error Free: – RTOS is error free that means it has no chances of error in performing tasks.

24-7 systems: – RTOS can be best used for any applications which run 24 hours and 7 days because it does less task shifting and give maximum output.

Real time operating system examples: – There are many real time operating system examples. They are used in vast areas like digital appliances, home video games, wind power systems, intelligent transport system, and robots in industry

Memory Allocation: – Memory allocation is best managed in these type of systems.

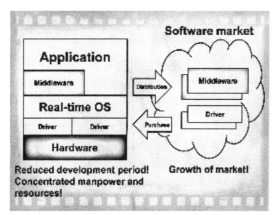

Pros and Cons of real time operating systems

Disadvantages of Real Time Operating System

There are some disadvantages of RTOS also. So every system has pros and cons so here are some of bad things about RTOS.

Limited Tasks: – There are only limited tasks run at the same time and the concentration of these system are on few application to avoid errors and other task have to wait. Sometime there is no time limit of how much the waiting tasks have to wait.

Use heavy system resources: – RTOS used lot of system resources which is not as good and is also expensive.

Low multi-tasking: – Multi tasking is done few of times and this is the main disadvantage of RTOS because these systems run few tasks and stay focused on them. So it is not best for systems which use lot of multi-threading because of poor thread priority.

Complex Algorithms: – RTOS uses complex algorithms to achieve a desired output and it is very difficult to write that algorithms for a designer.

Device driver and interrupt signals: – RTOS must need specific device drivers and interrupt signals to response fast to interrupts.

Thread Priority: – Thread priority is not good as RTOS do less switching of tasks.

Expensive: – RTOS are usually very expensive because of the resources they need to work.

Not easy to program: – The designer have to write proficient program for real time operating system which is not easy as a piece of cake.

Low Priority Tasks: – The low priority tasks may not get time to run because these systems have to keep accuracy of current running programs.

Precision of code: – Event handling of tasks is strict so more precision in code needed for designer to program. Event must be responded quickly and this is not easy for exact precision for the designer.

Other factors: – There are lot of factors needed to consider like memory management, CPU and error handling.

Difference between in GPOS and RTOS

General-Purpose Operating System (GPOS)	Real-Time Operating System (RTOS)
1) It used for desktop pc, laptop.	1) It applied for the embedded application.
2) Process-based Scheduling used.	2) Time-based scheduling used like round robin.
3) Interrupt latency is not considered as much crucial as in RTOS.	3) Interrupt lag is minimal, measured in few microseconds.
4) No priority inversion mechanism is present in the system.	4) Priority inversion mechanism is current. Once priority set by the programmer, it can't be changed by the system itself.
5) Kernel operations may or may not be preempted.	5) Kernel operation can be preempted.

Major Operating Systems

Unix and Linux

The Unix operating system is a set of programs that act as a link between the computer and the user.

The computer programs that allocate the system resources and coordinate all the details of the computer's internals is called the operating system or the kernel.

Users communicate with the kernel through a program known as the shell. The shell is a command line interpreter; it translates commands entered by the user and converts them into a language that is understood by the kernel.

- Unix was originally developed in 1969 by a group of AT&T employees Ken Thompson, Dennis Ritchie, Douglas Mcilroy, and Joe Ossanna at Bell Labs.

- There are various Unix variants available in the market. Solaris Unix, AIX, HP Unix and BSD are a few examples. Linux is also a flavor of Unix which is freely available.

- Several people can use a Unix computer at the same time; hence Unix is called a multiuser system.

- A user can also run multiple programs at the same time; hence Unix is a multitasking environment.

Unix Architecture

The main concept that unites all the versions of Unix is the following four basics –

- Kernel – The kernel is the heart of the operating system. It interacts with the hardware and most of the tasks like memory management, task scheduling and file management.

- Shell – The shell is the utility that processes your requests. When you type in a command at your terminal, the shell interprets the command and calls the program that you want. The shell uses standard syntax for all commands. C Shell, Bourne Shell and Korn Shell are the most famous shells which are available with most of the Unix variants.

- Commands and Utilities – There are various commands and utilities which you can make use of in your day to day activities. cp, mv, cat and grep, etc. are few examples of commands and utilities. There are over 250 standard commands plus numerous others provided through 3rd party software. All the commands come along with various options.

- Files and Directories – All the data of Unix is organized into files. All files are then organized into directories. These directories are further organized into a tree-like structure called the file system.

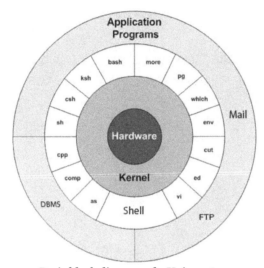

Basic block diagram of a Unix system

System Boot up

If you have a computer which has the Unix operating system installed in it, then you simply need to turn on the system to make it live.

As soon as you turn on the system, it starts booting up and finally it prompts you to log into the system, which is an activity to log into the system and use it for your day-to-day activities.

Login Unix

When you first connect to a Unix system, you usually see a prompt such as the following –

```
login:
```

To log in

- Have your user id (user identification) and password ready. Contact your system administrator if you don't have these yet.

- Type your user id at the login prompt, and then press ENTER. Your user id is case-sensitive, so be sure you type it exactly as your system administrator has instructed.

- Type your password at the password prompt, and then press 'enter'. Your password is also case-sensitive.

- If you provide the correct user id and password, then you will be allowed to enter into the system. Read the information and messages that comes up on the screen, which is as follows.

-    `login : amrood`

-    `amrood's password:`

-    `Last login: Sun Jun 14 09:32:32 2009 from 62.61.164.73`

-    `$`

-

You will be provided with a command prompt (sometime called the $ prompt) where you type all your commands. For example, to check calendar, you need to type the cal command as follows –

```
$ cal
     June 2009
Su Mo Tu We Th Fr Sa
    1  2  3  4  5  6
 7  8  9 10 11 12 13
14 15 16 17 18 19 20
21 22 23 24 25 26 27
28 29 30


$
```

Change Password

All Unix systems require passwords to help ensure that your files and data remain your own and that the system itself is secure from hackers and crackers. Following are the steps to change your password:

Step 1 – To start, type password at the command prompt as shown below.

Step 2 – Enter your old password, the one you're currently using.

Step 3 – Type in your new password. Always keep your password complex enough so that nobody can guess it. But make sure, you remember it.

Step 4 – You must verify the password by typing it again.

```
$ passwd

Changing password for amrood

(current) Unix password:******

New UNIX password:*******

Retype new UNIX password:*******

passwd: all authentication tokens updated  successfully


$
```

We have added asterisk (*) here just to show the location where you need to enter the current and new passwords otherwise at your system. It does not show you any character when you type.

Listing Directories and Files

All data in Unix is organized into files. All files are organized into directories. These directories are organized into a tree-like structure called the file system.

You can use the ls command to list out all the files or directories available in a directory. Following is the example of using ls command with -l option.

```
$ ls -l

total 19621

drwxrwxr-x   2 amrood amrood        4096 Dec 25 09:59 uml

-rw-rw-r--   1 amrood amrood        5341 Dec 25 08:38 uml.jpg

drwxr-xr-x   2 amrood amrood        4096 Feb 15  2006 univ

drwxr-xr-x   2 root   root          4096 Dec  9  2007 urlspedia

-rw-r--r--   1 root   root        276480 Dec  9  2007 urlspedia.tar

drwxr-xr-x   8 root   root          4096 Nov 25  2007 usr

-rwxr-xr-x   1 root   root          3192 Nov 25  2007 webthumb.php

-rw-rw-r--   1 amrood amrood       20480 Nov 25  2007 webthumb.tar

-rw-rw-r--   1 amrood amrood        5654 Aug  9  2007 yourfile.mid

-rw-rw-r--   1 amrood amrood      166255 Aug  9  2007 yourfile.swf


$
```

Here entries starting with 'd' Represent directories. For example, uml, univ and urlspedia are directories and rests of the entries are files.

Who Are You?

While you're logged into the system, you might be willing to know : Who am I?

The easiest way to find out "who you are" is to enter the whoami command:

```
$ whoami
  amrood


$
```

Try it on your system. This command lists the account name associated with the current login. You can try whoami command as well to get information about yourself.

Who is Logged in?

Sometime you might be interested to know who is logged in to the computer at the same time.

There are three commands available to get you this information, based on how much you wish to know about the other users: users, who, and w.

```
$ users
  amrood bablu qadir


$ who
amrood ttyp0 Oct 8 14:10 (limbo)
bablu  ttyp2 Oct 4 09:08 (calliope)
qadir  ttyp4 Oct 8 12:09 (dent)


$
```

Try the w command on your system to check the output. This lists down information associated with the users logged in the system.

Logging Out

When you finish your session, you need to log out of the system. This is to ensure that nobody else accesses your files.

To Log out

- Just type the logout command at the command prompt, and the system will clean up everything and break the connection.

System Shutdown

The most consistent way to shut down a Unix system properly via the command line is to use one of the following commands –

Sr.No.	Command & Description
1	**halt** Brings the system down immediately
2	**init 0** Powers off the system using predefined scripts to synchronize and clean up the system prior to shutting down
3	**init 6** Reboots the system by shutting it down completely and then restarting it
4	**poweroff** Shuts down the system by powering off
5	**reboot** Reboots the system
6	**shutdown** Shuts down the system

You typically need to be the super user or root (the most privileged account on a Unix system) to shut down the system. However, on some standalone or personally-owned Unix boxes, an administrative user and sometimes regular users can do so.

File Management

All data in Unix is organized into files. All files are organized into directories. These directories are organized into a tree-like structure called the file system.

When you work with Unix, one way or another, you spend most of your time working with files. We will show here how to create and remove files, copy and rename them, create links to them, etc.

In Unix, there are three basic types of files :

- Ordinary Files: An ordinary file is a file on the system that contains data, text, or program instructions.

- Directories: Directories store both special and ordinary files. For users familiar with Windows or Mac OS, Unix directories are equivalent to folders.

- Special Files: Some special files provide access to hardware such as hard drives, CD-ROM drives, modems, and Ethernet adapters. Other special files are similar to aliases or shortcuts and enable you to access a single file using different names.

Listing Files

To list the files and directories stored in the current directory, use the following command –

```
$ls
```

Here is the sample output of the above command –

```
ls
```

```
bin          hosts  lib     res.03
ch07         hw1    pub     test_results
ch07.bak     hw2    res.01  users
docs         hw3    res.02  work
```

The command ls supports the -l option which would help you to get more information about the listed files –$ls -l

```
total 1962188
```

```
drwxrwxr-x  2 amrood amrood      4096 Dec 25 09:59 uml
-rw-rw-r--  1 amrood amrood      5341 Dec 25 08:38 uml.jpg
drwxr-xr-x  2 amrood amrood      4096 Feb 15  2006 univ
drwxr-xr-x  2 root   root        4096 Dec  9  2007 urlspedia
-rw-r--r--  1 root   root      276480 Dec  9  2007 urlspedia.tar
drwxr-xr-x  8 root   root        4096 Nov 25  2007 usr
drwxr-xr-x  2    200    300      4096 Nov 25  2007 webthumb-1.01
-rwxr-xr-x  1 root   root        3192 Nov 25  2007 webthumb.php
-rw-rw-r--  1 amrood amrood     20480 Nov 25  2007 webthumb.tar
-rw-rw-r--  1 amrood amrood      5654 Aug  9  2007 yourfile.mid
-rw-rw-r--  1 amrood amrood    166255 Aug  9  2007 yourfile.swf
drwxr-xr-x 11 amrood amrood      4096 May 29  2007 zlib-1.2.3
$
```

Here is the information about all the listed columns –

- **First Column** – Represents the file type and the permission given on the file. Below is the description of all type of files.

- Second Column – Represents the number of memory blocks taken by the file or directory.

- Third Column – Represents the owner of the file. This is the Unix user who created this file.

- Fourth Column – Represents the group of the owner. Every Unix user will have an associated group.

- Fifth Column – Represents the file size in bytes.

- Sixth Column – Represents the date and the time when this file was created or modified for the last time.

- Seventh Column – Represents the file or the directory name.

In the ls -l listing example, every file line begins with a d, -, or l. These characters indicate the type of the file that's listed.

Sr.No.	Prefix & Description
1	**-** Regular file, such as an ASCII text file, binary executable, or hard link.
2	**b** Block special file. Block input/output device file such as a physical hard drive.
3	**c** Character special file. Raw input/output device file such as a physical hard drive.
4	**d** Directory file that contains a listing of other files and directories.
5	**l** Symbolic link file. Links on any regular file.
6	**p** Named pipe. A mechanism for interprocess communications.
7	**s** Socket used for interprocess communication.

Metacharacters

Metacharacters have a special meaning in Unix. For example, * and ? are metacharacters. We use * to match 0 or more characters, a question mark (?) matches with a single character.

For Example –

```
$ls ch*.doc
```

Displays all the files, the names of which start with ch and end with .doc –

```
ch01-1.doc    ch010.doc    ch02.doc     ch03-2.doc

ch04-1.doc    ch040.doc    ch05.doc     ch06-2.doc

ch01-2.doc ch02-1.doc c
```

Here, * works as meta character which matches with any character. If you want to display all the files ending with just .doc, then you can use the following command –

```
$ls *.doc
```

Hidden Files

An invisible file is one, the first character of which is the dot or the period character (.). Unix programs (including the shell) use most of these files to store configuration information.

Some common examples of the hidden files include the files –

- .profile – The Bourne shell (sh) initialization script
- .kshrc – The Korn shell (ksh) initialization script
- .cshrc – The C shell (csh) initialization script
- .rhosts – The remote shell configuration file

To list the invisible files, specify the -a option to ls –

```
$ ls -a
```

```
.            .profile     docs     lib      test_results
..           .rhosts      hosts    pub      users
.emacs       bin          hw1      res.01   work
.exrc        ch07         hw2      res.02
.kshrc       ch07.bak     hw3      res.03
$
```

- Single dot (.) – This represents the current directory.
- Double dot (..) – This represents the parent directory.

Creating Files

You can use the vi editor to create ordinary files on any Unix system. You simply need to give the following command –

```
$ vi filename
```

The above command will open a file with the given filename. Now, press the key i to come into the edit mode. Once you are in the edit mode, you can start writing your content in the file as in the following program –

```
This is unix file....I created it for the first time.....
I'm going to save this content in this file.
```

Once you are done with the program, follow these steps –

- Press the key esc to come out of the edit mode.

- Press two keys Shift + ZZ together to come out of the file completely.

You will now have a file created with filename in the current directory.

```
$ vi filename
$
```

Editing Files

You can edit an existing file using the vi editor. We will discuss in short how to open an existing file –

```
$ vi filename
```

Once the file is opened, you can come in the edit mode by pressing the key i and then you can proceed by editing the file. If you want to move here and there inside a file, then first you need to come out of the edit mode by pressing the key Esc. After this, you can use the following keys to move inside a file –

- l key to move to the right side.

- h key to move to the left side.

- k key to move upside in the file.

- j key to move downside in the file.

So using the above keys, you can position your cursor wherever you want to edit. Once you are positioned, then you can use the i key to come in the edit mode. Once you are done with the editing in your file, press Esc and finally two keys Shift + ZZ together to come out of the file completely.

Display Content of a File

You can use the cat command to see the content of a file. Following is a simple example to see the content of the above created file –

```
$ cat filename
This is unix file....I created it for the first time.....
I'm going to save this content in this file.
$
```

You can display the line numbers by using the -b option along with the cat command as follows

```
$ cat -b filename
1    This is unix file....I created it for the first time.....
2    I'm going to save this content in this file.
$
```

Counting Words in a File

You can use the wc command to get a count of the total number of lines, words, and characters contained in a file. Following is a simple example to see the information about the file created above –

```
$ wc filename
2   19 103 filename
$
```

Here is the detail of all the four columns –

- First Column – Represents the total number of lines in the file.
- Second Column – Represents the total number of words in the file.
- Third Column – Represents the total number of bytes in the file. This is the actual size of the file.
- Fourth Column – Represents the file name.

You can give multiple files and get information about those files at a time. Following is simple syntax –

```
$ wc filename1 filename2 filename3
```

Copying Files

To make a copy of a file use the cp command. The basic syntax of the command is –

```
$ cp source_file destination_file
```

Following is the example to create a copy of the existing file filename

```
$ cp filename copyfile
$
```

You will now find one more file copyfile in your current directory. This file will exactly be the same as the original file filename.

Renaming Files

To change the name of a file, use the mv command. Following is the basic syntax –

```
$ mv old_file new_file
```

The following program will rename the existing file filename to newfile.

```
$ mv filename newfile
$
```

The mv command will move the existing file completely into the new file. In this case, you will find only newfile in your current directory.

Deleting Files

To delete an existing file, use the rm command. Following is the basic syntax –

```
$ rm filename
```

Caution – A file may contain useful information. It is always recommended to be careful while using this Delete command. It is better to use the -i option along with rm command.

Following is the example which shows how to completely remove the existing file filename.

```
$ rm filename
$
```

You can remove multiple files at a time with the command given below –

```
$ rm filename1 filename2 filename3
$
```

Standard Unix Streams

Under normal circumstances, every Unix program has three streams (files) opened for it when it starts up –

- stdin – This is referred to as the standard input and the associated file descriptor is 0. This is also represented as STDIN. The Unix program will read the default input from STDIN.

- stdout – This is referred to as the standard output and the associated file descriptor is 1. This is also represented as STDOUT. The Unix program will write the default output at STDOUT

- stderr – This is referred to as the standard error and the associated file descriptor is 2. This is also represented as STDERR. The Unix program will write all the error messages at STDERR.

Directory Management

A directory is a file the solo job of which is to store the file names and the related information. All the files, whether ordinary, special, or directory, are contained in directories.

Unix uses a hierarchical structure for organizing files and directories. This structure is often referred to as a directory tree. The tree has a single root node, the slash character (/), and all other directories are contained below it.

Home Directory

The directory in which you find yourself when you first login is called your home directory.

You will be doing much of your work in your home directory and subdirectories that you'll be creating to organize your files.

You can go in your home directory anytime using the following command –

```
$cd ~
$
```

Here ~ indicates the home directory. Suppose you have to go in any other user's home directory, use the following command –

```
$cd ~username
$
```

To go in your last directory, you can use the following command –

```
$cd -
$
```

Absolute/Relative Pathnames

Directories are arranged in a hierarchy with root (/) at the top. The position of any file within the hierarchy is described by its pathname.

Elements of a pathname are separated by a /. A pathname is absolute, if it is described in relation to root, thus absolute pathnames always begin with a /.

Following are some examples of absolute filenames.

```
/etc/passwd
```

```
/users/sjones/chem/notes
```

```
/dev/rdsk/0s3
```

A pathname can also be relative to your current working directory. Relative pathnames never begin with /. Relative to user amrood's home directory, some pathnames might look like this –

```
chem/notes
```

```
personal/res
```

To determine where you are within the filesystem hierarchy at any time, enter the command pwd to print the current working directory –

```
$pwd
```

```
/user0/home/amrood
```

```
$
```

Listing Directories

To list the files in a directory, you can use the following syntax –

```
$ls dirname
```

Following is the example to list all the files contained in /usr/local directory –

```
$ls /usr/local
```

X11	bin	gimp	jikes	sbin
ace	doc	include	lib	share
atalk	etc	info	man	ami

Creating Directories

We will now understand how to create directories. Directories are created by the following command –

```
$mkdir dirname
```

Here, directory is the absolute or relative pathname of the directory you want to create. For example, the command –

```
$mkdir mydir
```

```
$
```

Creates the directory mydir in the current directory. Here is another example –

```
$mkdir /tmp/test-dir
```

```
$
```

This command creates the directory test-dir in the /tmp directory. The mkdir command produces no output if it successfully creates the requested directory.

If you give more than one directory on the command line, mkdir creates each of the directories. For example, –

```
$mkdir docs pub

$
```

Creates the directories docs and pub under the current directory.

Creating Parent Directories

We will now understand how to create parent directories. Sometimes when you want to create a directory, its parent directory or directories might not exist. In this case, mkdir issues an error message as follows –

```
$mkdir /tmp/amrood/test

mkdir: Failed to make directory "/tmp/amrood/test";

No such file or directory

$
```

In such cases, you can specify the -p option to the mkdir command. It creates all the necessary directories for you. For example –

```
$mkdir -p /tmp/amrood/test

$
```

The above command creates all the required parent directories.

Removing Directories

Directories can be deleted using the rmdir command as follows –

```
$rmdir dirname

$
```

To remove a directory, make sure it is empty which means there should not be any file or sub-directory inside this directory.

You can remove multiple directories at a time as follows –

```
$rmdir dirname1 dirname2 dirname3

$
```

The above command removes the directories dirname1, dirname2, and dirname3, if they are empty. The rmdir command produces no output if it is successful.

Changing Directories

You can use the cd command to do more than just change to a home directory. You can use it to change to any directory by specifying a valid absolute or relative path. The syntax is as given below –

```
$cd dirname
$
```

Here, dirname is the name of the directory that you want to change to. For example, the command –

```
$cd /usr/local/bin
$
```

Changes to the directory /usr/local/bin. From this directory, you can cd to the directory /usr/home/amrood using the following relative path –

```
$cd ../../home/amrood
$
```

Renaming Directories

The mv (move) command can also be used to rename a directory. The syntax is as follows –

```
$mv olddir newdir
$
```

You can rename a directory mydir to yourdir as follows –

```
$mv mydir yourdir
$
```

Directories . (dot) and .. (dot dot)

The filename . (dot) represents the current working directory; and the filename .. (dot dot) represents the directory one level above the current working directory, often referred to as the parent directory.

If we enter the command to show a listing of the current working directories/files and use the -a option to list all the files and the -l option to provide the long listing, we will receive the following result.

```
$ls -la

drwxrwxr-x    4    teacher    class    2048  Jul 16 17.56 .
drwxr-xr-x   60    root                1536  Jul 13 14:18 ..
```

```
----------    1    teacher   class   4210   May 1  08:27 .profile
-rwxr-xr-x    1    teacher   class   1948   May 12 13:42 memo
$
```

File Permission / Access Modes

File ownership is an important component of Unix that provides a secure method for storing files. Every file in Unix has the following attributes:

Owner permissions – The owner's permissions determine what actions the owner of the file can perform on the file.

Group permissions – The group's permissions determine what actions a user, who is a member of the group that a file belongs to, can perform on the file.

Other (world) permissions – The permissions for others indicate what action all other users can perform on the file.

Permission Indicators

While using ls -l command, it displays various information related to file permission as follows –

```
$ls -l /home/amrood

-rwxr-xr--  1 amrood   users 1024  Nov 2 00:10  myfile
drwxr-xr---  1 amrood   users 1024  Nov 2 00:10  mydir
```

Here, the first column represents different access modes, i.e., the permission associated with a file or a directory.

The permissions are broken into groups of threes, and each position in the group denotes a specific permission, in this order: read (r), write (w), execute (x) –

- The first three characters (2-4) represent the permissions for the file's owner. For example, -rwxr-xr-- represents that the owner has read (r), write (w) and execute (x) permission.

- The second group of three characters (5-7) consists of the permissions for the group to which the file belongs. For example, -rwxr-xr-- represents that the group has read (r) and execute (x) permission, but no write permission.

- The last group of three characters (8-10) represents the permissions for everyone else. For example, -rwxr-xr-- represents that there is read (r) only permission.

File Access Modes

The permissions of a file are the first line of defense in the security of a Unix system. The basic building blocks of Unix permissions are the read, write, and execute permissions, which have been described below –

Read

Grants the capability to read, i.e., view the contents of the file.

Write

Grants the capability to modify, or remove the content of the file.

Execute

User with execute permissions can run a file as a program.

Directory Access Modes

Directory access modes are listed and organized in the same manner as any other file. There are a few differences that need to be mentioned:

Read: Access to a directory means that the user can read the contents. The user can look at the filenames inside the directory.

Write: Access means that the user can add or delete files from the directory.

Execute: Executing a directory doesn't really make sense, so think of this as a traverse permission. A user must have execute access to the bin directory in order to execute the ls or the cd command.

Changing Permissions

To change the file or the directory permissions, you use the chmod (change mode) command. There are two ways to use chmod — the symbolic mode and the absolute mode.

Using chmod in Symbolic Mode

The easiest way for a beginner to modify file or directory permissions is to use the symbolic mode. With symbolic permissions you can add, delete, or specify the permission set you want by using the operators in the following table.

Sr. No.	Chmod operator & Description
1	+ Adds the designated permission(s) to a file or directory.
2	- Removes the designated permission(s) from a file or directory.
3	= Sets the designated permission(s).

Here's an example using testfile. Running ls -1 on the testfile shows that the file's permissions are as follows –

```
$ls -l testfile
```

```
-rwxrwxr-- 1 amrood   users 1024  Nov 2 00:10  testfile
```

Then each example chmod command from the preceding table is run on the testfile, followed by ls –l, so you can see the permission changes –

```
$chmod o+wx testfile
```

```
$ls -l testfile
```

```
-rwxrwxrwx 1 amrood   users 1024  Nov 2 00:10  testfile
```

```
$chmod u-x testfile
```

```
$ls -l testfile
```

```
-rw-rwxrwx 1 amrood   users 1024  Nov 2 00:10  testfile
```

```
$chmod g = rx testfile
```

```
$ls -l testfile
```

```
-rw-r-xrwx 1 amrood   users 1024  Nov 2 00:10  testfile
```

Here's how you can combine these commands on a single line –

```
$chmod o+wx,u-x,g = rx testfile
```

```
$ls -l testfile
```

```
-rw-r-xrwx 1 amrood   users 1024  Nov 2 00:10  testfile
```

Using chmod with Absolute Permissions

The second way to modify permissions with the chmod command is to use a number to specify each set of permissions for the file.

Each permission is assigned a value, as the following table shows, and the total of each set of permissions provides a number for that set.

Number	Octal Permission Representation	Ref
0	No permission	---
1	Execute permission	--x
2	Write permission	-w-
3	Execute and write permission: 1 (execute) + 2 (write) = 3	-wx
4	Read permission	r--
5	Read and execute permission: 4 (read) + 1 (execute) = 5	r-x

| 6 | Read and write permission: 4 (read) + 2 (write) = 6 | rw- |
| 7 | All permissions: 4 (read) + 2 (write) + 1 (execute) = 7 | rwx |

Here's an example using the testfile. Running ls -1 on the testfile shows that the file's permissions are as follows –

```
$ls -l testfile

-rwxrwxr--  1 amrood    users 1024  Nov 2 00:10  testfile
```

Then each example chmod command from the preceding table is run on the testfile, followed by ls –l, so you can see the permission changes –

```
$ chmod 755 testfile

$ls -l testfile

-rwxr-xr-x  1 amrood    users 1024  Nov 2 00:10  testfile

$chmod 743 testfile

$ls -l testfile

-rwxr---wx  1 amrood    users 1024  Nov 2 00:10  testfile

$chmod 043 testfile

$ls -l testfile

----r---wx  1 amrood    users 1024  Nov 2 00:10  testfile
```

Changing Owners and Groups

While creating an account on Unix, it assigns a owner ID and a group ID to each user. All the permissions mentioned above are also assigned based on the Owner and the Groups.

Two commands are available to change the owner and the group of files –

- Chown – The chown command stands for "change owner" and is used to change the owner of a file.

- Chgrp – The chgrp command stands for "change group" and is used to change the group of a file.

Changing Ownership

The chown command changes the ownership of a file. The basic syntax is as follows –

```
$ chown user filelist
```

The value of the user can be either the name of a user on the system or the user id (uid) of a user on the system.

The following example will help you understand the concept –

```
$ chown amrood testfile
$
```

Changes the owner of the given file to the user amrood.

The super user, root, has the unrestricted capability to change the ownership of any file but normal users can change the ownership of only those files that they own.

Changing Group Ownership

The chgrp command changes the group ownership of a file. The basic syntax is as follows –

```
$ chgrp group filelist
```

The value of group can be the name of a group on the system or the group ID (GID) of a group on the system.

Following example helps you understand the concept –

```
$ chgrp special testfile
$
```

Changes the group of the given file to special group.

SUID and SGID File Permission

Often when a command is executed, it will have to be executed with special privileges in order to accomplish its task.

As an example, when you change your password with the passwd command, your new password is stored in the file /etc./shadow.

As a regular user, you do not have read or write access to this file for security reasons, but when you change your password, you need to have the write permission to this file. This means that the passwd program has to give you additional permissions so that you can write to the file /etc/shadow.

Additional permissions are given to programs via a mechanism known as the Set User ID (SUID) and Set Group ID (SGID) bits.

When you execute a program that has the SUID bit enabled, you inherit the permissions of that program's owner. Programs that do not have the SUID bit set are run with the permissions of the user who started the program.

This is the case with SGID as well. Normally, programs execute with your group permissions, but instead your group will be changed just for this program to the group owner of the program.

The SUID and SGID bits will appear as the letter "s" if the permission is available. The SUID "s" bit will be located in the permission bits where the owners' execute permission normally resides.

For example, the command –

```
$ ls -l /usr/bin/passwd

-r-sr-xr-x  1   root   bin   19031 Feb 7 13:47   /usr/bin/passwd*

$
```

Shows that the SUID bit is set and that the command is owned by the root. A capital letter S in the execute position instead of a lowercase s indicates that the execute bit is not set.

If the sticky bit is enabled on the directory, files can only be removed if you are one of the following users –

- The owner of the sticky directory
- The owner of the file being removed
- The super user, root

To set the SUID and SGID bits for any directory try the following command:

```
$ chmod ug+s dirname

$ ls -l

drwsr-sr-x 2 root root  4096 Jun 19 06:45 dirname

$
```

Environment

An important Unix concept is the environment, which is defined by environment variables. Some are set by the system, others by you, yet others by the shell, or any program that loads another program.

A variable is a character string to which we assign a value. The value assigned could be a number, text, filename, device, or any other type of data.

For example, first we set a variable TEST and then we access its value using the echo command-

```
$TEST="Unix Programming"

$echo $TEST
```

It produces the following result.

```
Unix Programming
```

Note that the environment variables are set without using the $ sign but while accessing them we use the $ sign as prefix. These variables retain their values until we come out of the shell.

When you log in to the system, the shell undergoes a phase called initialization to set up the environment. This is usually a two-step process that involves the shell reading the following files –

- /etc/profile
- profile

The process is as follows –

- The shell checks to see whether the file /etc/profile exists.
- If it exists, the shell reads it. Otherwise, this file is skipped. No error message is displayed.
- The shell checks to see whether the file .profile exists in your home directory. Your home directory is the directory that you start out in after you log in.
- If it exists, the shell reads it; otherwise, the shell skips it. No error message is displayed.

As soon as both of these files have been read, the shell displays a prompt –

$

This is the prompt where you can enter commands in order to have them executed.

The shell initialization process detailed here applies to all Bourne type shells, but some additional files are used by bash and ksh.

.Profile (Dot Profile) File

The file /etc/profile is maintained by the system administrator of your Unix machine and contains shell initialization information required by all users on a system.

The file .profile is under your control. You can add as much shell customization information as you want to this file. The minimum set of information that you need to configure includes –

- The type of terminal you are using.
- A list of directories in which to locate the commands.
- A list of variables affecting the look and feel of your terminal.

You can check your .profile available in your home directory. Open it using the vi editor and check all the variables set for your environment.

Setting the Terminal Type

Usually, the type of terminal you are using is automatically configured by either the login or getty programs. Sometimes, the auto configuration process guesses your terminal incorrectly.

If your terminal is set incorrectly, the output of the commands might look strange, or you might not be able to interact with the shell properly.

To make sure that this is not the case, most users set their terminal to the lowest common denominator in the following way –

```
$TERM=vt100

$
```

Setting the PATH

When you type any command on the command prompt, the shell has to locate the command before it can be executed.

The PATH variable specifies the locations in which the shell should look for commands. Usually the Path variable is set as follows –

```
$PATH=/bin:/usr/bin

$
```

Here, each of the individual entries separated by the colon character (:) are directories. If you request the shell to execute a command and it cannot find it in any of the directories given in the PATH variable, a message similar to the following appears –

```
$hello

hello: not found

$
```

PS1 and PS2 Variables

The characters that the shell displays as your command prompt are stored in the variable PS1. You can change this variable to be anything you want. As soon as you change it, it'll be used by the shell from that point on.

For example, if you issued the command –

```
$PS1='=>'

=>

=>

=>
```

Your prompt will become =>. To set the value of PS1 so that it shows the working directory, issue the command –

```
=>PS1="[\u@\h \w]\$"

[root@ip-72-167-112-17 /var/www/dummywebsite/unix]$

[root@ip-72-167-112-17 /var/www/dummywebsite/unix]$
```

The result of this command is that the prompt displays the user's username, the machine's name (hostname), and the working directory.

There are quite a few escape sequences that can be used as value arguments for PS1; try to limit yourself to the most critical so that the prompt does not overwhelm you with information.

Sr. No.	Escape Sequence & Description
1	\t Current time, expressed as HH:MM:SS
2	\d Current date, expressed as Weekday Month Date
3	\n Newline
4	\s Current shell environment
5	\W Working directory
6	\w Full path of the working directory
7	\u Current user's username
8	\h Hostname of the current machine
9	\# Command number of the current command. Increases when a new command is entered
10	\$ If the effective UID is 0 (that is, if you are logged in as root), end the prompt with the # character; otherwise, use the $ sign

You can make the change yourself every time you log in, or you can have the change made automatically in PS1 by adding it to your .profile file.

When you issue a command that is incomplete, the shell will display a secondary prompt and wait for you to complete the command and hit Enter again.

The default secondary prompt is > (the greater than sign), but can be changed by re-defining the PS2 shell variable –

Following is the example which uses the default secondary prompt –

```
$ echo "this is a
> test"
this is a
test
```

```
$
```

The example given below re-defines PS2 with a customized prompt –

```
$ PS2="secondary prompt->"
$ echo "this is a
secondary prompt->test"
this is a
test
$
```

Environment Variables

Following is the partial list of important environment variables. These variables are set and accessed as mentioned below –

Sr. No.	Variable & Description
1	DISPLAY Contains the identifier for the display that X11 programs should use by default.
2	HOME Indicates the home directory of the current user: the default argument for the cd built-in command.
3	IFS Indicates the Internal Field Separator that is used by the parser for word splitting after expansion.
4	LANG LANG expands to the default system locale; LC_ALL can be used to override this. For example, if its value is pt_BR, then the language is set to (Brazilian) Portuguese and the locale to Brazil.
5	LD_LIBRARY_PATH A Unix system with a dynamic linker, contains a colonseparated list of directories that the dynamic linker should search for shared objects when building a process image after exec, before searching in any other directories.
6	PATH Indicates the search path for commands. It is a colon-separated list of directories in which the shell looks for commands.
7	PWD Indicates the current working directory as set by the cd command.
8	RANDOM Generates a random integer between 0 and 32,767 each time it is referenced.
9	SHLVL Increments by one each time an instance of bash is started. This variable is useful for determining whether the built-in exit command ends the current session.
10	TERM Refers to the display type.

11	TZ
	Refers to Time zone. It can take values like GMT, AST, etc.
12	UID
	Expands to the numeric user ID of the current user, initialized at the shell startup.

Following is the sample example showing few environment variables –

```
$ echo $HOME
/root
]$ echo $DISPLAY

$ echo $TERM
xterm
$ echo $PATH
/usr/local/bin:/bin:/usr/bin:/home/amrood/bin:/usr/local/bin
$
```

Printing Files

Before you print a file on a Unix system, you may want to reformat it to adjust the margins, highlight some words, and so on. Most files can also be printed without reformatting, but the raw printout may not be that appealing.

Many versions of Unix include two powerful text formatters, nroff and troff.

pr Command

The pr command does minor formatting of files on the terminal screen or for a printer. For example, if you have a long list of names in a file, you can format it onscreen into two or more columns.

Following is the syntax for the pr command –

```
pr option(s) filename(s)
```

The pr changes the format of the file only on the screen or on the printed copy; it doesn't modify the original file. Following table lists some pr options –

Sr.No.	Option & Description
1	**-k**
	Produces **k** columns of output
2	**-d**
	Double-spaces the output (not on all **pr** versions)

3	**-h "header"** Takes the next item as a report header
4	**-t** Eliminates the printing of header and the top/bottom margins
5	**-l PAGE_LENGTH** Sets the page length to PAGE_LENGTH (66) lines. The default number of lines of text is 56
6	**-o MARGIN** Offsets each line with MARGIN (zero) spaces
7	**-w PAGE_WIDTH** Sets the page width to PAGE_WIDTH (72) characters for multiple text-column output only

Before using pr, here are the contents of a sample file named food.

```
$cat food

Sweet Tooth

Bangkok Wok

Mandalay

Afghani Cuisine

Isle of Java

Big Apple Deli

Sushi and Sashimi

Tio Pepe's Peppers

. . . . . . . .

$
```

Let's use the pr command to make a two-column report with the header Restaurants –

```
$pr -2 -h "Restaurants" food

Nov  7  9:58 1997  Restaurants    Page 1


Sweet Tooth             Isle of Java

Bangkok Wok             Big Apple Deli

Mandalay                Sushi and Sashimi

Afghani Cuisine         Tio Pepe's Peppers

. . . . . . . .

$
```

lp and lpr Commands

The command lp or lpr prints a file onto paper as opposed to the screen display. Once you are ready with formatting using the pr command, you can use any of these commands to print your file on the printer connected to your computer.

Your system administrator has probably set up a default printer at your site. To print a file named food on the default printer, use the lp or lpr command, as in the following example –

```
$lp food

request id is laserp-525   (1 file)

$
```

The lp command shows an ID that you can use to cancel the print job or check its status.

- If you are using the lp command, you can use the -nNum option to print Num number of copies. Along with the command lpr, you can use -Num for the same.

- If there are multiple printers connected with the shared network, then you can choose a printer using -dprinter option along with lp command and for the same purpose you can use -Pprinter option along with lpr command. Here printer is the printer name.

lpstat and lpq Commands

The lpstat command shows what's in the printer queue: request IDs, owners, file sizes, when the jobs were sent for printing, and the status of the requests.

Use lpstat -o if you want to see all output requests other than just your own. Requests are shown in the order they'll be printed –

```
$lpstat -o

laserp-573   john   128865   Nov 7   11:27   on laserp

laserp-574   grace   82744   Nov 7   11:28

laserp-575   john    23347   Nov 7   11:35

$
```

The lpq gives slightly different information than lpstat -o –

```
$lpq

laserp is ready and printing

Rank     Owner      Job   Files                 Total Size

active   john       573   report.ps             128865 bytes

1st      grace      574   ch03.ps ch04.ps       82744 bytes

2nd      john       575   standard input        23347 bytes

$
```

Here the first line displays the printer status. If the printer is disabled or running out of paper, you may see different messages on this first line.

Cancel and lprm Commands

The cancel command terminates a printing request from the lp command. The lprm command terminates all lpr requests. You can specify either the ID of the request (displayed by lp or lpq) or the name of the printer.

```
$cancel laserp-575

request "laserp-575" cancelled

$
```

To cancel whatever request is currently printing, regardless of its ID, simply enter cancel and the printer name –

```
$cancel laserp

request "laserp-573" cancelled

$
```

The lprm command will cancel the active job if it belongs to you. Otherwise, you can give job numbers as arguments, or use a dash (-) to remove all of your jobs –

```
$lprm 575

dfA575diamond dequeued

cfA575diamond dequeued

$
```

The lprm command tells you the actual filenames removed from the printer queue.

Sending Email

You use the Unix mail command to send and receive mail. Here is the syntax to send an email –

```
$mail [-s subject] [-c cc-addr] [-b bcc-addr] to-addr
```

Here are important options related to mail command –s

Sr. No.	Option & Description
1	**-s** Specifies subject on the command line.
2	**-c** Sends carbon copies to the list of users. List should be a comma separated list of names.
3	**-b** Sends blind carbon copies to list. List should be a comma separated list of names.

Following is an example to send a test message to admin@yahoo.com.

```
$mail -s "Test Message" admin@yahoo.com
```

You are then expected to type in your message, followed by "control-D" at the beginning of a line. To stop, simply type dot (.) as follows –

```
Hi,

This is a test

.

Cc:
```

You can send a complete file using a redirect < operator as follows –

```
$mail -s "Report 05/06/07" admin@yahoo.com < demo.txt
```

To check incoming email at your Unix system, you simply type email as follows –

```
$mail

no email
```

Pipes and Filters

You can connect two commands together so that the output from one program becomes the input of the next program. Two or more commands connected in this way form a pipe.

To make a pipe, put a vertical bar (|) on the command line between two commands.

When a program takes its input from another program, it performs some operation on that input, and writes the result to the standard output. It is referred to as a filter.

Grep Command

The grep command searches a file or files for lines that have a certain pattern. The syntax is –

```
$grep pattern file(s)
```

The name "grep" comes from the ed (a Unix line editor) command g/re/p which means "globally search for a regular expression and print all lines containing it".

A regular expression is either some plain text (a word, for example) and/or special characters used for pattern matching.

The simplest use of grep is to look for a pattern consisting of a single word. It can be used in a pipe so that only those lines of the input files containing a given string are sent to the standard output. If you don't give grep a filename to read, it reads its standard input; that's the way all filter programs work –

```
$ls -l | grep "Aug"
-rw-rw-rw-    1 john    doc        11008 Aug   6 14:10 ch02
-rw-rw-rw-    1 john    doc         8515 Aug   6 15:30 ch07
-rw-rw-r--    1 john    doc         2488 Aug  15 10:51 intro
-rw-rw-r--    1 carol doc           1605 Aug  23 07:35 macros
$
```

There are various options which you can use along with the grep command –

Sr. No.	Option & Description
1	**-v** Prints all lines that do not match pattern.
2	**-n** Prints the matched line and its line number.
3	**-l** Prints only the names of files with matching lines (letter "l")
4	**-c** Prints only the count of matching lines.
5	**-i** Matches either upper or lowercase.

Let us now use a regular expression that tells grep to find lines with "carol", followed by zero or other characters abbreviated in a regular expression as ".*"), then followed by "Aug".–

Here, we are using the -i option to have case insensitive search –

```
$ls -l | grep -i "carol.*aug"
-rw-rw-r--    1 carol doc           1605 Aug  23 07:35 macros
$
```

Sort Command

The sort command arranges lines of text alphabetically or numerically. The following example sorts the lines in the food file –

```
$sort food
Afghani Cuisine
Bangkok Wok
Big Apple Deli
Isle of Java
```

```
Mandalay

Sushi and Sashimi

Sweet Tooth

Tio Pepe's Peppers

$
```

The sort command arranges lines of text alphabetically by default. There are many options that control the sorting –

Sr. No.	Description
1	**-n** Sorts numerically (example: 10 will sort after 2), ignores blanks and tabs.
2	**-r** Reverses the order of sort.
3	**-f** Sorts upper and lowercase together.
4	**+x** Ignores first **x** fields when sorting.

More than two commands may be linked up into a pipe. Taking a previous pipe example using grep, we can further sort the files modified in August by the order of size.

The following pipe consists of the commands ls, grep, and sort –

```
$ls -l | grep "Aug" | sort +4n

-rw-rw-r--  1 carol  doc        1605 Aug 23 07:35 macros

-rw-rw-r--  1 john   doc        2488 Aug 15 10:51 intro

-rw-rw-rw-  1 john   doc        8515 Aug  6 15:30 ch07

-rw-rw-rw-  1 john   doc       11008 Aug  6 14:10 ch02

$
```

This pipe sorts all files in your directory modified in August by the order of size, and prints them on the terminal screen. The sort option +4n skips four fields (fields are separated by blanks) then sorts the lines in numeric order.

pg and more Commands

A long output can normally be zipped by you on the screen, but if you run text through more or use the pg command as a filter; the display stops once the screen is full of text.

Let's assume that you have a long directory listing. To make it easier to read the sorted listing, pipe the output through more as follows –

```
$ls -l | grep "Aug" | sort +4n | more
-rw-rw-r--  1 carol doc       1605 Aug 23 07:35 macros
-rw-rw-r--  1 john  doc       2488 Aug 15 10:51 intro
-rw-rw-rw-  1 john  doc       8515 Aug  6 15:30 ch07
-rw-rw-r--  1 john  doc      14827 Aug  9 12:40 ch03
            .
            .
            .
-rw-rw-rw-  1 john  doc      16867 Aug  6 15:56 ch05
--More--(74%)
```

The screen will fill up once the screen is full of text consisting of lines sorted by the order of the file size. At the bottom of the screen is the more prompt, where you can type a command to move through the sorted text.

Processes Management

When you execute a program on your Unix system, the system creates a special environment for that program. This environment contains everything needed for the system to run the program as if no other program were running on the system.

Whenever you issue a command in Unix, it creates, or starts, a new process. When you tried out the ls command to list the directory contents, you started a process. A process, in simple terms, is an instance of a running program.

The operating system tracks processes through a five-digit ID number known as the pid or the process ID. Each process in the system has a unique pid.

Pids eventually repeat because all the possible numbers are used up and the next pid rolls or starts over. At any point of time, no two processes with the same pid exist in the system because it is the pid that Unix uses to track each process.

Starting a Process

When you start a process (run a command), there are two ways you can run it –

- Foreground Processes
- Background Processes

Foreground Processes

By default, every process that you start runs in the foreground. It gets its input from the keyboard and sends its output to the screen.

You can see this happen with the ls command. If you wish to list all the files in your current directory, you can use the following command –

```
$ls ch*.doc
```

This would display all the files, the names of which start with ch and end with .doc –

```
ch01-1.doc    ch010.doc    ch02.doc      ch03-2.doc

ch04-1.doc    ch040.doc    ch05.doc      ch06-2.doc

ch01-2.doc    ch02-1.doc
```

The process runs in the foreground, the output is directed to my screen, and if the ls command wants any input (which it does not), it waits for it from the keyboard.

While a program is running in the foreground and is time-consuming, no other commands can be run (start any other processes) because the prompt would not be available until the program finishes processing and comes out.

Background Processes

A background process runs without being connected to your keyboard. If the background process requires any keyboard input, it waits.

The advantage of running a process in the background is that you can run other commands; you do not have to wait until it completes to start another.

The simplest way to start a background process is to add an ampersand (&) at the end of the command.

```
$ls ch*.doc &
```

This displays all those files the names of which start with ch and end with .doc –

```
ch01-1.doc    ch010.doc    ch02.doc      ch03-2.doc

ch04-1.doc    ch040.doc    ch05.doc      ch06-2.doc

ch01-2.doc    ch02-1.doc
```

Here, if the ls command wants any input (which it does not), it goes into a stop state until we move it into the foreground and give it the data from the keyboard.

That first line contains information about the background process - the job number and the process ID. You need to know the job number to manipulate it between the background and the foreground.

Press the Enter key and you will see the following –

```
[1]    +    Done                      ls ch*.doc &
$
```

The first line tells you that the ls command background process finishes successfully. The second is a prompt for another command.

Listing Running Processes

It is easy to see your own processes by running the ps (process status) command as follows –

```
$ps
PID          TTY          TIME          CMD
18358        ttyp3        00:00:00      sh
18361        ttyp3        00:01:31      abiword
18789        ttyp3        00:00:00      ps
```

One of the most commonly used flags for ps is the -f (f for full) option, which provides more information as shown in the following example –

```
$ps -f
UID        PID   PPID C STIME       TTY     TIME CMD
amrood     6738  3662 0 10:23:03 pts/6 0:00 first_one
amrood     6739  3662 0 10:22:54 pts/6 0:00 second_one
amrood     3662  3657 0 08:10:53 pts/6 0:00 -ksh
amrood     6892  3662 4 10:51:50 pts/6 0:00 ps -f
```

Here is the description of all the fields displayed by ps -f command –

Sr. No.	Column & Description
1	**UID** User ID that this process belongs to (the person running it)
2	**PID** Process ID
3	**PPID** Parent process ID (the ID of the process that started it)
4	**C** CPU utilization of process
5	**STIME** Process start time
6	**TTY** Terminal type associated with the process

7	**TIME** CPU time taken by the process
8	**CMD** The command that started this process

There are other options which can be used along with ps command –

Sr.No.	Option & Description
1	**-a** Shows information about all users
2	**-x** Shows information about processes without terminals
3	**-u** Shows additional information like -f option
4	**-e** Displays extended information

Stopping Processes

Ending a process can be done in several different ways. Often, from a console-based command, sending a CTRL + C keystroke (the default interrupt character) will exit the command. This works when the process is running in the foreground mode.

If a process is running in the background, you should get its Job ID using the ps command. After that, you can use the kill command to kill the process as follows –

```
$ps -f

UID       PID  PPID C STIME     TTY    TIME CMD

amrood    6738 3662 0 10:23:03  pts/6  0:00 first_one

amrood    6739 3662 0 10:22:54  pts/6  0:00 second_one

amrood    3662 3657 0 08:10:53  pts/6  0:00 -ksh

amrood    6892 3662 4 10:51:50  pts/6  0:00 ps -f

$kill 6738

Terminated
```

Here, the kill command terminates the first_one process. If a process ignores a regular kill command, you can use kill -9 followed by the process ID as follows –

```
$kill -9 6738

Terminated
```

Parent and Child Processes

Each unix process has two ID numbers assigned to it: The Process ID (pid) and the Parent process ID (ppid). Each user process in the system has a parent process.

Most of the commands that you run have the shell as their parent. Check the ps -f example where this command listed both the process ID and the parent process ID.

Zombie and Orphan Processes

Normally, when a child process is killed, the parent process is updated via a SIGCHLD signal. Then the parent can do some other task or restart a new child as needed. However, sometimes the parent process is killed before its child is killed. In this case, the "parent of all processes," the init process, becomes the new PPID (parent process ID). In some cases, these processes are called orphan processes.

When a process is killed, a ps listing may still show the process with a Z state. This is a zombie or defunct process. The process is dead and not being used. These processes are different from the orphan processes. They have completed execution but still find an entry in the process table.

Daemon Processes

Daemons are system-related background processes that often run with the permissions of root and services requests from other processes.

A daemon has no controlling terminal. It cannot open /dev/tty. If you do a "ps -ef" and look at the tty field, all daemons will have a ? for the tty.

To be precise, a daemon is a process that runs in the background, usually waiting for something to happen that it is capable of working with. For example, a printer daemon waiting for print commands.

If you have a program that calls for lengthy processing, then it's worth to make it a daemon and run it in the background.

Top Command

The top command is a very useful tool for quickly showing processes sorted by various criteria.

It is an interactive diagnostic tool that updates frequently and shows information about physical and virtual memory, CPU usage, load averages, and your busy processes.

Here is the simple syntax to run top command and to see the statistics of CPU utilization by different processes –

```
$top
```

Job ID versus Process ID

Background and suspended processes are usually manipulated via job number (job ID). This number is different from the process ID and is used because it is shorter.

In addition, a job can consist of multiple processes running in a series or at the same time, in parallel. Using the job ID is easier than tracking individual processes.

Network Communication Utilities

When you work in a distributed environment, you need to communicate with remote users and you also need to access remote Unix machines.

There are several Unix utilities that help users compute in a networked, distributed environment.

Ping Utility

The ping command sends an echo request to a host available on the network. Using this command, you can check if your remote host is responding well or not.

The ping command is useful for the following –

- Tracking and isolating hardware and software problems.

- Determining the status of the network and various foreign hosts.

- Testing, measuring, and managing networks.

Syntax

Following is the simple syntax to use the ping command –

```
$ping hostname or ip-address
```

The above command starts printing a response after every second. To come out of the command, you can terminate it by pressing CNTRL + C keys.

Example

Following is an example to check the availability of a host available on the network –

```
$ping google.com
PING google.com (74.125.67.100) 56(84) bytes of data.
64 bytes from 74.125.67.100: icmp_seq = 1 ttl = 54 time = 39.4 ms
64 bytes from 74.125.67.100: icmp_seq = 2 ttl = 54 time = 39.9 ms
64 bytes from 74.125.67.100: icmp_seq = 3 ttl = 54 time = 39.3 ms
64 bytes from 74.125.67.100: icmp_seq = 4 ttl = 54 time = 39.1 ms
64 bytes from 74.125.67.100: icmp_seq = 5 ttl = 54 time = 38.8 ms
```

```
--- google.com ping statistics,-

22 packets transmitted, 22 received, 0% packet loss, time 21017ms

rtt min/avg/max/mdev = 38.867/39.334/39.900/0.396 ms

$
```

If a host does not exist, you will receive the following output –

```
$ping giiiiiigle.com

ping: unknown host giiiiigle.com

$
```

ftp Utility

Here, ftp stands for File Transfer Protocol. This utility helps you upload and download your file from one computer to another computer.

The ftp utility has its own set of Unix-like commands. These commands help you perform tasks such as –

- Connect and login to a remote host.

- Navigate directories.

- List directory contents.

- Put and get files.

- Transfer files as ascii, ebcdic or binary.

Syntax

Following is the simple syntax to use the ping command –

```
$ftp hostname or ip-address
```

The above command would prompt you for the login ID and the password. Once you are authenticated, you can access the home directory of the login account and you would be able to perform various commands.

The following tables lists out a few important commands –

Sr. No.	Command & Description
1	**put filename** Uploads filename from the local machine to the remote machine.
2	**get filename** Downloads filename from the remote machine to the local machine.

3	**mput file list** Uploads more than one file from the local machine to the remote machine.
4	**mget file list** Downloads more than one file from the remote machine to the local machine.
5	**prompt off** Turns the prompt off. By default, you will receive a prompt to upload or download files using **mput** or **mget** commands.
6	**prompt on** Turns the prompt on.
7	**dir** Lists all the files available in the current directory of the remote machine.
8	**cd dirname** Changes directory to dirname on the remote machine.
9	**lcd dirname** Changes directory to dirname on the local machine.
10	**quit** Helps logout from the current login.

It should be noted that all the files would be downloaded or uploaded to or from the current directories. If you want to upload your files in a particular directory, you need to first change to that directory and then upload the required files.

Example

Following is the example to show the working of a few commands –

```
$ftp amrood.com

Connected to amrood.com.

220 amrood.com FTP server (Ver 4.9 Thu Sep 2 20:35:07 CDT 2009)

Name (amrood.com:amrood): amrood

331 Password required for amrood.

Password:

230 User amrood logged in.

ftp> dir

200 PORT command successful.

150 Opening data connection for /bin/ls.

total 1464

drwxr-sr-x    3 amrood    group          1024 Mar 11 20:04 Mail

drwxr-sr-x    2 amrood    group          1536 Mar  3 18:07 Misc
```

```
drwxr-sr-x    5 amrood     group          512 Dec  7 10:59 OldStuff
drwxr-sr-x    2 amrood     group         1024 Mar 11 15:24 bin
drwxr-sr-x    5 amrood     group         3072 Mar 13 16:10 mpl
-rw-r--r--    1 amrood     group       209671 Mar 15 10:57 myfile.out
drwxr-sr-x    3 amrood     group          512 Jan  5 13:32 public
drwxr-sr-x    3 amrood     group          512 Feb 10 10:17 pvm3
226 Transfer complete.
ftp> cd mpl
250 CWD command successful.
ftp> dir
200 PORT command successful.
150 Opening data connection for /bin/ls.
total 7320
-rw-r--r--    1 amrood     group         1630 Aug  8 1994  dboard.f
-rw-r-----    1 amrood     group         4340 Jul 17 1994  vttest.c
-rwxr-xr-x    1 amrood     group       525574 Feb 15 11:52 wave_shift
-rw-r--r--    1 amrood     group         1648 Aug  5 1994  wide.list
-rwxr-xr-x    1 amrood     group         4019 Feb 14 16:26 fix.c
226 Transfer complete.
ftp> get wave_shift
200 PORT command successful.
150 Opening data connection for wave_shift (525574 bytes).
226 Transfer complete.
528454 bytes received in 1.296 seconds (398.1 Kbytes/s)
ftp> quit
221 Goodbye.
$
```

Telnet Utility

There are times when we are required to connect to a remote Unix machine and work on that machine remotely. Telnet is a utility that allows a computer user at one site to make a connection, login and then conduct work on a computer at another site.

Once you login using Telnet, you can perform all the activities on your remotely connected machine. The following is an example of Telnet session –

```
C:>telnet amrood.com

Trying...

Connected to amrood.com.

Escape character is '^]'.


login: amrood

amrood's Password:

* * * * * * * * * * * * * * * * * * * * * * * * * * * * * * * * * * * * * * * * * *

*                                                     *

*                                                     *

*     WELCOME TO AMROOD.COM                           *

*                                                     *

*                                                     *

* * * * * * * * * * * * * * * * * * * * * * * * * * * * * * * * * * * * * * * * * *


Last unsuccessful login: Fri Mar  3 12:01:09 IST 2009

Last login: Wed Mar  8 18:33:27 IST 2009 on pts/10


    {  do your work }


$ logout

Connection closed.

C:>
```

Finger Utility

The finger command displays information about users on a given host. The host can be either local or remote.

Finger may be disabled on other systems for security reasons.

Following is the simple syntax to use the finger command –

Check all the logged-in users on the local machine –

```
$ finger
Login       Name        Tty        Idle  Login Time    Office
amrood                  pts/0            Jun 25 08:03  (62.61.164.115)
```

Get information about a specific user available on the local machine –

```
$ finger amrood
Login: amrood                          Name: (null)
Directory: /home/amrood                Shell: /bin/bash
On since Thu Jun 25 08:03 (MST) on pts/0 from 62.61.164.115
No mail.
No Plan.
```

Check all the logged-in users on the remote machine –

```
$ finger @avtar.com
Login       Name        Tty        Idle  Login Time    Office
amrood                  pts/0            Jun 25 08:03  (62.61.164.115)
```

Get the information about a specific user available on the remote machine –

```
$ finger amrood@avtar.com
Login: amrood                          Name: (null)
Directory: /home/amrood                Shell: /bin/bash
On since Thu Jun 25 08:03 (MST) on pts/0 from 62.61.164.115
No mail.
No Plan.
```

vi Editor

There are many ways to edit files in Unix. Editing files using the screen-oriented text editor vi is one of the best ways. This editor enables you to edit lines in context with other lines in the file.

An improved version of the vi editor which is called the VIM has also been made available now. Here, VIM stands for Vi Improved.

vi is generally considered the de facto standard in Unix editors because –

- It's usually available on all the flavors of Unix system.

- Its implementations are very similar across the board.

- It requires very few resources.

- It is more user-friendly than other editors such as the ed or the ex.

You can use the vi editor to edit an existing file or to create a new file from scratch. You can also use this editor to just read a text file.

Starting the vi Editor

The following table lists out the basic commands to use the vi editor –

Sr. No.	Command & Description
1	**vi filename** Creates a new file if it already does not exist, otherwise opens an existing file.
2	**vi -R filename** Opens an existing file in the read-only mode.
3	**view filename** Opens an existing file in the read-only mode.

Following is an example to create a new file testfile if it already does not exist in the current working directory –

```
$vi testfile
```

The above command will generate the following output –

```
|
~
~
~
~
~
~
~
~
~
~
```

~

~

```
"testfile" [New File]
```

You will notice a tilde (~) on each line following the cursor. A tilde represents an unused line. If a line does not begin with a tilde and appears to be blank, there is a space, tab, newline, or some other non-viewable character present.

You now have one open file to start working on. Before proceeding further, let us understand a few important concepts.

Operation Modes

While working with the vi editor, we usually come across the following two modes –

- Command mode – This mode enables you to perform administrative tasks such as saving the files, executing the commands, moving the cursor, cutting (yanking) and pasting the lines or words, as well as finding and replacing. In this mode, whatever you type is interpreted as a command.

- Insert mode – This mode enables you to insert text into the file. Everything that's typed in this mode is interpreted as input and placed in the file.

vi always starts in the command mode. To enter text, you must be in the insert mode for which simply type i. To come out of the insert mode, press the Esc key, which will take you back to the command mode.

Hint – If you are not sure which mode you are in, press the Esc key twice; this will take you to the command mode. You open a file using the vi editor. Start by typing some characters and then come to the command mode to understand the difference.

Getting Out of vi

The command to quit out of vi is: q. Once in the command mode, type colon, and 'q', followed by return. If your file has been modified in any way, the editor will warn you of this, and not let you quit. To ignore this message, the command to quit out of vi without saving is :q!. This lets you exit vi without saving any of the changes.

The command to save the contents of the editor is :w. You can combine the above command with the quit command, or use :wq and return.

The easiest way to save your changes and exit vi is with the ZZ command. When you are in the command mode, type ZZ. The ZZ command works the same way as the :wq command.

If you want to specify/state any particular name for the file, you can do so by specifying it after the :w. For example, if you wanted to save the file you were working on as another filename called filename2, you would type :w filename2 and return.

Moving within a File

To move around within a file without affecting your text, you must be in the command mode (press Esc twice). The following table lists out a few commands you can use to move around one character at a time –

Sr. No.	Command & Description
1	**k** Moves the cursor up one line
2	**j** Moves the cursor down one line
3	**h** Moves the cursor to the left one character position
4	**l** Moves the cursor to the right one character position

The following points need to be considered to move within a file –

- vi is case-sensitive. You need to pay attention to capitalization when using the commands.
- Most commands in vi can be prefaced by the number of times you want the action to occur. For example, 2j moves the cursor two lines down the cursor location.

There are many other ways to move within a file in vi. Remember that you must be in the command mode (press Esc twice).

Control Commands

The following commands can be used with the control key to perform functions as given in the table below –

Given below is the list of control commands.

Editing Files

To edit the file, you need to be in the insert mode. There are many ways to enter the insert mode from the command mode –

Sr.No.	Command & Description
1	**i** Inserts text before the current cursor location
2	**I** Inserts text at the beginning of the current line
3	**a** Inserts text after the current cursor location
4	**A** Inserts text at the end of the current line

5	**o** Creates a new line for text entry below the cursor location
6	**O** Creates a new line for text entry above the cursor location

Deleting Characters

Here is a list of important commands, which can be used to delete characters and lines in an open file –

Sr.No.	Command & Description
1	**x** Deletes the character under the cursor location
2	**X** Deletes the character before the cursor location
3	**dw** Deletes from the current cursor location to the next word
4	**d^** Deletes from the current cursor position to the beginning of the line
5	**d$** Deletes from the current cursor position to the end of the line
6	**D** Deletes from the cursor position to the end of the current line
7	**dd** Deletes the line the cursor is on

As mentioned above, most commands in vi can be prefaced by the number of times you want the action to occur. For example, 2x deletes two characters under the cursor location and 2dd deletes two lines the cursor is on.

It is recommended that the commands are practiced before we proceed further.

Change Commands

You also have the capability to change characters, words, or lines in vi without deleting them. Here are the relevant commands –

Sr.No.	Command & Description
1	**cc** Removes the contents of the line, leaving you in insert mode.
2	**cw** Changes the word the cursor is on from the cursor to the lowercase w end of the word.

3	**r** Replaces the character under the cursor. vi returns to the command mode after the replacement is entered.
4	**R** Overwrites multiple characters beginning with the character currently under the cursor. You must use **Esc** to stop the overwriting.
5	**s** Replaces the current character with the character you type. Afterward, you are left in the insert mode.
6	**S** Deletes the line the cursor is on and replaces it with the new text. After the new text is entered, vi remains in the insert mode.

Copy and Paste Commands

You can copy lines or words from one place and then you can paste them at another place using the following commands –

Sr.No.	Command & Description
1	**yy** Copies the current line.
2	**yw** Copies the current word from the character the lowercase w cursor is on, until the end of the word.
3	**p** Puts the copied text after the cursor.
4	**P** Puts the yanked text before the cursor.

Advanced Commands

There are some advanced commands that simplify day-to-day editing and allow for more efficient use of vi –

Given below is the list advanced commands.

Word and Character Searching

The vi editor has two kinds of searches: string and character. For a string search, the / and ? commands are used. When you start these commands, the command just typed will be shown on the last line of the screen, where you type the particular string to look for.

These two commands differ only in the direction where the search takes place –

- The / command searches forwards (downwards) in the file.
- The ? command searches backwards (upwards) in the file.

The n and N commands repeat the previous search command in the same or the opposite direction, respectively. Some characters have special meanings. These characters must be preceded by a backslash (\) to be included as part of the search expression.

Sr. No.	Character &Description
1	^ Searches at the beginning of the line (Use at the beginning of a search expression).
2	. Matches a single character.
3	* Matches zero or more of the previous character.
4	$ End of the line (Use at the end of the search expression).
5	[Starts a set of matching or non-matching expressions.
6	< This is put in an expression escaped with the backslash to find the ending or the beginning of a word.
7	> This helps see the '<' character description above.

The character search searches within one line to find a character entered after the command. The f and F commands search for a character on the current line only. f searches forwards and F searches backwards and the cursor moves to the position of the found character.

The t and T commands search for a character on the current line only, but for t, the cursor moves to the position before the character, and T searches the line backwards to the position after the character.

Set Commands

You can change the look and feel of your vi screen using the following :set commands. Once you are in the command mode, type :set followed by any of the following commands.

Sr. No.	Command & Description
1	**:set ic** Ignores the case when searching
2	**:set ai** Sets autoindent
3	**:set noai** Unsets autoindent
4	**:set nu** Displays lines with line numbers on the left side

5	**:set sw** Sets the width of a software tabstop. For example, you would set a shift width of 4 with this command — **:set sw = 4**
6	**:set ws** If *wrapscan* is set, and the word is not found at the bottom of the file, it will try searching for it at the beginning
7	**:set wm** If this option has a value greater than zero, the editor will automatically "word wrap". For example, to set the wrap margin to two characters, you would type this: **:set wm = 2**
8	**:set ro** Changes file type to "read only"
9	**:set term** Prints terminal type
10	**:set bf** Discards control characters from input

Running Commands

The vi has the capability to run commands from within the editor. To run a command, you only need to go to the command mode and type :! command.

For example, if you want to check whether a file exists before you try to save your file with that filename, you can type :! ls and you will see the output of ls on the screen.

You can press any key (or the command's escape sequence) to return to your vi session.

Replacing Text

The substitution command (:s/) enables you to quickly replace words or groups of words within your files. Following is the syntax to replace text –

```
:s/search/replace/g
```

The g stands for globally. The result of this command is that all occurrences on the cursor's line are changed.

Important Points aboute vi

The following points will add to your success with vi:

- You must be in command mode to use the commands. (Press Esc twice at any time to ensure that you are in command mode.)

- You must be careful with the commands. These are case-sensitive.

- You must be in insert mode to enter text.

Shells

A Shell provides you with an interface to the Unix system. It gathers input from you and executes programs based on that input. When a program finishes executing, it displays that program's output.

Shell is an environment in which we can run our commands, programs, and shell scripts. There are different flavors of a shell, just as there are different flavors of operating systems. Each flavor of shell has its own set of recognized commands and functions.

Shell Prompt

The prompt, $, which is called the command prompt, is issued by the shell. While the prompt is displayed, you can type a command.

Shell reads your input after you press Enter. It determines the command you want executed by looking at the first word of your input. A word is an unbroken set of characters. Spaces and tabs separate words.

Following is a simple example of the date command, which displays the current date and time –

```
$date
Thu Jun 25 08:30:19 MST 2009
```

You can customize your command prompt using the environment variable PS1.

Shell Types

In Unix, there are two major types of shells –

- Bourne shell – If you are using a Bourne-type shell, the $ character is the default prompt.
- C shell – If you are using a C-type shell, the % character is the default prompt.

The Bourne Shell has the following subcategories –

- Bourne shell (sh)
- Korn shell (ksh)
- Bourne Again shell (bash)
- POSIX shell (sh)

The different C-type shells follow –

- C shell (csh)
- TENEX/TOPS C shell (tcsh)

The original Unix shell was written in the mid-1970s by Stephen R. Bourne while he was at the AT&T Bell Labs in New Jersey.

Bourne shell was the first shell to appear on Unix systems, thus it is referred to as "the shell".

Bourne shell is usually installed as /bin/sh on most versions of Unix. For this reason, it is the shell of choice for writing scripts that can be used on different versions of Unix.

Shell Scripts

The basic concept of a shell script is a list of commands, which are listed in the order of execution. A good shell script will have comments, preceded by # sign, describing the steps.

There are conditional tests, such as value A is greater than value B, loops allowing us to go through massive amounts of data, files to read and store data, and variables to read and store data, and the script may include functions.

It would be a simple text file in which we would put all our commands and several other required constructs that tell the shell environment what to do and when to do it.

Shell scripts and functions are both interpreted. This means they are not compiled.

Example Script

Assume we create a test.sh script. Note all the scripts would have the .sh extension. Before you add anything else to your script, you need to alert the system that a shell script is being started. This is done using the shebang construct. For example –

```
#!/bin/sh
```

This tells the system that the commands that follow are to be executed by the Bourne shell. It's called a shebang because the # symbol is called a hash, and the ! symbol is called a bang.

To create a script containing these commands, you put the shebang line first and then add the commands –

```
#!/bin/bash
pwd
ls
```

Shell Comments

You can put your comments in your script as follows –

```
#!/bin/bash


# Script follows here:
pwd
ls
```

Save the above content and make the script executable –

```
$chmod +x test.sh
```

The shell script is now ready to be executed –

```
$./test.sh
```

Upon execution, you will receive the following result –

```
/home/amrood
index.htm   unix-basic_utilities.htm   unix-directories.htm
test.sh     unix-communication.htm     unix-environment.htm
```

To execute a program available in the current directory, use ./program_name

Extended Shell Scripts

Shell scripts have several required constructs that tell the shell environment what to do and when to do it. Of course, most scripts are more complex than the above one.

The shell is, after all, a real programming language, complete with variables, control structures, and so forth. No matter how complicated a script gets, it is still just a list of commands executed sequentially.

The following script uses the read command which takes the input from the keyboard and assigns it as the value of the variable PERSON and finally prints it on STDOUT.

```
#!/bin/sh


# Script follows here:


echo "What is your name?"
read PERSON
echo "Hello, $PERSON"
```

Here is a sample run of the script –

```
$./test.sh
What is your name?
Zara Ali
Hello, Zara Ali
$
```

Using Shell Variables

A variable is a character string to which we assign a value. The value assigned could be a number, text, filename, device, or any other type of data.

A variable is nothing more than a pointer to the actual data. The shell enables you to create, assign, and delete variables.

Variable Names

The name of a variable can contain only letters (a to z or A to Z), numbers (0 to 9) or the under-score character (_).

By convention, Unix shell variables will have their names in UPPERCASE.

The following examples are valid variable names –

```
_ALI
TOKEN_A
VAR_1
VAR_2
```

Following are the examples of invalid variable names –

```
2_VAR
-VARIABLE
VAR1-VAR2
VAR_A!
```

The reason you cannot use other characters such as !, *, or - is that these characters have a special meaning for the shell.

Defining Variables

Variables are defined as follows –

```
variable_name=variable_value
```

For example –

```
NAME="Zara Ali"
```

The above example defines the variable NAME and assigns the value "Zara Ali" to it. Variables of this type are called scalar variables. A scalar variable can hold only one value at a time.

Shell enables you to store any value you want in a variable. For example –

```
VAR1="Zara Ali"
VAR2=100
```

Accessing Values

To access the value stored in a variable, prefix its name with the dollar sign ($) –

For example, the following script will access the value of defined variable NAME and print it on STDOUT –

```
#!/bin/sh
```

```
NAME="Zara Ali"
echo $NAME
```

The above script will produce the following value –

```
Zara Ali
```

Read-only Variables

Shell provides a way to mark variables as read-only by using the read-only command. After a variable is marked read-only, its value cannot be changed.

For example, the following script generates an error while trying to change the value of NAME –

```
#!/bin/sh
```

```
NAME="Zara Ali"
readonly NAME
NAME="Qadiri"
```

The above script will generate the following result –

```
/bin/sh: NAME: This variable is read only.
```

Unsetting Variables

Unsetting or deleting a variable directs the shell to remove the variable from the list of variables that it tracks. Once you unset a variable, you cannot access the stored value in the variable.

Following is the syntax to unset a defined variable using the unset command –

```
unset variable_name
```

The above command unsets the value of a defined variable. Here is a simple example that demonstrates how the command works –

```
#!/bin/sh
```

```
NAME="Zara Ali"
unset NAME
echo $NAME
```

The above example does not print anything. You cannot use the unset command to unset variables that are marked readonly.

Variable Types

When a shell is running, three main types of variables are present –

- Local Variables – A local variable is a variable that is present within the current instance of the shell. It is not available to programs that are started by the shell. They are set at the command prompt.

- Environment Variables – An environment variable is available to any child process of the shell. Some programs need environment variables in order to function correctly. Usually, a shell script defines only those environment variables that are needed by the programs that it runs.

- Shell Variables – A shell variable is a special variable that is set by the shell and is required by the shell in order to function correctly. Some of these variables are environment variables whereas others are local variables.

Special Variables

We should be careful when we use certain non alphanumeric characters in variable names. This is because those characters are used in the names of special Unix variables. These variables are reserved for specific functions.

For example, the $ character represents the process ID number, or PID, of the current shell –

```
$echo $$
```

The above command writes the PID of the current shell –

```
29949
```

The following table shows a number of special variables that you can use in your shell scripts –

Sr. No.	Variable & Description
1	**$0** The filename of the current script.

2	**$n** These variables correspond to the arguments with which a script was invoked. Here **n** is a positive decimal number corresponding to the position of an argument (the first argument is $1, the second argument is $2, and so on).
3	**$#** The number of arguments supplied to a script.
4	**$*** All the arguments are double quoted. If a script receives two arguments, $* is equivalent to $1 $2.
5	**$@** All the arguments are individually double quoted. If a script receives two arguments, $@ is equivalent to $1 $2.
6	**$?** The exit status of the last command executed.
7	**$$** The process number of the current shell. For shell scripts, this is the process ID under which they are executing.
8	**$!** The process number of the last background command.

Command-Line Arguments

The command-line arguments $1, $2, $3, ...$9 are positional parameters, with $0 pointing to the actual command, program, shell script, or function and $1, $2, $3, ...$9 as the arguments to the command.

Following script uses various special variables related to the command line –

```
#!/bin/sh


echo "File Name: $0"

echo "First Parameter : $1"

echo "Second Parameter : $2"

echo "Quoted Values: $@"

echo "Quoted Values: $*"

echo "Total Number of Parameters : $#"
```

Here is a sample run for the above script –

```
$./test.sh Zara Ali
File Name : ./test.sh
First Parameter : Zara
Second Parameter : Ali
Quoted Values: Zara Ali
Quoted Values: Zara Ali
Total Number of Parameters : 2
```

Special Parameters $* and $@

There are special parameters that allow accessing all the command-line arguments at once. $* and $@ both will act the same unless they are enclosed in double quotes, "".

Both the parameters specify the command-line arguments. However, the "$*" special parameter takes the entire list as one argument with spaces between and the "$@" special parameter takes the entire list and separates it into separate arguments.

We can write the shell script as shown below to process an unknown number of command line arguments with either the $* or $@ special parameters –

```
#!/bin/sh

for TOKEN in $*
do
    echo $TOKEN
done
```

Here is a sample run for the above script –

```
$./test.sh Zara Ali 10 Years Old
Zara
Ali
10
Years
Old
```

Here, do...done is a kind of loop.

Exit Status

The $? variable represents the exit status of the previous command.

Exit status is a numerical value returned by every command upon its completion. As a rule, most commands return an exit status of 0 if they were successful, and 1 if they were unsuccessful.

Some commands return additional exit statuses for particular reasons. For example, some commands differentiate between kinds of errors and will return various exit values depending on the specific type of failure.

Following is the example of successful command –

```
$./test.sh Zara Ali

File Name : ./test.sh

First Parameter : Zara

Second Parameter : Ali

Quoted Values: Zara Ali

Quoted Values: Zara Ali

Total Number of Parameters : 2

$echo $?

0

$
```

Using Shell Arrays

A shell variable is capable enough to hold a single value. These variables are called scalar variables.

Shell supports a different type of variable called an array variable. This can hold multiple values at the same time. Arrays provide a method of grouping a set of variables. Instead of creating a new name for each variable that is required, you can use a single array variable that stores all the other variables.

All the naming rules discussed for Shell Variables would be applicable while naming arrays.

Defining Array Values

The difference between an array variable and a scalar variable can be explained as follows.

Suppose you are trying to represent the names of various students as a set of variables. Each of the individual variables is a scalar variable as follows –

```
NAME01="Zara"
```

```
NAME02="Qadir"
```

```
NAME03="Mahnaz"
```

```
NAME04="Ayan"
```

```
NAME05="Daisy"
```

We can use a single array to store all the above mentioned names. Following is the simplest method of creating an array variable. This helps assign a value to one of its indices.

```
array_name[index]=value
```

Here array_name is the name of the array, index is the index of the item in the array that you want to set, and value is the value you want to set for that item.

As an example, the following commands –

```
NAME[0]="Zara"
```

```
NAME[1]="Qadir"
```

```
NAME[2]="Mahnaz"
```

```
NAME[3]="Ayan"
```

```
NAME[4]="Daisy"
```

If you are using the ksh shell, here is the syntax of array initialization –

```
set -A array_name value1 value2 ... valuen
```

If you are using the bash shell, here is the syntax of array initialization –

```
array_name=(value1 ... valuen)
```

Accessing Array Values

After you have set any array variable, you access it as follows –

```
${array_name[index]}
```

Here array_name is the name of the array, and index is the index of the value to be accessed. Following is an example to understand the concept –

```
#!/bin/sh
```

```
NAME[0]="Zara"
```

```
NAME[1]="Qadir"
```

```
NAME[2]="Mahnaz"
```

```
NAME[3]="Ayan"
```

```
NAME[4]="Daisy"
echo "First Index: ${NAME[0]}"
echo "Second Index: ${NAME[1]}"
```

The above example will generate the following result –

```
$./test.sh
First Index: Zara
Second Index: Qadir
```

You can access all the items in an array in one of the following ways –

```
${array_name[*]}
${array_name[@]}
```

Here array_name is the name of the array you are interested in. Following example will help you understand the concept –

```
#!/bin/sh


NAME[0]="Zara"
NAME[1]="Qadir"
NAME[2]="Mahnaz"
NAME[3]="Ayan"
NAME[4]="Daisy"
echo "First Method: ${NAME[*]}"
echo "Second Method: ${NAME[@]}"
```

The above example will generate the following result –

```
$./test.sh
First Method: Zara Qadir Mahnaz Ayan Daisy
Second Method: Zara Qadir Mahnaz Ayan Daisy
```

Shell Basic Operators

There are various operators supported by each shell.

We will now discuss the following operators –

- Arithmetic Operators
- Relational Operators

- Boolean Operators
- String Operators
- File Test Operators

Bourne shell didn't originally have any mechanism to perform simple arithmetic operations but it uses external programs, either awk or expr.

The following example shows how to add two numbers –

```
#!/bin/sh
```

```
val=`expr 2 + 2`
echo "Total value : $val"
```

The above script will generate the following result –

```
Total value : 4
```

The following points need to be considered while adding –

- There must be spaces between operators and expressions. For example, 2+2 is not correct; it should be written as 2 + 2.
- The complete expression should be enclosed between ' ', called the backtick.

Arithmetic Operators

The following arithmetic operators are supported by Bourne Shell.

Assume variable a holds 10 and variable b holds 20 then –

Examples

Operator	Description	Example
+ (Addition)	Adds values on either side of the operator	`expr $a + $b` will give 30
- (Subtraction)	Subtracts right hand operand from left hand operand	`expr $a - $b` will give -10
* (Multiplication)	Multiplies values on either side of the operator	`expr $a \* $b` will give 200
/ (Division)	Divides left hand operand by right hand operand	`expr $b / $a` will give 2
% (Modulus)	Divides left hand operand by right hand operand and returns remainder	`expr $b % $a` will give 0
= (Assignment)	Assigns right operand in left operand	a = $b would assign value of b into a
== (Equality)	Compares two numbers, if both are same then returns true.	[$a == $b] would return false.
!= (Not Equality)	Compares two numbers, if both are different then returns true.	[$a != $b] would return true.

It is very important to understand that all the conditional expressions should be inside square braces with spaces around them, for example [$a == $b] is correct whereas, [$a==$b] is incorrect.

All the arithmetical calculations are done using long integers.

Relational Operators

Bourne Shell supports the following relational operators that are specific to numeric values. These operators do not work for string values unless their value is numeric.

For example, following operators will work to check a relation between 10 and 20 as well as in between "10" and "20" but not in between "ten" and "twenty".

Assume variable a holds 10 and variable b holds 20 then –

Examples

Operator	Description	Example
-eq	Checks if the value of two operands are equal or not; if yes, then the condition becomes true.	[$a -eq $b] is not true.
-ne	Checks if the value of two operands are equal or not; if values are not equal, then the condition becomes true.	[$a -ne $b] is true.
-gt	Checks if the value of left operand is greater than the value of right operand; if yes, then the condition becomes true.	[$a -gt $b] is not true.
-lt	Checks if the value of left operand is less than the value of right operand; if yes, then the condition becomes true.	[$a -lt $b] is true.
-ge	Checks if the value of left operand is greater than or equal to the value of right operand; if yes, then the condition becomes true.	[$a -ge $b] is not true.
-le	Checks if the value of left operand is less than or equal to the value of right operand; if yes, then the condition becomes true.	[$a -le $b] is true.

It is very important to understand that all the conditional expressions should be placed inside square braces with spaces around them. For example, [$a <= $b] is correct whereas, [$a <= $b] is incorrect.

Boolean Operators

The following Boolean operators are supported by the Bourne Shell.

Assume variable a holds 10 and variable b holds 20 then –

Show Examples

Operator	Description	Example
!	This is logical negation. This inverts a true condition into false and vice versa.	[! false] is true.
-o	This is logical OR. If one of the operands is true, then the condition becomes true.	[$a -lt 20 -o $b -gt 100] is true.
-a	This is logical AND. If both the operands are true, then the condition becomes true otherwise false.	[$a -lt 20 -a $b -gt 100] is false.

String Operators

The following string operators are supported by Bourne Shell.

Assume variable a holds "abc" and variable b holds "efg" then –

Examples

Operator	Description	Example
=	Checks if the value of two operands are equal or not; if yes, then the condition becomes true.	[$a = $b] is not true.
!=	Checks if the value of two operands are equal or not; if values are not equal then the condition becomes true.	[$a != $b] is true.
-z	Checks if the given string operand size is zero; if it is zero length, then it returns true.	[-z $a] is not true.
-n	Checks if the given string operand size is non-zero; if it is nonzero length, then it returns true.	[-n $a] is not false.
str	Checks if **str** is not the empty string; if it is empty, then it returns false.	[$a] is not false.

File Test Operators

We have a few operators that can be used to test various properties associated with a Unix file.

Assume a variable file holds an existing file name "test" the size of which is 100 bytes and has read, write and execute permission on –

Examples

Operator	Description	Example
-b file	Checks if file is a block special file; if yes, then the condition becomes true.	[-b $file] is false.
-c file	Checks if file is a character special file; if yes, then the condition becomes true.	[-c $file] is false.
-d file	Checks if file is a directory; if yes, then the condition becomes true.	[-d $file] is not true.
-f file	Checks if file is an ordinary file as opposed to a directory or special file; if yes, then the condition becomes true.	[-f $file] is true.
-g file	Checks if file has its set group ID (SGID) bit set; if yes, then the condition becomes true.	[-g $file] is false.
-k file	Checks if file has its sticky bit set; if yes, then the condition becomes true.	[-k $file] is false.
-p file	Checks if file is a named pipe; if yes, then the condition becomes true.	[-p $file] is false.
-t file	Checks if file descriptor is open and associated with a terminal; if yes, then the condition becomes true.	[-t $file] is false.
-u file	Checks if file has its Set User ID (SUID) bit set; if yes, then the condition becomes true.	[-u $file] is false.
-r file	Checks if file is readable; if yes, then the condition becomes true.	[-r $file] is true.
-w file	Checks if file is writable; if yes, then the condition becomes true.	[-w $file] is true.
-x file	Checks if file is executable; if yes, then the condition becomes true.	[-x $file] is true.
-s file	Checks if file has size greater than 0; if yes, then condition becomes true.	[-s $file] is true.
-e file	Checks if file exists; is true even if file is a directory but exists.	[-e $file] is true.

Shell Decision Making

While writing a shell script, there may be a situation when you need to adopt one path out of the given two paths. So you need to make use of conditional statements that allow your program to make correct decisions and perform the right actions.

Unix Shell supports conditional statements which are used to perform different actions based on different conditions. We will now understand two decision-making statements here –

- The if...else statement
- The case...esac statement

if...else statements

If else statements are useful decision-making statements which can be used to select an option from a given set of options.

Unix Shell supports following forms of if...else statement –

- if...fi statement
- if...else...fi statement
- if...elif...else...fi statement

Most of the if statements check relations using relational operators.

Case...esac Statement

You can use multiple if...elif statements to perform a multiway branch. However, this is not always the best solution, especially when all of the branches depend on the value of a single variable.

Unix Shell supports case...esac statement which handles exactly this situation, and it does so more efficiently than repeated if...elif statements.

There is only one form of case...esac statement which has been described in detail here –

- case...esac statement

The case...esac statement in the Unix shell is very similar to the switch...case statement we have in other programming languages like C or C++ and PERL, etc.

Shell Loop Types

A loop is a powerful programming tool that enables you to execute a set of commands repeatedly. The following types of loops are available to shell programmers:

- The while loop
- The for loop
- The until loop
- The select loop

You will use different loops based on the situation. For example, the while loop executes the given commands until the given condition remains true; the until loop executes until a given condition becomes true.

Once you have good programming practice you will gain the expertise and thereby, start using appropriate loop based on the situation. Here, while and for loops are available in most of the other programming languages like C, C++ and PERL, etc.

Nesting Loops

All the loops support nesting concept which means you can put one loop inside another similar one or different loops. This nesting can go up to unlimited number of times based on your requirement.

Here is an example of nesting while loop. The other loops can be nested based on the programming requirement in a similar way –

Nesting while Loops

It is possible to use a while loop as part of the body of another while loop.

Syntax

```
while command1 ; # this is loop1, the outer loop
do

   Statement(s) to be executed if command1 is true


   while command2 ; # this is loop2, the inner loop
   do
      Statement(s) to be executed if command2 is true
   done


   Statement(s) to be executed if command1 is true
done
```

Example

Here is a simple example of loop nesting. Let's add another countdown loop inside the loop that you used to count to nine –

```
#!/bin/sh
```

```
a=0
while [ "$a" -lt 10 ]     # this is loop1
do
    b="$a"
    while [ "$b" -ge 0 ]  # this is loop2
    do
        echo -n "$b "
        b=`expr $b - 1`
    done
    echo
    a=`expr $a + 1`
done
```

This will produce the following result. It is important to note how echo -n works here. Here -n option lets echo avoid printing a new line character.

```
0
1 0
2 1 0
3 2 1 0
4 3 2 1 0
5 4 3 2 1 0
6 5 4 3 2 1 0
7 6 5 4 3 2 1 0
8 7 6 5 4 3 2 1 0
9 8 7 6 5 4 3 2 1 0
```

Shell Loop Control

So far you have looked at creating loops and working with loops to accomplish different tasks. Sometimes you need to stop a loop or skip iterations of the loop.

Following two statements are used to control shell loops:

- The break statement

- The continue statement

Infinite Loop

All the loops have a limited life and they come out once the condition is false or true depending on the loop.

A loop may continue forever if the required condition is not met. A loop that executes forever without terminating executes for an infinite number of times. For this reason, such loops are called infinite loops.

Example

Here is a simple example that uses the while loop to display the numbers zero to nine –

```
#!/bin/sh


a=10


until [ $a -lt 10 ]
do
    echo $a
    a=expr $a + 1`
done
```

This loop continues forever because a is always greater than or equal to 10 and it is never less than 10.

Break Statement

The break statement is used to terminate the execution of the entire loop, after completing the execution of all of the lines of code up to the break statement. It then steps down to the code following the end of the loop.

Syntax

The following break statement is used to come out of a loop –

```
break
```

The break command can also be used to exit from a nested loop using this format –

```
break n
```

Here n specifies the nth enclosing loop to the exit from.

Example

Here is a simple example which shows that loop terminates as soon as a becomes 5 –

```
#!/bin/sh


a=0


while [ $a -lt 10 ]
do
    echo $a
    if [ $a -eq 5 ]
    then
        break
    fi
    a=`expr $a + 1`
done
```

Upon execution, you will receive the following result –

```
0
1
2
3
4
5
```

Here is a simple example of nested for loop. This script breaks out of both loops if var1 equals 2 and var2 equals 0 –

```
#!/bin/sh


for var1 in 1 2 3
do
    for var2 in 0 5
    do
```

```
        if [ $var1 -eq 2 -a $var2 -eq 0 ]

        then

            break 2

        else

            echo "$var1 $var2"

        fi

    done

done
```

Upon execution, you will receive the following result. In the inner loop, you have a break command with the argument 2. This indicates that if a condition is met you should break out of outer loop and ultimately from the inner loop as well.

```
1 0

1 5
```

Continue Statement

The continue statement is similar to the break command, except that it causes the current iteration of the loop to exit, rather than the entire loop.

This statement is useful when an error has occurred but you want to try to execute the next iteration of the loop.

Syntax

```
continue
```

Like with the break statement, an integer argument can be given to the continue command to skip commands from nested loops.

```
continue n
```

Here n specifies the nth enclosing loop to continue from.

Example

The following loop makes use of the continue statement which returns from the continue statement and starts processing the next statement –

```
#!/bin/sh
```

```
NUMS="1 2 3 4 5 6 7"
```

```
for NUM in $NUMS
do
    Q=`expr $NUM % 2`
    if [ $Q -eq 0 ]
    then
        echo "Number is an even number!!"
        continue
    fi
    echo "Found odd number"
done
```

Upon execution, you will receive the following result –

```
Found odd number
Number is an even number!!
Found odd number
Number is an even number!!
Found odd number
Number is an even number!!
Found odd number
```

Shell Substitution

The shell performs substitution when it encounters an expression that contains one or more special characters.

Example

Here, the printing value of the variable is substituted by its value. Same time, "\n" is substituted by a new line –

```
#!/bin/sh


a=10

echo -e "Value of a is $a \n"
```

You will receive the following result. Here the -e option enables the interpretation of backslash escapes.

```
Value of a is 10
```

Following is the result without -e option −

```
Value of a is 10\n
```

Here are following escape sequences which can be used in echo command −

Sr.No.	Escape & Description
1	\\ backslash
2	\a alert (BEL)
3	\b backspace
4	\c suppress trailing newline
5	\f form feed
6	\n new line
7	\r carriage return
8	\t horizontal tab
9	\v vertical tab

You can use the -E option to disable the interpretation of the backslash escapes (default).

You can use the -n option to disable the insertion of a new line.

Command Substitution

Command substitution is the mechanism by which the shell performs a given set of commands and then substitutes their output in the place of the commands.

Syntax

The command substitution is performed when a command is given as −

```
`command`
```

When performing the command substitution make sure that you use the backquote, not the single quote character.

Example

Command substitution is generally used to assign the output of a command to a variable. Each of the following examples demonstrates the command substitution –

```
#!/bin/sh


DATE=`date`
echo "Date is $DATE"


USERS=`who | wc -l`
echo "Logged in user are $USERS"


UP=`date ; uptime`
echo "Uptime is $UP"
```

Upon execution, you will receive the following result –

```
Date is Thu Jul  2 03:59:57 MST 2009
Logged in user are 1
Uptime is Thu Jul  2 03:59:57 MST 2009
03:59:57 up 20 days, 14:03,  1 user,  load avg: 0.13, 0.07, 0.15
```

Variable Substitution

Variable substitution enables the shell programmer to manipulate the value of a variable based on its state.

Here is the following table for all the possible substitutions –

Sr. No.	Form & Description
1	**${var}** Substitute the value of *var*.
2	**${var:-word}** If *var* is null or unset, *word* is substituted for **var**. The value of *var* does not change.
3	**${var:=word}** If *var* is null or unset, *var* is set to the value of **word**.

4	**${var:?message}** If *var* is null or unset, *message* is printed to standard error. This checks that variables are set correctly.
5	**${var:+word}** If *var* is set, *word* is substituted for var. The value of *var* does not change.

Example

Following is the example to show various states of the above substitution –

```sh
#!/bin/sh

echo ${var:-"Variable is not set"}
echo "1 - Value of var is ${var}"


echo ${var:="Variable is not set"}
echo "2 - Value of var is ${var}"


unset var
echo ${var:+"This is default value"}
echo "3 - Value of var is $var"


var="Prefix"
echo ${var:+"This is default value"}
echo "4 - Value of var is $var"


echo ${var:?"Print this message"}
echo "5 - Value of var is ${var}"
```

Upon execution, you will receive the following result –

```
Variable is not set
1 - Value of var is
Variable is not set
2 - Value of var is Variable is not set
```

```
3 - Value of var is

This is default value

4 - Value of var is Prefix

Prefix

5 - Value of var is Prefix
```

Shell Quoting Mechanisms

Here, we will discuss in detail about the Shell quoting mechanisms. We will start by metacharacters.

Metacharacters

Unix Shell provides various metacharacters which have special meaning while using them in any Shell Script and causes termination of a word unless quoted.

For example, ? matches with a single character while listing files in a directory and an * matches more than one character. Here is a list of most of the shell special characters (also called metacharacters) –

* ? [ ] ' " \ $; & ( ) | ^ < > new-line space tab

A character may be quoted (i.e., made to stand for itself) by preceding it with a \.

Example

Following example shows how to print a * or a ? –

```
#!/bin/sh
```

```
echo Hello; Word
```

Upon execution, you will receive the following result –

```
Hello
./test.sh: line 2: Word: command not found
```

```
shell returned 127
```

Let us now try using a quoted character –

```
#!/bin/sh
```

```
echo Hello\; Word
```

Upon execution, you will receive the following result –

```
Hello; Word
```

The $ sign is one of the metacharacters, so it must be quoted to avoid special handling by the shell –

```
#!/bin/sh
```

```
echo "I have \$1200"
```

Upon execution, you will receive the following result –

```
I have $1200
```

The following table lists the four forms of quoting –

Sr. No.	Quoting & Description
1	**Single quote** All special characters between these quotes lose their special meaning.
2	**Double quote** Most special characters between these quotes lose their special meaning with these exceptions – • $ • ` • \$ • \' • \" • \\
3	**Backslash** Any character immediately following the backslash loses its special meaning.
4	**Back quote** Anything in between back quotes would be treated as a command and would be executed.

Single Quotes

Consider an echo command that contains many special shell characters –

```
echo <-$1500.**>; (update?) [y|n]
```

Putting a backslash in front of each special character is tedious and makes the line difficult to read –

```
echo \<-\$1500.\*\*\>\; \(update\?\) \[y\|n\]
```

There is an easy way to quote a large group of characters. Put a single quote (') at the beginning and at the end of the string –

```
echo '<-$1500.**>; (update?) [y|n]'
```

Characters within single quotes are quoted just as if a backslash is in front of each character. With this, the echo command displays in a proper way.

If a single quote appears within a string to be output, you should not put the whole string within single quotes instead you should precede that using a backslash (\) as follows –

```
echo 'It\'s Shell Programming'
```

Double Quotes

Try to execute the following shell script. This shell script makes use of single quote –

```
VAR=ZARA
```

```
echo '$VAR owes <-$1500.**>; [ as of (`date +%m/%d`) ]'
```

Upon execution, you will receive the following result –

```
$VAR owes <-$1500.**>; [ as of (`date +%m/%d`) ]
```

This is not what had to be displayed. It is obvious that single quotes prevent variable substitution. If you want to substitute variable values and to make inverted commas work as expected, then you would need to put your commands in double quotes as follows –

```
VAR=ZARA
```

```
echo "$VAR owes <-\$1500.**>; [ as of (`date +%m/%d`) ]"
```

Upon execution, you will receive the following result –

```
ZARA owes <-$1500.**>; [ as of (07/02) ]
```

Double quotes take away the special meaning of all characters except the following –

- $ for parameter substitution
- Backquotes for command substitution
- \$ to enable literal dollar signs
- \` to enable literal backquotes
- \" to enable embedded double quotes
- \\ to enable embedded backslashes
- All other \ characters are literal (not special)

Characters within single quotes are quoted just as if a backslash is in front of each character. This helps the echo command display properly.

If a single quote appears within a string to be output, you should not put the whole string within single quotes instead you should precede that using a backslash (\) as follows –

```
echo 'It\'s Shell Programming'
```

Backquotes

Putting any Shell command in between backquotes executes the command.

Syntax

Here is the simple syntax to put any Shell command in between backquotes –

```
var=`command`
```

Example

The date command is executed in the following example and the produced result is stored in DATA variable.

```
DATE=`date`
```

```
echo "Current Date: $DATE"
```

Upon execution, you will receive the following result –

```
Current Date: Thu Jul  2 05:28:45 MST 2009
```

Shell Input/Output Redirections

Most Unix system commands take input from your terminal and send the resulting output back to your terminal. A command normally reads its input from the standard input, which happens to be your terminal by default. Similarly, a command normally writes its output to standard output, which is again your terminal by default.

Output Redirection

The output from a command normally intended for standard output can be easily diverted to a file instead. This capability is known as output redirection.

If the notation > file is appended to any command that normally writes its output to standard output, the output of that command will be written to file instead of your terminal.

Check the following who command which redirects the complete output of the command in the users file.

```
$ who > users
```

Notice that no output appears at the terminal. This is because the output has been redirected from the default standard output device (the terminal) into the specified file. You can check the users file for the complete content –

```
$ cat users
oko          tty01    Sep 12 07:30
ai           tty15    Sep 12 13:32
ruth         tty21    Sep 12 10:10
pat          tty24    Sep 12 13:07
steve        tty25    Sep 12 13:03
$
```

If a command has its output redirected to a file and the file already contains some data, that data will be lost. Consider the following example –

```
$ echo line 1 > users
$ cat users
line 1
$
```

You can use >> operator to append the output in an existing file as follows –

```
$ echo line 2 >> users
$ cat users
line 1
line 2
$
```

Input Redirection

Just as the output of a command can be redirected to a file, so can the input of a command be redirected from a file. As the greater-than character > is used for output redirection, the less-than character < is used to redirect the input of a command.

The commands that normally take their input from the standard input can have their input redirected from a file in this manner. For example, to count the number of lines in the file users generated above, you can execute the command as follows –

```
$ wc -l users
```

```
2 users

$
```

Upon execution, you will receive the following output. You can count the number of lines in the file by redirecting the standard input of the wc command from the file users –

```
$ wc -l < users

2

$
```

Note that there is a difference in the output produced by the two forms of the wc command. In the first case, the name of the file users is listed with the line count; in the second case, it is not.

In the first case, wc knows that it is reading its input from the file users. In the second case, it only knows that it is reading its input from standard input so it does not display file name.

Here Document

A here document is used to redirect input into an interactive shell script or program.

We can run an interactive program within a shell script without user action by supplying the required input for the interactive program, or interactive shell script.

The general form for a here document is –

```
command << delimiter

document

delimiter
```

Here the shell interprets the << operator as an instruction to read input until it finds a line containing the specified delimiter. All the input lines up to the line containing the delimiter are then fed into the standard input of the command.

The delimiter tells the shell that the here document has completed. Without it, the shell continues to read the input forever. The delimiter must be a single word that does not contain spaces or tabs.

Following is the input to the command wc -l to count the total number of lines –

```
$wc -l << EOF

    This is a simple lookup program

        for good (and bad) restaurants

        in Cape Town.

EOF

3
```

```
$
```

You can use the here document to print multiple lines using your script as follows –

```
#!/bin/sh


cat << EOF
This is a simple lookup program
for good (and bad) restaurants
in Cape Town.
EOF
```

Upon execution, you will receive the following result –

```
This is a simple lookup program
for good (and bad) restaurants
in Cape Town.
```

The following script runs a session with the vi text editor and saves the input in the file test.txt.

```
#!/bin/sh


filename=test.txt
vi $filename <<EndOfCommands
i
This file was created automatically from
a shell script
^[
ZZ
EndOfCommands
```

If you run this script with vim acting as vi, then you will likely see output like the following –

```
$ sh test.sh
Vim: Warning: Input is not from a terminal
$
```

After running the script, you should see the following added to the file test.txt –

```
$ cat test.txt
```

```
This file was created automatically from

a shell script

$
```

Discard the output

Sometimes you will need to execute a command, but you don't want the output displayed on the screen. In such cases, you can discard the output by redirecting it to the file /dev/null –

```
$ command > /dev/null
```

Here command is the name of the command you want to execute. The file /dev/null is a special file that automatically discards all its input.

To discard both output of a command and its error output, use standard redirection to redirect STDERR to STDOUT –

```
$ command > /dev/null 2>&1
```

Here 2 represents STDERR and 1 represents STDOUT. You can display a message on to STDERR by redirecting STDOUT into STDERR as follows –

```
$ echo message 1>&2
```

Redirection Commands

Following is a complete list of commands which you can use for redirection –

Sr. No.	Command & Description
1	**pgm > file** Output of pgm is redirected to file
2	**pgm < file** Program pgm reads its input from file
3	**pgm >> file** Output of pgm is appended to file
4	**n > file** Output from stream with descriptor **n** redirected to file
5	**n >> file** Output from stream with descriptor **n** appended to file

6	**n >& m** Merges output from stream **n** with stream **m**
7	**n <& m** Merges input from stream **n** with stream **m**
8	**<< tag** Standard input comes from here through next tag at the start of line
9	**|** Takes output from one program, or process, and sends it to another

Note that the file descriptor 0 is normally standard input (STDIN), 1 is standard output (STD-OUT), and 2 is standard error output (STDERR).

Shell Functions

Functions enable you to break down the overall functionality of a script into smaller, logical subsections, which can then be called upon to perform their individual tasks when needed.

Using functions to perform repetitive tasks is an excellent way to create code reuse. This is an important part of modern object-oriented programming principles.

Shell functions are similar to subroutines, procedures, and functions in other programming languages.

Creating Functions

To declare a function, simply use the following syntax –

```
function_name () {
   list of commands
}
```

The name of your function is function_name, and that's what you will use to call it from elsewhere in your scripts. The function name must be followed by parentheses, followed by a list of commands enclosed within braces.

Example

Following example shows the use of function –

```
#!/bin/sh


# Define your function here
Hello () {
```

```
    echo "Hello World"
}
```

```
# Invoke your function
Hello
```

Upon execution, you will receive the following output –

```
$./test.sh
Hello World
```

Pass Parameters to a Function

You can define a function that will accept parameters while calling the function. These parameters would be represented by $1, $2 and so on.

Following is an example where we pass two parameters Zara and Ali and then we capture and print these parameters in the function.

```
#!/bin/sh
```

```
# Define your function here
Hello () {
    echo "Hello World $1 $2"
}
```

```
# Invoke your function
Hello Zara Ali
```

Upon execution, you will receive the following result –

```
$./test.sh
Hello World Zara Ali
```

Returning Values from Functions

If you execute an exit command from inside a function, its effect is not only to terminate execution of the function but also of the shell program that called the function.

If you instead want to just terminate execution of the function, then there is way to come out of a defined function.

Based on the situation you can return any value from your function using the return command whose syntax is as follows –

```
return code
```

Here code can be anything you choose here, but obviously you should choose something that is meaningful or useful in the context of your script as a whole.

Example

Following function returns a value 10 –

```
#!/bin/sh


# Define your function here
Hello () {
   echo "Hello World $1 $2"
   return 10
}


# Invoke your function
Hello Zara Ali


# Capture value returnd by last command
ret=$?


echo "Return value is $ret"
```

Upon execution, you will receive the following result –

```
$./test.sh
Hello World Zara Ali
Return value is 10
```

Nested Functions

One of the more interesting features of functions is that they can call themselves and also other functions. A function that calls itself is known as a recursive function.

Following example demonstrates nesting of two functions –

```sh
#!/bin/sh


# Calling one function from another
number_one () {
    echo "This is the first function speaking..."
    number_two
}


number_two () {
    echo "This is now the second function speaking..."
}


# Calling function one.
number_one
```

Upon execution, you will receive the following result –

```
This is the first function speaking...
This is now the second function speaking...
```

Function Call from Prompt

You can put definitions for commonly used functions inside your .profile. These definitions will be available whenever you log in and you can use them at the command prompt.

Alternatively, you can group the definitions in a file, say test.sh, and then execute the file in the current shell by typing –

```
$. test.sh
```

This has the effect of causing functions defined inside test.sh to be read and defined to the current shell as follows –

```
$ number_one
```

```
This is the first function speaking...

This is now the second function speaking...

$
```

To remove the definition of a function from the shell, use the unset command with the .f option. This command is also used to remove the definition of a variable to the shell.

```
$ unset -f function_name
```

Shell Man Page Help

All the Unix commands come with a number of optional and mandatory options. It is very common to forget the complete syntax of these commands.

Because no one can possibly remember every Unix command and all its options, we have online help available to mitigate this right from when Unix was at its development stage.

Unix's version of Help files are called man pages. If there is a command name and you are not sure how to use it, then Man Pages help you out with every step.

Syntax

Here is the simple command that helps you get the detail of any Unix command while working with the system –

```
$man command
```

Example

Suppose there is a command that requires you to get help; assume that you want to know about pwd then you simply need to use the following command –

```
$man pwd
```

The above command helps you with the complete information about the pwd command. Try it yourself at your command prompt to get more detail.

You can get complete detail on man command itself using the following command –

```
$man man
```

Man Page Sections

Man pages are generally divided into sections, which generally vary by the man page author's preference. Following table lists some common sections –

Sr. No.	Section & Description
1	**NAME** Name of the command
2	**SYNOPSIS** General usage parameters of the command
3	**DESCRIPTION** Describes what the command does
4	**OPTIONS** Describes all the arguments or options to the command
5	**SEE ALSO** Lists other commands that are directly related to the command in the man page or closely resemble its functionality
6	**BUGS** Explains any known issues or bugs that exist with the command or its output
7	**EXAMPLES** Common usage examples that give the reader an idea of how the command can be used
8	**AUTHORS** The author of the man page/command

To sum it up, man pages are a vital resource and the first avenue of research when you need information about commands or files in a Unix system.

Regular Expressions with SED

A regular expression is a string that can be used to describe several sequences of characters. Regular expressions are used by several different Unix commands, including ed, sed, awk, grep, and to a more limited extent, vi.

Here SED stands for stream editor. This stream-oriented editor was created exclusively for executing scripts. Thus, all the input you feed into it passes through and goes to STDOUT and it does not change the input file.

Invoking Sed

Before we start, let us ensure we have a local copy of /etc/passwd text file to work with sed.

As mentioned previously, sed can be invoked by sending data through a pipe to it as follows –

```
$ cat /etc/passwd | sed

Usage: sed [OPTION]... {script-other-script} [input-file]...


  -n,,quiet,,silent
```

```
            suppress automatic printing of pattern space

  -e script,,expression = script
```

. . . .

The cat command dumps the contents of /etc/passwd to sed through the pipe into sed's pattern space. The pattern space is the internal work buffer that sed uses for its operations.

Sed General Syntax

Following is the general syntax for sed –

```
/pattern/action
```

Here, pattern is a regular expression, and action is one of the commands given in the following table. If pattern is omitted, action is performed for every line as we have seen above.

The slash character (/) that surrounds the pattern are required because they are used as delimiters.

Sr. No.	Range & Description
1	**p** Prints the line
2	**d** Deletes the line
3	**s/pattern1/pattern2/** Substitutes the first occurrence of pattern1 with pattern2

Deleting All Lines with sed

We will now understand how to delete all lines with sed. Invoke sed again; but the sed is now supposed to use the editing command delete line, denoted by the single letter d –

```
$ cat /etc/passwd | sed 'd'
$
```

Instead of invoking sed by sending a file to it through a pipe, the sed can be instructed to read the data from a file, as in the following example.

The following command does exactly the same as in the previous example, without the cat command –

```
$ sed -e 'd' /etc/passwd
$
```

Sed Addresses

The sed also supports addresses. Addresses are either particular locations in a file or a range where a particular editing command should be applied. When the sed encounters no addresses, it performs its operations on every line in the file.

The following command adds a basic address to the sed command you've been using –

```
$ cat /etc/passwd | sed '1d' |more
daemon:x:1:1:daemon:/usr/sbin:/bin/sh
bin:x:2:2:bin:/bin:/bin/sh
sys:x:3:3:sys:/dev:/bin/sh
sync:x:4:65534:sync:/bin:/bin/sync
games:x:5:60:games:/usr/games:/bin/sh
man:x:6:12:man:/var/cache/man:/bin/sh
mail:x:8:8:mail:/var/mail:/bin/sh
news:x:9:9:news:/var/spool/news:/bin/sh
backup:x:34:34:backup:/var/backups:/bin/sh
$
```

Notice that the number 1 is added before the delete edit command. This instructs the sed to perform the editing command on the first line of the file. In this example, the sed will delete the first line of /etc/password and print the rest of the file.

Sed Address Ranges

We will now understand how to work with the sed address ranges. So what if you want to remove more than one line from a file? You can specify an address range with sed as follows –

```
$ cat /etc/passwd | sed '1, 5d' |more
games:x:5:60:games:/usr/games:/bin/sh
man:x:6:12:man:/var/cache/man:/bin/sh
mail:x:8:8:mail:/var/mail:/bin/sh
news:x:9:9:news:/var/spool/news:/bin/sh
backup:x:34:34:backup:/var/backups:/bin/sh
$
```

The above command will be applied on all the lines starting from 1 through 5. This deletes the first five lines.

Try out the following address ranges –

Sr. No.	Range & Description
1	**'4,10d'** Lines starting from the 4th till the 10th are deleted
2	**'10,4d'** Only 10th line is deleted, because the sed does not work in reverse direction
3	**'4,+5d'** This matches line 4 in the file, deletes that line, continues to delete the next five lines, and then ceases its deletion and prints the rest
4	**'2,5!d'** This deletes everything except starting from 2nd till 5th line
5	**'1~3d'** This deletes the first line, steps over the next three lines, and then deletes the fourth line. Sed continues to apply this pattern until the end of the file.
6	**'2~2d'** This tells sed to delete the second line, step over the next line, delete the next line, and repeat until the end of the file is reached
7	**'4,10p'** Lines starting from 4th till 10th are printed
8	**'4,d'** This generates the syntax error
9	**',10d'** This would also generate syntax error

While using the p action, you should use the -n option to avoid repetition of line printing. Check the difference in between the following two commands –

```
$ cat /etc/passwd | sed -n '1,3p'
```

Check the above command without -n as follows –

```
$ cat /etc/passwd | sed '1,3p'
```

Substitution Command

The substitution command, denoted by s, will substitute any string that you specify with any other string that you specify.

To substitute one string with another, the sed needs to have the information on where the first string ends and the substitution string begins. For this, we proceed with bookending the two strings with the forward slash (/) character.

The following command substitutes the first occurrence on a line of the string root with the string amrood.

```
$ cat /etc/passwd | sed 's/root/amrood/'
amrood:x:0:0:root user:/root:/bin/sh
daemon:x:1:1:daemon:/usr/sbin:/bin/sh
. . . . . . . . . . . . . . . . . . . . . . . .
```

It is very important to note that sed substitutes only the first occurrence on a line. If the string root occurs more than once on a line only the first match will be replaced.

For the sed to perform a global substitution, add the letter g to the end of the command as follows –

```
$ cat /etc/passwd | sed 's/root/amrood/g'
amrood:x:0:0:amrood user:/amrood:/bin/sh
daemon:x:1:1:daemon:/usr/sbin:/bin/sh
bin:x:2:2:bin:/bin:/bin/sh
sys:x:3:3:sys:/dev:/bin/sh
. . . . . . . . . . . . . . . . . . . . . . . . .
```

Substitution Flags

There are a number of other useful flags that can be passed in addition to the g flag, and you can specify more than one at a time.

Sr. No.	Flag & Description
1	**g** Replaces all matches, not just the first match
2	**NUMBER** Replaces only NUMBER[th] match
3	**p** If substitution was made, then prints the pattern space
4	**w FILENAME** If substitution was made, then writes result to FILENAME
5	**I or i** Matches in a case-insensitive manner
6	**M or m** In addition to the normal behavior of the special regular expression characters ^ and $, this flag causes ^ to match the empty string after a newline and $ to match the empty string before a newline

Using an Alternative String Separator

Suppose you have to do a substitution on a string that includes the forward slash character. In this case, you can specify a different separator by providing the designated character after the s.

```
$ cat /etc/passwd | sed 's:/root:/amrood:g'
amrood:x:0:0:amrood user:/amrood:/bin/sh
daemon:x:1:1:daemon:/usr/sbin:/bin/sh
```

In the above example, we have used : as the delimiter instead of slash / because we were trying to search /root instead of the simple root.

Replacing with Empty Space

Use an empty substitution string to delete the root string from the /etc/passwd file entirely –

```
$ cat /etc/passwd | sed 's/root//g'
:x:0:0::/:/bin/sh
daemon:x:1:1:daemon:/usr/sbin:/bin/sh
```

Address Substitution

If you want to substitute the string sh with the string quiet only on line 10, you can specify it as follows –

```
$ cat /etc/passwd | sed '10s/sh/quiet/g'
root:x:0:0:root user:/root:/bin/sh
daemon:x:1:1:daemon:/usr/sbin:/bin/sh
bin:x:2:2:bin:/bin:/bin/sh
sys:x:3:3:sys:/dev:/bin/sh
sync:x:4:65534:sync:/bin:/bin/sync
games:x:5:60:games:/usr/games:/bin/sh
man:x:6:12:man:/var/cache/man:/bin/sh
mail:x:8:8:mail:/var/mail:/bin/sh
news:x:9:9:news:/var/spool/news:/bin/sh
backup:x:34:34:backup:/var/backups:/bin/quiet
```

Similarly, to do an address range substitution, you could do something like the following –

```
$ cat /etc/passwd | sed '1,5s/sh/quiet/g'
```

```
root:x:0:0:root user:/root:/bin/quiet

daemon:x:1:1:daemon:/usr/sbin:/bin/quiet

bin:x:2:2:bin:/bin:/bin/quiet

sys:x:3:3:sys:/dev:/bin/quiet

sync:x:4:65534:sync:/bin:/bin/sync

games:x:5:60:games:/usr/games:/bin/sh

man:x:6:12:man:/var/cache/man:/bin/sh

mail:x:8:8:mail:/var/mail:/bin/sh

news:x:9:9:news:/var/spool/news:/bin/sh

backup:x:34:34:backup:/var/backups:/bin/sh
```

As you can see from the output, the first five lines had the string sh changed to quiet, but the rest of the lines were left untouched.

Matching Command

You would use the p option along with the -n option to print all the matching lines as follows –

```
$ cat testing | sed -n '/root/p'

root:x:0:0:root user:/root:/bin/sh

[root@ip-72-167-112-17 amrood]# vi testing

root:x:0:0:root user:/root:/bin/sh

daemon:x:1:1:daemon:/usr/sbin:/bin/sh

bin:x:2:2:bin:/bin:/bin/sh

sys:x:3:3:sys:/dev:/bin/sh

sync:x:4:65534:sync:/bin:/bin/sync

games:x:5:60:games:/usr/games:/bin/sh

man:x:6:12:man:/var/cache/man:/bin/sh

mail:x:8:8:mail:/var/mail:/bin/sh

news:x:9:9:news:/var/spool/news:/bin/sh

backup:x:34:34:backup:/var/backups:/bin/sh
```

Using Regular Expression

While matching patterns, you can use the regular expression which provides more flexibility.

Check the following example which matches all the lines starting with daemon and then deletes them –

```
$ cat testing | sed '/^daemon/d'
root:x:0:0:root user:/root:/bin/sh
bin:x:2:2:bin:/bin:/bin/sh
sys:x:3:3:sys:/dev:/bin/sh
sync:x:4:65534:sync:/bin:/bin/sync
games:x:5:60:games:/usr/games:/bin/sh
man:x:6:12:man:/var/cache/man:/bin/sh
mail:x:8:8:mail:/var/mail:/bin/sh
news:x:9:9:news:/var/spool/news:/bin/sh
backup:x:34:34:backup:/var/backups:/bin/sh
```

Following is the example which deletes all the lines ending with sh –

```
$ cat testing | sed '/sh$/d'
sync:x:4:65534:sync:/bin:/bin/sync
```

The following table lists four special characters that are very useful in regular expressions.

Sr. No.	Character & Description
1	^ Matches the beginning of lines
2	$ Matches the end of lines
3	. Matches any single character
4	* Matches zero or more occurrences of the previous character
5	[chars] Matches any one of the characters given in chars, where chars is a sequence of characters. You can use the - character to indicate a range of characters.

Matching Characters

Look at a few more expressions to demonstrate the use of meta characters. For example, the following pattern –

Sr. No.	Expression & Description
1	/a.c/ Matches lines that contain strings such as **a+c**, **a-c**, **abc**, **match**, and **a3c**

2	**/a*c/** Matches the same strings along with strings such as **ace**, **yacc**, and **arctic**	
3	**/[tT]he/** Matches the string **The** and **the**	
4	**/^$/** Matches blank lines	
5	**/^.*$/** Matches an entire line whatever it is	
6	**/ */** Matches one or more spaces	
7	**/^$/** Matches **blank** lines	

Following table shows some frequently used sets of characters –

Sr. No.	Set & Description
1	**[a-z]** Matches a single lowercase letter
2	**[A-Z]** Matches a single uppercase letter
3	**[a-zA-Z]** Matches a single letter
4	**[0-9]** Matches a single number
5	**[a-zA-Z0-9]** Matches a single letter or number

Character Class Keywords

Some special keywords are commonly available to regexps, especially GNU utilities that employ regexps. These are very useful for sed regular expressions as they simplify things and enhance readability.

For example, the characters a through z and the characters A through Z, constitute one such class of characters that has the keyword [[:alpha:]]

Using the alphabet character class keyword, this command prints only those lines in the /etc/syslog.conf file that start with a letter of the alphabet –

```
$ cat /etc/syslog.conf | sed -n '/^[[:alpha:]]/p'

authpriv.*                    /var/log/secure

mail.*                        -/var/log/maillog
```

```
cron.*                              /var/log/cron

uucp,news.crit                      /var/log/spooler

local7.*                            /var/log/boot.log
```

The following table is a complete list of the available character class keywords in GNU sed.

Sr. No.	Character Class & Description
1	**[[:alnum:]]** Alphanumeric [a-z A-Z 0-9]
2	**[[:alpha:]]** Alphabetic [a-z A-Z]
3	**[[:blank:]]** Blank characters (spaces or tabs)
4	**[[:cntrl:]]** Control characters
5	**[[:digit:]]** Numbers [0-9]
6	**[[:graph:]]** Any visible characters (excludes whitespace)
7	**[[:lower:]]** Lowercase letters [a-z]
8	**[[:print:]]** Printable characters (non-control characters)
9	**[[:punct:]]** Punctuation characters
10	**[[:space:]]** Whitespace
11	**[[:upper:]]** Uppercase letters [A-Z]
12	**[[:xdigit:]]** Hex digits [0-9 a-f A-F]

Ampersand Referencing

The sed metacharacter & represents the contents of the pattern that was matched. For instance, say you have a file called phone.txt full of phone numbers, such as the following:

```
5555551212

5555551213

5555551214

6665551215
```

```
6665551216
7775551217
```

You want to make the area code (the first three digits) surrounded by parentheses for easier reading. To do this, you can use the ampersand replacement character:

```
$ sed -e 's/^[[:digit:]][[:digit:]][[:digit:]]/(&)/g' phone.txt
(555)5551212
(555)5551213
(555)5551214
(666)5551215

(666)5551216
(777)5551217
```

Here in the pattern part you are matching the first 3 digits and then using & you are replacing those 3 digits with the surrounding parentheses.

Using Multiple Sed Commands

You can use multiple sed commands in a single sed command as follows −

```
$ sed -e 'command1' -e 'command2' ... -e 'commandN' files
```

Here command1 through commandN are sed commands of the type discussed previously. These commands are applied to each of the lines in the list of files given by files.

Using the same mechanism, we can write the above phone number example as follows −

```
$ sed -e 's/^[[:digit:]]\{3\}/(&)/g'  \
    -e 's/)[[:digit:]]\{3\}/&-/g' phone.txt
(555)555-1212
(555)555-1213
(555)555-1214
(666)555-1215
(666)555-1216
(777)555-1217
```

In the above example, instead of repeating the character class keyword [[:digit:]] three times, we replaced it with \{3\}, which means the preceding regular expression is matched three times. We have also used \ to give line break and this has to be removed before the command is run.

Back References

The ampersand metacharacter is useful, but even more useful is the ability to define specific regions in regular expressions. These special regions can be used as reference in your replacement strings. By defining specific parts of a regular expression, you can then refer back to those parts with a special reference character.

To do back references, you have to first define a region and then refer back to that region. To define a region, you insert backslashed parentheses around each region of interest. The first region that you surround with backslashes is then referenced by \1, the second region by \2, and so on.

Assuming phone.txt has the following text –

```
(555) 555-1212
(555) 555-1213
(555) 555-1214
(666) 555-1215
(666) 555-1216
(777) 555-1217
```

Try the following command –

```
$ cat phone.txt | sed 's/\(.*\)\)\(.*-\)\(.*$\)/Area \
   code: \1 Second: \2 Third: \3/'
Area code: (555) Second: 555- Third: 1212
Area code: (555) Second: 555- Third: 1213
Area code: (555) Second: 555- Third: 1214
Area code: (666) Second: 555- Third: 1215
Area code: (666) Second: 555- Third: 1216
Area code: (777) Second: 555- Third: 1217
```

Note – In the above example, each regular expression inside the parenthesis would be back referenced by \1, \2 and so on. We have used \ to give line break here. This should be removed before running the command.

File System Basics

A file system is a logical collection of files on a partition or disk. A partition is a container for information and can span an entire hard drive if desired.

Your hard drive can have various partitions which usually contain only one file system, such as one file system housing the /file system or another containing the /home file system.

One file system per partition allows for the logical maintenance and management of differing file systems.

Everything in Unix is considered to be a file, including physical devices such as DVD-ROMs, USB devices, and floppy drives.

Directory Structure

Unix uses a hierarchical file system structure, much like an upside-down tree, with root (/) at the base of the file system and all other directories spreading from there.

A Unix filesystem is a collection of files and directories that has the following properties –

- It has a root directory (/) that contains other files and directories.

- Each file or directory is uniquely identified by its name, the directory in which it resides, and a unique identifier, typically called an inode.

- By convention, the root directory has an inode number of 2 and the lost+found directory has an inode number of 3. Inode numbers 0 and 1 are not used. File inode numbers can be seen by specifying the -i option to ls command.

- It is self-contained. There are no dependencies between one filesystem and another.

The directories have specific purposes and generally hold the same types of information for easily locating files. Following are the directories that exist on the major versions of Unix –

Sr.No.	Directory & Description
1	**/** This is the root directory which should contain only the directories needed at the top level of the file structure
2	**/bin** This is where the executable files are located. These files are available to all users
3	**/dev** These are device drivers
4	**/etc** Supervisor directory commands, configuration files, disk configuration files, valid user lists, groups, ethernet, hosts, where to send critical messages
5	**/lib** Contains shared library files and sometimes other kernel-related files
6	**/boot** Contains files for booting the system
7	**/home** Contains the home directory for users and other accounts
8	**/mnt** Used to mount other temporary file systems, such as **cdrom** and **floppy** for the **CD-ROM** drive and **floppy diskette drive**, respectively

9	**/proc** Contains all processes marked as a file by **process number** or other information that is dynamic to the system
10	**/tmp** Holds temporary files used between system boots
11	**/usr** Used for miscellaneous purposes, and can be used by many users. Includes administrative commands, shared files, library files, and others
12	**/var** Typically contains variable-length files such as log and print files and any other type of file that may contain a variable amount of data
13	**/sbin** Contains binary (executable) files, usually for system administration. For example, *fdisk* and *ifconfig* utlities
14	**/kernel** Contains kernel files

Navigating the File System

Now that you understand the basics of the file system, you can begin navigating to the files you need. The following commands are used to navigate the system –

Sr. No.	Command & Description
1	**cat filename** Displays a filename
2	**cd dirname** Moves you to the identified directory
3	**cp file1 file2** Copies one file/directory to the specified location
4	**file filename** Identifies the file type (binary, text, etc)
5	**find filename dir** Finds a file/directory
6	**head filename** Shows the beginning of a file
7	**less filename** Browses through a file from the end or the beginning
8	**ls dirname** Shows the contents of the directory specified
9	**mkdir dirname** Creates the specified directory
10	**more filename** Browses through a file from the beginning to the end

11	**mv file1 file2** Moves the location of, or renames a file/directory
12	**pwd** Shows the current directory the user is in
13	**rm filename** Removes a file
14	**rmdir dirname** Removes a directory
15	**tail filename** Shows the end of a file
16	**touch filename** Creates a blank file or modifies an existing file or its attributes
17	**whereis filename** Shows the location of a file
18	**which filename** Shows the location of a file if it is in your PATH

df Command

The first way to manage your partition space is with the df (disk free) command. The command df -k (disk free) displays the disk space usage in kilobytes, as shown below –

```
$df -k

Filesystem       1K-blocks       Used    Available  Use% Mounted on

/dev/vzfs        10485760     7836644      2649116   75% /

/devices                0           0            0    0% /devices

$
```

Some of the directories, such as /devices, shows 0 in the kbytes, used, and avail columns as well as 0% for capacity. These are special (or virtual) file systems, and although they reside on the disk under /, by themselves they do not consume disk space.

The df -k output is generally the same on all Unix systems. Here's what it usually includes –

Sr. No.	Column & Description
1	**Filesystem** The physical file system name
2	**kbytes** Total kilobytes of space available on the storage medium
3	**used** Total kilobytes of space used (by files)

4	**avail** Total kilobytes available for use
5	**capacity** Percentage of total space used by files
6	**Mounted on** What the file system is mounted on

You can use the -h (human readable) option to display the output in a format that shows the size in easier-to-understand notation.

du Command

The du (disk usage) command enables you to specify directories to show disk space usage on a particular directory.

This command is helpful if you want to determine how much space a particular directory is taking. The following command displays number of blocks consumed by each directory. A single block may take either 512 Bytes or 1 Kilo Byte depending on your system.

```
$du /etc
10      /etc/cron.d
126     /etc/default
6       /etc/dfs
...
$
```

The -h option makes the output easier to comprehend –

```
$du -h /etc
5k      /etc/cron.d
63k     /etc/default
3k      /etc/dfs
...
$
```

Mounting the File System

A file system must be mounted in order to be usable by the system. To see what is currently mounted (available for use) on your system, use the following command –

```
$ mount
```

```
/dev/vzfs on / type reiserfs (rw,usrquota,grpquota)
```

```
proc on /proc type proc (rw,nodiratime)
```

```
devpts on /dev/pts type devpts (rw)
```

```
$
```

The /mnt directory, by the Unix convention, is where temporary mounts (such as CDROM drives, remote network drives, and floppy drives) are located. If you need to mount a file system, you can use the mount command with the following syntax –

```
mount -t file_system_type device_to_mount directory_to_mount_to
```

For example, if you want to mount a CD-ROM to the directory /mnt/cdrom, you can type –

```
$ mount -t iso9660 /dev/cdrom /mnt/cdrom
```

This assumes that your CD-ROM device is called /dev/cdrom and that you want to mount it to /mnt/cdrom. Type mount -h at the command line for help information.

After mounting, you can use the cd command to navigate the newly available file system through the mount point you just made.

Unmounting the File System

To unmount (remove) the file system from your system, use the umounts command by identifying the mount point or device.

For example, to unmount cdrom, use the following command –

```
$ umount /dev/cdrom
```

The mount command enables you to access your file systems, but on most modern Unix systems, the automount function makes this process invisible to the user and requires no intervention.

User and Group Quotas

The user and group quotas provide the mechanisms by which the amount of space used by a single user or all users within a specific group can be limited to a value defined by the administrator.

Quotas operate around two limits that allow the user to take some action if the amount of space or number of disk blocks start to exceed the administrator defined limits –

- Soft Limit – If the user exceeds the limit defined, there is a grace period that allows the user to free up some space.

- Hard Limit – When the hard limit is reached, regardless of the grace period, no further files or blocks can be allocated.

There are a number of commands to administer quotas –

Sr. No.	Command & Description
1	**quota** Displays disk usage and limits for a user of group
2	**edquota** This is a quota editor. Users or Groups quota can be edited using this command
3	**quotacheck** Scans a filesystem for disk usage, creates, checks and repairs quota files
4	**setquota** This is a command line quota editor
5	**quotaon** This announces to the system that disk quotas should be enabled on one or more filesystems
6	**quotaoff** This announces to the system that disk quotas should be disabled for one or more filesystems
7	**repquota** This prints a summary of the disc usage and quotas for the specified file systems

User Administration

There are three types of accounts on a Unix system.

Root Account

This is also called superuser and would have complete and unfettered control of the system. A superuser can run any commands without any restriction. This user should be assumed as a system administrator.

System Accounts

System accounts are those needed for the operation of system-specific components for example mail accounts and the sshd accounts. These accounts are usually needed for some specific function on your system, and any modifications to them could adversely affect the system.

User Accounts

User accounts provide interactive access to the system for users and groups of users. General users are typically assigned to these accounts and usually have limited access to critical system files and directories.

Unix supports a concept of Group Account which logically groups a number of accounts. Every account would be a part of another group account. A Unix group plays important role in handling file permissions and process management.

Managing Users and Groups

There are four main user administration files –

- /etc/passwd – Keeps the user account and password information. This file holds the majority of information about accounts on the Unix system.

- /etc/shadow – Holds the encrypted password of the corresponding account. Not all the systems support this file.

- /etc/group – This file contains the group information for each account.

- /etc/gshadow – This file contains secure group account information.

Check all the above files using the cat command.

The following table lists out commands that are available on majority of Unix systems to create and manage accounts and groups –

Sr. No.	Command & Description
1	**useradd** Adds accounts to the system
2	**usermod** Modifies account attributes
3	**userdel** Deletes accounts from the system
4	**groupadd** Adds groups to the system
5	**groupmod** Modifies group attributes
6	**groupdel** Removes groups from the system

You can use Man page Help to check complete syntax for each command mentioned here.

Create a Group

We will now understand how to create a group. For this, we need to create groups before creating any account otherwise; we can make use of the existing groups in our system. We have all the groups listed in /etc/groups file.

All the default groups are system account specific groups and it is not recommended to use them for ordinary accounts. So, following is the syntax to create a new group account –

```
groupadd [-g gid [-o]] [-r] [-f] groupname
```

The following table lists out the parameters –

Sr. No.	Option & Description
1	**-g GID** The numerical value of the group's ID
2	**-o** This option permits to add group with non-unique GID
3	**-r** This flag instructs **groupadd** to add a system account
4	**-f** This option causes to just exit with success status, if the specified group already exists. With -g, if the specified GID already exists, other (unique) GID is chosen
5	**groupname** Actual group name to be created

If you do not specify any parameter, then the system makes use of the default values.

Following example creates a developers group with default values, which is very much acceptable for most of the administrators.

```
$ groupadd developers
```

Modify a Group

To modify a group, use the groupmod syntax –

```
$ groupmod -n new_modified_group_name old_group_name
```

To change the developers_2 group name to developer, type –

```
$ groupmod -n developer developer_2
```

Here is how you will change the financial GID to 545 –

```
$ groupmod -g 545 developer
```

Delete a Group

We will now understand how to delete a group. To delete an existing group, all you need is the groupdel command and the group name. To delete the financial group, the command is –

```
$ groupdel developer
```

This removes only the group, not the files associated with that group. The files are still accessible by their owners.

Create an Account

Let us see how to create a new account on your Unix system. Following is the syntax to create a user's account –

```
useradd -d homedir -g groupname -m -s shell -u userid accountname
```

The following table lists out the parameters –

Sr. No.	Option & Description
1	**-d homedir** Specifies home directory for the account
2	**-g groupname** Specifies a group account for this account
3	**-m** Creates the home directory if it doesn't exist
4	**-s shell** Specifies the default shell for this account
5	**-u userid** You can specify a user id for this account
6	**Account name** Actual account name to be created

If you do not specify any parameter, then the system makes use of the default values. The useradd command modifies the /etc/passwd, /etc/shadow, and /etc/group files and creates a home directory.

Following is the example that creates an account mcmohd, setting its home directory to /home/mcmohd and the group as developers. This user would have Korn Shell assigned to it.

```
$ useradd -d /home/mcmohd -g developers -s /bin/ksh mcmohd
```

Before issuing the above command, make sure you already have the developers group created using the groupadd command.

Once an account is created you can set its password using the passwd command as follows –

```
$ passwd mcmohd20

Changing password for user mcmohd20.

New UNIX password:

Retype new UNIX password:

passwd: all authentication tokens updated successfully.
```

When you type passwd account name, it gives you an option to change the password, provided you are a super user. Otherwise, you can change just your password using the same command but without specifying your account name.

Modify an Account

The usermod command enables you to make changes to an existing account from the command line. It uses the same arguments as the useradd command, plus the -l argument, which allows you to change the account name.

For example, to change the account name mcmohd to mcmohd20 and to change home directory accordingly, you will need to issue the following command –

```
$ usermod -d /home/mcmohd20 -m -l mcmohd mcmohd20
```

Delete an Account

The userdel command can be used to delete an existing user. This is a very dangerous command if not used with caution.

There is only one argument or option available for the command .r, for removing the account's home directory and mail file.

For example, to remove account mcmohd20, issue the following command –

```
$ userdel -r mcmohd20
```

If you want to keep the home directory for backup purposes, omit the -r option. You can remove the home directory as needed at a later time.

System Performance

We will introduce you to a few free tools that are available to monitor and manage performance on Unix systems. These tools also provide guidelines on how to diagnose and fix performance problems in the Unix environment.

Unix has following major resource types that need to be monitored and tuned –

- CPU
- Memory
- Disk space
- Communications lines
- I/O Time
- Network Time
- Applications programs

Performance Components

The following table lists out five major components which take up the system time –

Sr. No.	Component & Description
1	**User State CPU** The actual amount of time the CPU spends running the users' program in the user state. It includes the time spent executing library calls, but does not include the time spent in the kernel on its behalf
2	**System State CPU** This is the amount of time the CPU spends in the system state on behalf of this program. All **I/O routines** require kernel services. The programmer can affect this value by blocking I/O transfers
3	**I/O Time and Network Time** This is the amount of time spent moving data and servicing I/O requests
4	**Virtual Memory Performance** This includes context switching and swapping
5	**Application Program** Time spent running other programs - when the system is not servicing this application because another application currently has the CPU

Performance Tools

Unix provides following important tools to measure and fine tune Unix system performance –

Sr. No.	Command & Description
1	**nice/renice** Runs a program with modified scheduling priority
2	**netstat** Prints network connections, routing tables, interface statistics, masquerade connections, and multicast memberships
3	**time** Helps time a simple command or give resource usage
4	**uptime** This is System Load Average
5	**ps** Reports a snapshot of the current processes
6	**vmstat** Reports virtual memory statistics
7	**gprof** Displays call graph profile data
8	**prof** Facilitates Process Profiling
9	**top** Displays system tasks

You can use Man page Help to check complete syntax for each command mentioned here.

System Logging

Unix systems have a very flexible and powerful logging system, which enables you to record almost anything you can imagine and then manipulate the logs to retrieve the information you require.

Many versions of Unix provide a general-purpose logging facility called syslog. Individual programs that need to have information logged, send the information to syslog.

Unix syslog is a host-configurable, uniform system logging facility. The system uses a centralized system logging process that runs the program /etc/syslogd or /etc/syslog.

The operation of the system logger is quite straightforward. Programs send their log entries to syslogd, which consults the configuration file /etc/syslogd.conf or /etc/syslog and, when a match is found, writes the log message to the desired log file.

There are four basic syslog terms that you should understand –

Sr. No.	Term & Description
1	**Facility** The identifier used to describe the application or process that submitted the log message. For example, mail, kernel, and ftp.
2	**Priority** An indicator of the importance of the message. Levels are defined within syslog as guidelines, from debugging information to critical events.
3	**Selector** A combination of one or more facilities and levels. When an incoming event matches a selector, an action is performed.
4	**Action** What happens to an incoming message that matches a selector — Actions can write the message to a log file, echo the message to a console or other device, write the message to a logged in user, or send the message along to another syslog server.

Syslog Facilities

We will now understand about the syslog facilities. Here are the available facilities for the selector. Not all facilities are present on all versions of Unix.

Facility	Description
1	**auth** Activity related to requesting name and password (getty, su, login)
2	**authpriv** Same as auth but logged to a file that can only be read by selected users
3	**console** Used to capture messages that are generally directed to the system console
4	**cron** Messages from the cron system scheduler

5	**daemon** System daemon catch-all
6	**ftp** Messages relating to the ftp daemon
7	**kern** Kernel messages
8	**localo.local7** Local facilities defined per site
9	**lpr** Messages from the line printing system
10	**mail** Messages relating to the mail system
11	**mark** Pseudo-event used to generate timestamps in log files
12	**news** Messages relating to network news protocol (nntp)
13	**ntp** Messages relating to network time protocol
14	**user** Regular user processes
15	**uucp** UUCP subsystem

Syslog Priorities

The syslog priorities are summarized in the following table –

Sr.No.	Priority & Description
1	**emerg** Emergency condition, such as an imminent system crash, usually broadcast to all users
2	**alert** Condition that should be corrected immediately, such as a corrupted system database
3	**crit** Critical condition, such as a hardware error
4	**err** Ordinary error
5	**Warning** Warning
6	**notice** Condition that is not an error, but possibly should be handled in a special way
7	**info** Informational message

8	**debug** Messages that are used when debugging programs
9	**none** Pseudo level used to specify not to log messages

The combination of facilities and levels enables you to be discerning about what is logged and where that information goes.

As each program sends its messages dutifully to the system logger, the logger makes decisions on what to keep track of and what to discard based on the levels defined in the selector.

When you specify a level, the system will keep track of everything at that level and higher.

The /etc/syslog.conf file

The /etc/syslog.conf file controls where messages are logged. A typical syslog.conf file might look like this –

```
*.err;kern.debug;auth.notice  /dev/console

daemon,auth.notice            /var/log/messages

lpr.info                      /var/log/lpr.log

mail.*                        /var/log/mail.log

ftp.*                         /var/log/ftp.log

auth.*                        @prep.ai.mit.edu

auth.*                        root,amrood

netinfo.err                   /var/log/netinfo.log

install.*                     /var/log/install.log

*.emerg                       *

*.alert                       |program_name

mark.*                        /dev/console
```

Each line of the file contains two parts –

- A message selector that specifies which kind of messages to log. For example, all error messages or all debugging messages from the kernel.

- An action field that says what should be done with the message. For example, put it in a file or send the message to a user's terminal.

Following are the notable points for the above configuration –

- Message selectors have two parts: a facility and a priority. For example, kern.debug selects all debug messages (the priority) generated by the kernel (the facility).

- Message selector kern.debug selects all priorities that are greater than debug.

- An asterisk in place of either the facility or the priority indicates "all". For example, *.debug means all debug messages, while kern.* means all messages generated by the kernel.

- You can also use commas to specify multiple facilities. Two or more selectors can be grouped together by using a semicolon.

Logging Actions

The action field specifies one of five actions –

- Log message to a file or a device. For example, /var/log/lpr.log or /dev/console.

- Send a message to a user. You can specify multiple usernames by separating them with commas; for example, root, amrood.

- Send a message to all users. In this case, the action field consists of an asterisk; for example, *.

- Pipe the message to a program. In this case, the program is specified after the Unix pipe symbol (|).

- Send the message to the syslog on another host.

Logger Command

Unix provides the logger command, which is an extremely useful command to deal with system logging. The logger command sends logging messages to the syslogd daemon, and consequently provokes system logging.

This means we can check from the command line at any time the syslogd daemon and its configuration. The logger command provides a method for adding one-line entries to the system log file from the command line.

The format of the command is –

```
logger [-i] [-f file] [-p priority] [-t tag] [message]...
```

Here is the detail of the parameters –

Sr.No.	Option & Description
1	**-f filename** Uses the contents of file filename as the message to log.
2	**-i** Logs the process ID of the logger process with each line.
3	**-p priority** Enters the message with the specified priority (specified selector entry); the message priority can be specified numerically, or as a facility.priority pair. The default priority is user.notice.

4	**-t tag** Marks each line added to the log with the specified tag.
5	**message** The string arguments whose contents are concatenated together in the specified order, separated by the space.

Log Rotation

Log files have the propensity to grow very fast and consume large amounts of disk space. To enable log rotations, most distributions use tools such as newsyslog or logrotate.

These tools should be called on a frequent time interval using the cron daemon.

Important Log Locations

All the system applications create their log files in /var/log and its sub-directories. Here are few important applications and their corresponding log directories –

Application	Directory
httpd	/var/log/httpd
samba	/var/log/samba
cron	/var/log/
mail	/var/log/
mysql	/var/log/

Signals and Traps

Signals are software interrupts sent to a program to indicate that an important event has occurred. The events can vary from user requests to illegal memory access errors. Some signals, such as the interrupt signal, indicate that a user has asked the program to do something that is not in the usual flow of control.

The following table lists out common signals you might encounter and want to use in your programs –

Signal Name	Signal Number	Description
SIGHUP	1	Hang up detected on controlling terminal or death of controlling process
SIGINT	2	Issued if the user sends an interrupt signal (Ctrl + C)
SIGQUIT	3	Issued if the user sends a quit signal (Ctrl + D)
SIGFPE	8	Issued if an illegal mathematical operation is attempted
SIGKILL	9	If a process gets this signal it must quit immediately and will not perform any clean-up operations
SIGALRM	14	Alarm clock signal (used for timers)
SIGTERM	15	Software termination signal (sent by kill by default)

List of Signals

There is an easy way to list down all the signals supported by your system. Just issue the kill -l command and it would display all the supported signals –

```
$ kill -l
```

1) SIGHUP	2) SIGINT	3) SIGQUIT	4) SIGILL
5) SIGTRAP	6) SIGABRT	7) SIGBUS	8) SIGFPE
9) SIGKILL	10) SIGUSR1	11) SIGSEGV	12) SIGUSR2
13) SIGPIPE	14) SIGALRM	15) SIGTERM	16) SIGSTKFLT
17) SIGCHLD	18) SIGCONT	19) SIGSTOP	20) SIGTSTP
21) SIGTTIN	22) SIGTTOU	23) SIGURG	24) SIGXCPU
25) SIGXFSZ	26) SIGVTALRM	27) SIGPROF	28) SIGWINCH
29) SIGIO	30) SIGPWR	31) SIGSYS	34) SIGRTMIN
35) SIGRTMIN+1	36) SIGRTMIN+2	37) SIGRTMIN+3	38) SIGRTMIN+4
39) SIGRTMIN+5	40) SIGRTMIN+6	41) SIGRTMIN+7	42) SIGRTMIN+8
43) SIGRTMIN+9	44) SIGRTMIN+10	45) SIGRTMIN+11	46) SIGRTMIN+12
47) SIGRTMIN+13	48) SIGRTMIN+14	49) SIGRTMIN+15	50) SIGRTMAX-14
51) SIGRTMAX-13	52) SIGRTMAX-12	53) SIGRTMAX-11	54) SIGRTMAX-10
55) SIGRTMAX-9	56) SIGRTMAX-8	57) SIGRTMAX-7	58) SIGRTMAX-6
59) SIGRTMAX-5	60) SIGRTMAX-4	61) SIGRTMAX-3	62) SIGRTMAX-2
63) SIGRTMAX-1	64) SIGRTMAX		

The actual list of signals varies between Solaris, HP-UX, and Linux.

Default Actions

Every signal has a default action associated with it. The default action for a signal is the action that a script or program performs when it receives a signal.

Some of the possible default actions are –

- Terminate the process.
- Ignore the signal.
- Dump core. This creates a file called core containing the memory image of the process when it received the signal.
- Stop the process.
- Continue a stopped process.

Sending Signals

There are several methods of delivering signals to a program or script. One of the most common is for a user to type CONTROL-C or the INTERRUPT key while a script is executing.

When you press the Ctrl+C key, a SIGINT is sent to the script and as per defined default action script terminates.

The other common method for delivering signals is to use the kill command, the syntax of which is as follows –

```
$ kill -signal pid
```

Here signal is either the number or name of the signal to deliver and pid is the process ID that the signal should be sent to. For Example –

```
$ kill -1 1001
```

The above command sends the HUP or hang-up signal to the program that is running with process ID 1001. To send a kill signal to the same process, use the following command –

```
$ kill -9 1001
```

This kills the process running with process ID 1001.

Trapping Signals

When you press the Ctrl+C or Break key at your terminal during execution of a shell program, normally that program is immediately terminated, and your command prompt returns. This may not always be desirable. For instance, you may end up leaving a bunch of temporary files that won't get cleaned up.

Trapping these signals is quite easy, and the trap command has the following syntax –

```
$ trap commands signals
```

Here command can be any valid Unix command, or even a user-defined function, and signal can be a list of any number of signals you want to trap.

There are two common uses for trap in shell scripts –

- Clean up temporary files
- Ignore signals

Cleaning up Temporary Files

As an example of the trap command, the following shows how you can remove some files and then exit if someone tries to abort the program from the terminal –

```
$ trap "rm -f $WORKDIR/work1$$ $WORKDIR/dataout$$; exit" 2
```

From the point in the shell program that this trap is executed, the two files work1$$ and dataout$$ will be automatically removed if signal number 2 is received by the program.

Hence, if the user interrupts the execution of the program after this trap is executed, you can be assured that these two files will be cleaned up. The exit command that follows the rm is necessary because without it, the execution would continue in the program at the point that it left off when the signal was received.

Signal number 1 is generated for hangup. Either someone intentionally hangs up the line or the line gets accidentally disconnected.

You can modify the preceding trap to also remove the two specified files in this case by adding signal number 1 to the list of signals –

```
$ trap "rm $WORKDIR/work1$$ $WORKDIR/dataout$$; exit" 1 2
```

Now these files will be removed if the line gets hung up or if the *Ctrl+C* key gets pressed.

The commands specified to trap must be enclosed in quotes, if they contain more than one command. Also note that the shell scans the command line at the time that the trap command gets executed and also when one of the listed signals is received.

Thus, in the preceding example, the value of WORKDIR and $$ will be substituted at the time that the trap command is executed. If you wanted this substitution to occur at the time that either signal 1 or 2 was received, you can put the commands inside single quotes –

```
$ trap 'rm $WORKDIR/work1$$ $WORKDIR/dataout$$; exit' 1 2
```

Ignoring Signals

If the command listed for trap is null, the specified signal will be ignored when received. For example, the command –

```
$ trap '' 2
```

This specifies that the interrupt signal is to be ignored. You might want to ignore certain signals when performing an operation that you don't want to be interrupted. You can specify multiple signals to be ignored as follows –

```
$ trap '' 1 2 3 15
```

Note that the first argument must be specified for a signal to be ignored and is not equivalent to writing the following, which has a separate meaning of its own –

```
$ trap  2
```

If you ignore a signal, all subshells also ignore that signal. However, if you specify an action to be taken on the receipt of a signal, all subshells will still take the default action on receipt of that signal.

Resetting Traps

After you've changed the default action to be taken on receipt of a signal, you can change it back again with the trap if you simply omit the first argument; so –

```
$ trap 1 2
```

This resets the action to be taken on the receipt of signals 1 or 2 back to the default.

Microsoft Windows

Windows is Microsoft's flagship operating system (OS), the de facto standard for home and business computers. The graphical user interface (GUI)-based OS was introduced in 1985 and has been released in many versions since then, as described below. Microsoft got its start with the partnership of Bill Gates and Paul Allen in 1975. Gates and Allen co-developed Xenix (a version of Unix) and also collaborated on a BASIC interpreter for the Altair 8800. The company was incorporated in 1981.

Microsoft gained prominence in the tech field with the release of MS-DOS, a text-based command-line-driven operating system. DOS was mostly based on a purchased intellectual property, QDOS. GUI-based operating systems of that time included Xerox's Alto, released in 1979, and Apple's LISA and Macintosh systems, which came later. Die-hard fans of MS-DOS referred to such systems as WIMPs, which stood for "windows, icons, mouse and pull-down menus (or pointers)."

However, Gates saw the potential in GUI-based systems and started a project he called Interface Manager. Gates thought he could bring the GUI to a wider audience at a lower cost than the $9,000 LISA. The rest of Microsoft supported this idea, and, in a somewhat ironic move, the project team selected "Windows" as the name of the new operating system.

Microsoft announced the impending release of Windows 1.0 in 1983. The company used some features it licensed from Apple for portions of its interface. Microsoft released Windows 1.0 in 1985. Apple sued Microsoft and Hewlett-Packard for $5.5 billion in 1988 claiming it did not give the companies authorization to use certain GUI elements. In 1992, a federal court concluded Microsoft and Hewlett-Packard did not go beyond the 1985 agreement. Apple appealed that decision, which was upheld in 1994.

Competitors to Windows include Apple's macOS and the open source Linux operating system from Linus Torvalds. The free price gives Linux an edge in availability, while macOS is known for its stability and user experience. However, Microsoft Windows continues to maintain its dominance, a June 2018 report from the NetMarketShare site shows Windows installed on nearly 88% of desktops and laptops, with a steady rollout of new versions to support advances in hardware.

Windows versions through the years

Windows 1.0

Like many early versions of Microsoft's GUI operating systems, Windows 1.0 was essentially a program that ran on top of DOS. Microsoft did not release the system until two years after its first announcement, leading to suggestions that Windows was vaporware. The release was a shaky start for the tech giant. Users found the software unstable. However, the point-and-click interface made it easier for new users to operate a computer. The user-friendly nature of Windows also drew interest from customers who might have been intimidated by a command-line interface. Windows 1.0 offered many of the common components found in today's graphical user interface, such as scroll bars and "OK" buttons.

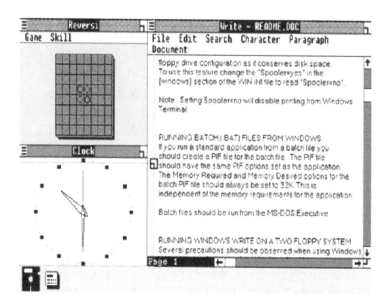

Windows 2.0 and 2.11

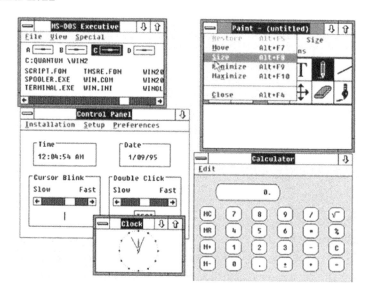

Windows 2.0 was faster, more stable and had more GUI features in common with the Apple LISA. The system introduced the control panel and ran the first versions of Excel and Word. Windows 2.0 supported extended memory, and Microsoft updated it for compatibility with Intel's 80386 processor. It was during this time that Microsoft became the largest software vendor in the world, just as computers were becoming more commonplace. The fact that Windows systems were user-friendly and relatively affordable was a contributing factor to the growing PC market.

Windows 3.0

Microsoft optimized the Windows 3.0 operating system, which still ran on top of DOS, for the 386 processor for a more responsive system. Windows 3.0 supported 16 colors and included the casual games familiar to most Windows users: Solitaire, Minesweeper and Hearts. Games that required more processing power still ran directly on MS-DOS. Exiting to DOS gave games direct hardware access made more system resources available that otherwise would have gone to Windows. Microsoft offered Windows 3.1 as a paid sub-release in 1993. Windows 3.1 features included support for TrueType fonts and peer-to-peer networking.

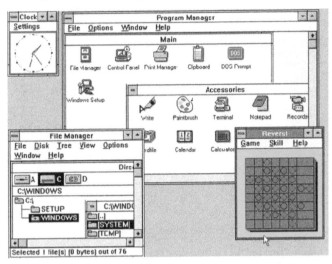

Windows NT

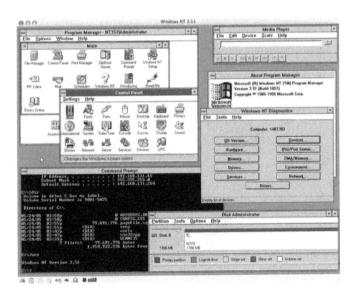

Windows NT's release marked the completion of a side project to build a new, advanced OS. NT was 32-bit and had a hardware abstraction layer. DOS was available through the command prompt, but it did not run the Windows OS. Microsoft designed NT as a workstation OS for businesses rather than home users. The system introduced the Start button.

Windows 95

Windows 95 introduced the Windows operating system to a wider audience with a marketing campaign that featured The Rolling Stones song "Start Me Up" to celebrate the Start button's arrival to the masses. Windows 95 facilitated hardware installation with its Plug and Play feature. Microsoft also unveiled 32-bit color depth, enhanced multimedia capabilities and TCP/IP network support.

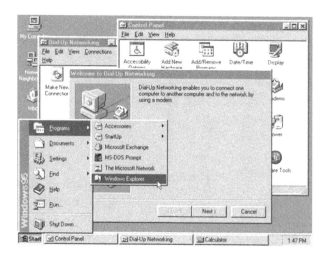

Windows 98

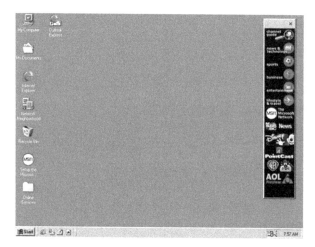

Microsoft improved speed and Plug and Play hardware support in Windows 98. The company also debuted USB support and the Quick Launch bar in this release. DOS gaming began to wane as Windows gaming technology improved. The popularity of the OS made it an attractive target for malware. Microsoft integrated web technology into the Windows user interface and built its own web browser into the desktop. This feature was one of the defining issues in the U.S. Justice Department's antitrust suit against Microsoft in the 1990s.

Windows ME

Windows ME (Millennium Edition) was the last use of the Windows 95 codebase. Its most notable new feature was System Restore. Many customers found this release to be unstable, and it was acknowledged as a poor release by Steve Ballmer and Microsoft. Some critics said ME stood for "mistake edition."

Microsoft released the professional desktop OS Windows 2000 the same year. Microsoft based this OS on the more stable Windows NT code. Some home users installed Windows 2000 for its greater reliability. Microsoft updated Plug and Play support, which spurred home users to switch to this OS.

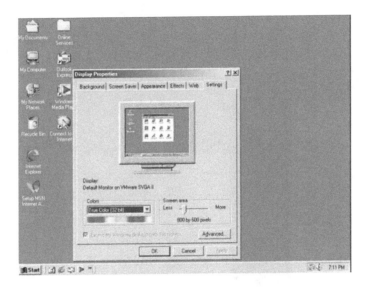

Windows XP

Microsoft delivered Windows XP as the first NT-based system with a version aimed squarely at the home user. Home users and critics rated XP highly. The system improved Windows appearance with colorful themes and provided a more stable platform.

Microsoft virtually ended gaming in DOS with this release. DirectX-enabled features in 3D gaming that OpenGL had difficulties with. XP offered the first Windows support for 64-bit computing, but it was not very well supported, lacking drivers and applications to run.

Windows Vista

Microsoft hyped Windows Vista after the company spent a lot of resources to develop a more polished appearance. Vista had interesting visual effects but the OS was slow to start and run. The 32-bit version, in particular, didn't enable enough RAM for the memory-hungry OS to operate properly.

Microsoft tightened licensing rights and made it more work to activate Windows. The company also peeled back user control of the operating system's internal workings.

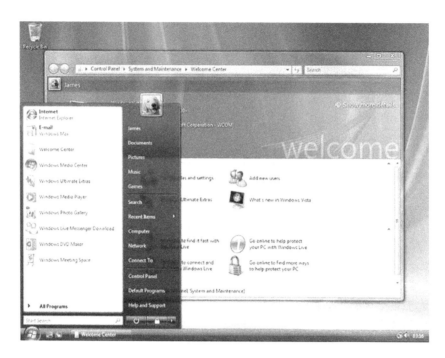

Microsoft lost market share to Apple and Linux variants. Vista's flaws, coupled with the fact that many older computers lacked the resources to run the system, led to many home and business users staying with XP.

Windows 7

Microsoft built Windows 7 on the Vista kernel. Windows 7 picked up Vista's visual capabilities but featured more stability. To many end users, the biggest changes between Vista and Windows 7 were faster boot times, new user interface and the addition of Internet Explorer 8.

With true 64-bit support and more Direct X features, Windows 7 proved to be a popular release for Windows users.

Windows 8

Microsoft released Windows 8 with a number of enhancements and debuted its tile-based Metro user interface. Windows 8 took better advantage of multicore processing, solid-state drives (SSD), touchscreens and other alternate input methods. Users found the switching from the traditional desktop to the tile-based interface awkward. Even after Microsoft's UI and other updates in 8.1, Windows 8 trailed not just Windows 7 but XP in user numbers into 2014.

Windows 10

Microsoft announced Windows 10 in September 2014, skipping Windows 9. Version 10 includes the Start menu, which was absent from Windows 8. A responsive design feature called Continuum adapts the interface depending on whether the user works with a touchscreen or a keyboard and mouse for input. New features like an onscreen back button simplified touch input. Microsoft designed the OS to have a consistent interface across devices including PCs, laptops and tablets.

Changes in Security

Microsoft did not implement many security methods in its operating systems until Windows NT and XP. For example, the default user on a Windows computer received administrator privileges until Vista.

Consumer editions of early versions of Windows did not have security measures built in since Microsoft designed the OS for single users without network connections. The company integrated security features in Windows NT, but they weren't in the forefront of Microsoft's design. The combination of lack of security and widespread popularity made Windows systems a target for malicious programs, such as viruses or system exploits.

Microsoft began to release monthly patches every second Tuesday of the month, known as Patch Tuesday, in 2003. Patches to update critical issues may be released on a faster schedule, known as out-of-band patches.

Windows Vista added User Account Control, a privilege evaluation feature based on a token system. The token allowed users only the most basic privileges, such as the ability to execute tasks that may modify system data. When an administrator logged on, they received two tokens, one that a standard user would receive and another that allowed administrator-level tasks.

Microsoft released its Windows Defender security application as a beta program for Windows XP in 2005. Windows Defender protects systems from spyware threats. Microsoft included Defender in later versions of Windows, such as Windows 10. Microsoft further buttressed system security with Windows Defender Credential Guard for virtualization-based security, System Guard to protect firmware components and configurations and Application Guard to protect against malware and hacking threats in the Microsoft Edge browser.

Differences in Windows Operating System Editions

Starting with Windows XP, Microsoft separated Windows to give different features to distinct audiences. Windows 10, for example, has multiple editions including Windows 10 Home, Pro and Enterprise editions.

Microsoft makes its consumer operating systems for users in an ordinary household setting. Enterprise operating system is designed for large organizations in a business setting. The enterprise software tends to have more customization abilities and features that an organization can utilize, such as security or language packs.

Microsoft designed Windows 10 Home for consumers and tailored to operate on PCs, tablets and 2-in-1 devices. Microsoft built Windows 10 Pro as a baseline OS for any business, while it developed Windows 10 Enterprise for businesses with higher security needs.

Security features differ from Windows 10 Home, Pro and Enterprise editions. Windows 10 Home includes basic security features such as Windows Defender, Device Encryption and Windows Information Protection. Windows 10 Pro adds more security features such as Bitlocker, Windows Defender System Guard, Windows Defender Exploit Guard and Windows Defender Antivirus. Windows 10 Enterprise is identical in features and functionality to Pro but adds more security features such as Windows Defender Credential Guard, Windows Defender Application Guard and Windows Defender Application Control.

File Systems of Windows

Microsoft Windows employs two major file systems: NTFS, the primary format most modern versions of this OS use by default, and FAT, which was inherited from old DOS and has exFAT as its later extension. In addition, the ReFS file system was developed by Microsoft as a new generation file system for server computers starting from Windows Server 2012.

FAT

FAT (File Allocation Table) is one of the simplest file system types, which has been around since the 1980s. It consists of the file system descriptor sector (boot sector or superblock), the file system block allocation table (referred as the File Allocation Table) and plain storage space for storing files and folders. Files in FAT are stored in directories. Each directory is an array of 32-byte records, each defining a file or extended attributes of a file (e.g. a long file name). A file record attributes the first block of a file. Any next block can be found through the block allocation table by using it as a linked list.

The block allocation table contains an array of block descriptors. A zero value indicates that the block is not used and a non-zero one relates to the next block of a file or a special value for the file end.

The numbers in FAT12, FAT16, FAT32 stand for the number of bits used to enumerate a file system block. This means that FAT12 can use up to 4096 different block references, while FAT16 and FAT32 can use up to 65536 and 4294967296 accordingly. The actual maximum count of blocks is even less and depends on the implementation of the file system driver.

FAT12 and FAT16 used to be applied to old floppy disks and do not find extensive employment nowadays. FAT32 is still widely used for memory cards and USB sticks. The system is supported by smartphones, digital cameras and other portable devices.

FAT32 can be used on Windows-compatible external storages or disk partitions with the size under 32 GB (Windows cannot create a FAT32 file system which would be larger than 32 GB, although Linux supports the size up to 2 TB) and doesn't allow to create files the size of which exceeds 4 GB. To address this issue, exFAT was introduced, which doesn't have any realistic limitations concerning the size of files or partitions.

NTFS

NTFS (New Technology File System) was introduced in 1993 with Windows NT and is currently the most common file system for end user computers based on Windows. Most operating systems of the Windows Server line use this format as well.

The file system is quite reliable thanks to journaling and supports many features, including access control, encryption, etc. Each file in NTFS is stored as a file descriptor in the Master File Table and file content. The Master file table contains entries with all information about files: size, allocation, name, etc. The first 16 entries of the Master File Table are retained for the BitMap, which keeps record of all free and used clusters, the Log used for journaling records and the BadClus containing information about bad clusters. The first and the last sectors of the file system contain file system settings (the boot record or the superblock). This file system uses 48 and 64 bit values to reference files, thus being able to support data storages with extremely high capacity.

ReFS

ReFS (Resilient File System) is the latest development of Microsoft introduced with Windows 8 and now available for Windows 10. The file system architecture absolutely differs from other Windows file systems and is mainly organized in a form of the B+-tree. ReFS has high tolerance to failures due to new features included into the system. And, namely, Copy-on-Write (CoW): no metadata is modified without being copied; data is not written over the existing data, but into new disk space. With any file modifications, a new copy of metadata is stored into free storage space, and then the system creates a link from older metadata to the newer one. Thus, the system stores significant quantity of older backups in different places providing easy file recovery unless this storage space is overwritten.

OS X

OS X is Apple's operating system that runs on Macintosh computers. It was first released in 2001 and over the next few years replaced Mac OS 9 (also known as Mac OS Classic) as the standard OS for Macs. It was called "Mac OS X" until version OS X 10.8, when Apple dropped "Mac" from the name.

OS X was originally built from NeXTSTEP, an operating system designed by NeXT, which Apple acquired when Steve Jobs returned to Apple in 1997. Like NeXTSTEP, OS X is based on Unix and uses the same Mach kernel. This kernel provides OS X with better multithreading capabilities and improved memory management compared to Mac OS Classic. While the change forced Mac developers to rewrite their software programs, it provided necessary performance improvements and scalability for future generations of Macs.

The OS X desktop interface is called the Finder and includes several standard features. OS X does not have a task bar like Windows, but instead includes a menu bar, which is fixed at the top of the screen. The menu bar options change depending on what application is currently running and is only hidden when full screen mode is enabled. The Finder also includes a Dock, which is displayed by default on the bottom of the screen. The Dock provides easy one-click access to frequently used applications and files. The Finder also displays a user-selectable desktop background that serves as a backdrop for icons and open windows.

When you start up a Mac, OS X loads automatically. It serves as the fundamental user interface, but also works behind the scenes, managing processes and applications. For example, when you double-click an application icon, OS X launches the corresponding program and provides memory to the application while it is running. It reallocates memory as necessary and frees up used memory when an application is quit. OS X also includes an extensive API, or library of functions, that developers can use when writing Mac programs.

While the OS X interface remains similar to the original version released in 2001, it has gone through several updates, which have each added numerous new features to the operating system. Below is a list of the different versions of OS X, along with their code names.

- Mac OS X 10.0 (Cheetah)

- Mac OS X 10.1 (Puma)

- Mac OS X 10.2 (Jaguar)

- Mac OS X 10.3 (Panther)

- Mac OS X 10.4 (Tiger)

- Mac OS X 10.5 (Leopard)

- Mac OS X 10.6 (Snow Leopard)

- Mac OS X 10.7 (Lion)

- OS X 10.8 (Mountain Lion)

- OS X 10.9 (Mavericks)

- OS X 10.10 (Yosemite)

Apple File System

APFS (Apple File System) is a system for organizing and structuring data on a storage system. APFS originally released with macOS Sierra replaces the 30-year-old HFS+.

HFS+ and HFS (a slightly earlier version of the Hierarchical File System) was originally created back in the days of floppy disks, which were the primary storage medium for the Mac when spinning hard drives were an expensive option offered by third parties.

In the past, Apple has flirted with replacing HFS+, but APFS which is already included in iOS, tvOS, and watchOS, is now the default file system for macOS High Sierra and later.

HFS+ was implemented when 800 kb floppies were king. Current Macs may not be using floppies, but spinning hard drives are beginning to seem just as archaic. With Apple emphasizing flash-based storage in all of its products, a file system optimized to work with rotational media, and the inherent latency in waiting for a disk to spin around just doesn't make a lot of sense.

APFS is designed from the get-go for SSD and other flash-based storage systems. Even though APFS is optimized for how solid-state storage works, it performs well with modern hard drives.

APFS supports a 64-bit inode number. The inode is a unique identifier that identifies a file system object. A file system object can be anything; a file, a folder. With a 64-bit inode, the APFS could hold roughly 9 quintillion file system objects blasting past the old limit of 2.1 billion.

Nine quintillion may seem like a pretty big number, and you may rightly ask what storage device is going to have enough space to actually hold that many objects. The answer requires a peek into storage trends. Consider this: Apple has already started moving enterprise-level storage technology to consumer-level products, such as the Mac and its ability to use tiered storage. This was first seen in Fusion drives that moved data between a high-performance SSD and a slower, but much larger, hard drive. Frequently accessed data was kept on the fast SSD, while files used less often were stored on the hard drive.

With macOS, Apple extended this concept by adding iCloud-based storage to the mix. Allowing movies and TV shows you've already watched to be stored in iCloud freeing up local storage. While this last example doesn't require a unified inode numbering system across all the disks in use by this tiered storage system, it does show a general direction Apple may be moving in; to bring together multiple storage technologies that best fit the needs of the user, and have the OS see them as a single file space.

APFS Features

APFS has a number of features that set it apart from older file systems.

- Clones – Clones allow almost instantaneous file copies without using additional space. Instead of copying a file bit by bit from one location to another, clones instead reference the original file, sharing the blocks of data that are identical between the two files. Make changes to one file, and only the block of data that has changed is written to the new clone, while both the original and the clone continue to share unchanged blocks of data. This not only makes file copying and saving especially fast, but also saves on storage space needs.

- Snapshots – APFS can create a volume snapshot that represents a point in time. Snapshots can be used to facilitate efficient backups as well as allow you to go back to how things were at a particular point in time. Snapshots are read-only pointers to the original volume and its data. A new snapshot takes up no real space, other than the amount of space needed to store a pointer to the original volume. As time goes by and changes are made to the original volume, the snapshot is updated with only the changes that occur.

- Encryption – APFS supports strong full disk encryption using AES-XTS or AES-CBC modes. Both files and metadata will be encrypted. Supported encryption methods include:

  ◦ Clear (no encryption).

  ◦ Single-key.

  ◦ Multi-key, with per-file keys for both data and metadata.

- Space Sharing – Space sharing puts an end to predefining partition sizes; instead, all volumes share the underlying free space on a drive. Space sharing will allow multiple volumes on a drive to grow and shrink dynamically as needed, without any need to repartition.

- Copy-On-Write – This data protection scheme allows data structures to be shared as long as no change is made. Once a change is requested (write), a new unique copy is made, ensuring the original is left intact. Only after the write is completed is the file information updated to point to the new data.

- Atomic Safe-Save – This is similar to the idea of copy-on-write but applies to any file operation, such as a renaming or moving a file or directory. Using rename as an example, the file that is about to be renamed is copied with the new data (the file name); not until the copy process is complete is the files system updated to point to the new data. This ensures that if for any reason, such as a power failure, or some type of CPU hiccup, the write isn't completed, the original file remains intact.

- Sparse Files – This more efficient way of allocating file space allows file space to grow only when actually needed. In non-sparse file systems, the file space must be reserved in advance, even when no data is ready to be stored.

iOS

iOS is a mobile operating system developed by Apple. It was originally named the iPhone OS, but was renamed to the iOS in June, 2009. The iOS currently runs on the iPhone, iPod touch, and iPad.

Like modern desktop operating systems, iOS uses a graphical user interface, or GUI. However, since it is a mobile operating system, iOS is designed around touchscreen input, rather than a keyboard and mouse. For example, applications, or "apps," can be opened by a single tap, rather than a double-click. Different screens can be viewed by swiping your finger across the screen, rather than clicking on open windows.

Since iOS is designed to be simple and easy to use, it does not include several features found in a traditional operating system. For example, you cannot manage files and folders like you can in Mac OS X or Windows. You also have limited access to iOS system settings. Instead of modifying application preferences from within each program, most settings need to be adjusted within the Settings app. additionally, while you can run multiple programs at once, you can only view one open program at a time.

Android

Android OS is a Linux-based platform for mobile phones. Android was released under the Apache v2 open source license.

Android was developed by Google and the Open Handset Alliance (OHA), a coalition of hardware, software and telecommunications companies. More than 30 companies were involved in the OHA, including Qualcomm, Broadcom, HTC, Intel, Samsung, Motorola, Sprint, Texas Instruments and Japanese wireless carriers KDDI and NTT DoCoMo.

Android began its life as a Palo Alto-based startup company, founded in 2003. That company was subsequently acquired by Google in 2005. The Android platform includes an operating system based upon Linux, a GUI, a Web browser and end user applications that can be downloaded. Although the initial demonstrations of Android featured a generic QWERTY smartphone and large VGA screen, the operating system was written to run on relatively inexpensive handsets with conventional numeric keypads.

Android runs on both of the most widely deployed cellular standards, GSM/HSDPA and CDMA/EV-DO. Android will also support:

- Bluetooth

- EDGE

- 3G communication protocols, like EV-DO and HSDPA

- WiFi

- SMS messaging

- MMS

- Video/still digital cameras

- Touchscreens

- GPS

- Compasses

- Accelerometers

- Accelerated 3D graphics

References

- Embedded-operating-systems-833068: lifewire.com, Retrieved 14 July 2018

- Real-time-operating-systems, disk-operating-system, fundamental: ecomputernotes.com, Retrieved 11 May 2018

- Advantages-disadvantages-real-time-operating-systems: itrelease.com, Retrieved 19 March 2018

- Unix-quick-guide: tutorialspoint.com, Retrieved 31 March 2018

- Apple-apfs-file-system-4117093: lifewire.com, Retrieved 23 June 2018

Computer Files, File Systems and Directories

A computer file records data in a computer storage device. All complete files are organized in a file system. It allows the easy access and manipulation of files. A file system cataloging structure that contains references to computer files and directories is called a directory. This chapter closely examines the different types of computer files, file systems and directories such as data files, binary and text files, sparse files, etc.

Computer File

When we use our computer to create things, those things are stored in units of information called files. A computer file can be a document we write with our word processor. A computer file can also be a graphical image from a digital camera or an image we create with a digital paintbrush, a piece of music, a video, or just about anything. Whatever it is, the computer stores that information as a file.

Examples of Files

An image we copy from our camera to our computer may be in the JPG or TIF format. These are files in the same way that videos in the MP4 format, or MP3 audio files, are files. The same holds true for DOCX files used with Microsoft Word, TXT files that hold plain text information, etc.

Though files are contained in folders for organization (like the photos in our Pictures folder or music files in our iTunes folder), some files are in compressed folders, but they're still considered files. For example, a ZIP file is basically a folder that holds other files and folders but it actually acts as a single file.

Another popular file type similar to ZIP is an ISO file, which is a representation of a physical disc. It's just a single file but it holds all the information we might find on a disc, like a video game or movie.

We can see even with these few examples that not all files are alike, but they all share a similar purpose of holding information together in one place.

File Format

A file format defines the structure and type of data stored in a file. The structure of a typical file may include a header, metadata, saved content, and an end-of-file (EOF) marker. The data stored in the file depends on the purpose of the file format. Some files, such as XML files, are used to store lists of items, while others, such as JPEG image files simply contain a block of data.

A file format also defines whether the data is stored in a plain text or binary format. Plain text files can be opened and viewed in a standard text editor. While text-based files are easy to create, they often use up more space than comparable binary files. They also lack security, since the contents can be easily viewed by dragging the file to a text editor. Binary file formats can be compressed and are well-suited for storing graphics, audio, and video data. If we attempt to view a binary file in a text editor, most of the data will appear garbled and unintelligible, but we may see some header text that identifies the file's contents.

Some file formats are proprietary, while others are universal, or open formats. Proprietary file formats can only be opened by one or more related programs. For example, a compressed StuffIt X (.SITX) archive can only be opened by StuffIt Deluxe or StuffIt Expander. If we try to open a StuffIt X archive with WinZip or another file decompression tool, the file will not be recognized. Conversely, open file formats are publicly available and are recognized by multiple programs. For example, StuffIt Deluxe can also save compressed archives in a standard zipped (.ZIP) format, which can be opened by nearly all decompression utilities.

When software developers create applications that save files, choosing an appropriate file format is important. For some programs, it might make sense to use an open format, which is compatible with other applications. In other cases, using a proprietary format may give the developer a competitive advantage, since the files created with the program can only be opened with the developer's software. However, most people prefer to have multiple software options, so many developers have moved away from proprietary file formats and now use open formats instead. For example, Microsoft Word, which used to save word processing documents in the proprietary .DOC format, now saves documents in the open .DOCX format, which is supported by multiple applications.

Some Common File Formats

Executable Formats

Files that run programs are known as executable. These files run and install upon clicking or through proper commands. An executable can be part of the OS itself, an application, or an installation package. The following table lists some common executable formats that are mostly used.

Extension	File Type
.app	A mac application bundle. In macOS it looks an application executable, but the bundle is actually a folder containing the application's files. Windows users just see the bundle as a folder.
.bat	A Batch file (or script) is a list of commands to be executed in sequential order.
.exe or .com	A Windows application. An .exe file may have multiple helper files that work with it; a. com file is normally a stand-alone application
.msi	An installer package file format used in Windows.
.scexe	A proprietary file extension used by HP for firmware updates.

Table: Different Common Executable Formats

Compression Formats

Groups of files can be compressed and combined into a single *compressed archive* file, which makes the group of files easier to distribute and transport. For example, suppose we want to send ten picture files to someone. We can attach all ten files separately to an e-mail, but it would be better to create a single compressed archive file that holds all of them and send it easily.

There are different types of compression files like .zip (the default compressed file in Windows) and many more in other platforms. Some of the common types of compression file formats and their purposes are shown in the following table.

Format	Purpose
7ZIP or 7Z	7ZIP is the default format for the file compression utility 7-Zip archiver. 7z is an updated version of the file format, offering better compression and security
DMG	The format of a macOS disc image; similar to ISO but for Mac.
GZIP or GZ	The default format for the gzip utility. The G stands for GNU. GNU is a Linux variant.
ISO	The format of a file that represents an optical disc image; use a DVD burning application to burn an ISO file to removable media such as a blank CD, DVD, or USB flash drive.
JAR	A compression format for Java classes and data. You may encounter this when you work with Java application.
RAR	The Linux and UNIX standard archive format. It's an acronym that stands for tape archive.
TAR	The Linux and UNIX standard archive format. It's an acronym that stands for tape archive.
ZIP	A popular compression format for windows computers. Originally developed for a command-line application called PKZIP, it is now most closely associated with WinZip.

Table: Common Compression files formats and their purposes

Audio and Video Formats

Usually, files containing audio (such as voice recordings, music, or audio books) and video (movies, music videos, presentations, TV shows, and so on) are often referred to as *media clips*. We can download some media clips and then play them, and we can also play *streaming media* through cloud computing like SoundCloud etc.

The playback software (which plays the clips) must have a *codec* installed for each format it supports. Codec stands for "compressor-decompressor," and it refers to the encoding and decoding of the clips. The following table shows most common file types of the Audio and Video Formats and their purposes.

Type	Format	Purpose
Audio	AAC	Advanced Audio Coding (AAC) was designed to replace MP3. It has better sound quality than MP3 at similar compression levels and file sizes.
Audio	FLAC	Free Lossless Audio Codec (FLAC) is similar to MP3, but the lossless compression yields a little higher Quality.
Audio	MAA	This format is used for music downloads from iTunes that have no copy protection on them. M4A is a container file, and the content inside the container is usually coded as AAC.

Audio	MP3	This is a common general format for music files. It's popular because it uses a high level of loss compression (so files are small), it lacks copy protection (so files can be freely shared), and almost all music player applications support it. The extension is short for moving Picture Experts Group Layer 3 Audio.
Audio	WAV	The raw data inside is usually uncompressed CD-quality sound. The files are large, so this format is not usually used for long clips. This is the default container format for the Sound Recorder application in Windows.
Audio	MID/ MIDI	This Format is not in the exam objectives, but it is in the exam acronyms list. A Musical Instrument Digital Interface (MIDI) file is a text file that takes advantage of the sound-processing hardware to enable the computing device to produce sound. Programmers use these small files to tell the sound card which notes to play; how long, how loud, and on which instruments to play them; and so forth. Think of a MDI files as a piece of electronic sheet music, with the instruments built into your sound card.
Video	AVI	Audio Video Interleave (AVI) is a Microsoft-created container format for audio and video. It's common format for short, homemade videos you might find online.
Video	FLV	Flash Video (FLV) is a Container file format designed to distribute video online using Adobe Flash Player as the playback application, usually within a Web page.
Video	MP4	This format uses MPEG-4 raw video data and usually AAC or MP3 audio data. The extension is short for Moving Picture Experts Group Layer 4.
Video	MPG/ MPEG	The MPG format is a container that can hold either MPEG-1 or MPEG-2 raw video data, plus accompanying audio data. It is an older format but still in use. The extension is an acronym for Moving Picture Experts Group.
Video	WMV	Windows Media Video (WMV) is used in some Microsoft programs that deal with user-created videos, such as Windows Movie Maker.

Table: Different Audio and Video Formats and their purposes

Image Formats

Files that store still images, like photos, drawings etc are called image formats. There are different types of image formats depending on their uses. Some of the common image formats use today are shown in the following table with their purposes.

Format	Purpose
Bmp	Short for bitmap, the BMP format is one of the oldest raster formats used in personal computing. In the early days of Windows, BMP was the only format that Microsoft's application Paint supported. BMP is widely used because there are other formats that are more appealing in terms of file size and quality.
GIF	Graphics File interchange (GIF) is an uncompressed format. It support only 256 colors, so it's not a great choice for photos, but it is popular for Web page ads because it can store and cycle through several graphics in a single file.
JPG/JPEG	Joint Photographic Experts Group (JPG or JPEG) is a lossy image compression format that sacrifices some image quality but has a very small file size. It's commonly used on the Web and in onscreen graphics, where you can't detect the reduced image quality
PNG	Portable Network Graphic (PNG) is the successor to GIF. It uses lossless compression and supports 16.7 million colors, a big improvement from GIF'S 256 Colors. It is one of the most popular formats used on Web pages and in game graphics.
TIF/TIFF	Tagged Image File Format (TFF or TIFF) uses lossless compression and is considered a high-quality format but with a rather large file Size. Some digital cameras capture images in this format, and photos in publications that will be printed on paper often use this format because of the high quality.

Table: Different Image formats and their purposes

Document Formats

These formats include various types of text files, spreadsheets, presentations, and page lawets and all types of data files that we create in business-oriented applications. The following Table shows different formats of Document files and their purposes.

Format	Purpose
TXT	A Plain-text file, with no formatting. This is the default format for the Notepad app in Windows, as well as most other text editors.
RTF	Rich Text Format (RTF) is a widely accepted generic word processing format Nearly all word processing application can read and write this format. It includes all the basic text formatting options, including fonts, attributes, paragraph indentation, margins, bullets and numbering, and headers/footers.
DOC/DOCX	The DOCX format is the current format for Microsoft Word documents and is also used by many other word processing applications for compatibility with Word. The Doc format is an earlier version, used in Word 2003 and earlier still supported.
XLS/XLSX	Microsoft Excel, the spreadsheet application, uses XLSX as its default format. The XLS format is an earlier version, used in Excel 2003 and earlier and still supported.
PPT/PPTX	Microsoft PowerPoint, the presentation application, uses PPTX as its default format. The PPT format is an earlier version, used in Power Point 2003 and earlier and still supported.
PDF	Portable Document Format (PDF) is the default format for Adobe Acrobat and Adobe Reader. This format is designed to make document formatting consistent when distributing documents across platforms, No matter what computer or device you open up a PDF file on, the file looks the same, without any variation in fonts or spacing. You can save to PDF in most Microsoft Office applications; you can also set up a PDF print driver that outputs print jobs to PDF files, useful in applications that do not save to PDF.

Table: Different Document Formats and their purposes

File Size

File size measures the size of a computer file and is typically measured in bytes with a prefix. The smallest unit in computers is bit and comes from binary digit. A bit has only two digits - zero and one. The zero is also known as false (off) state and the one is known as true (on).

The bits are combined in groups in order to form larger units. The next unit larger than the bit is the byte which is formed by the combination of eight bits and can represent a value from 0 to 255 which is 2 to the power of 8 - all the possible combinations of the 8 bits that it includes.

The next larger units after the byte are named kilobyte, megabyte, gigabyte, terrabyte and so on which lead to great deal of confusion. Though the kilo prefix in the metric system means 1000 (e.g grams) in computers it means 1024 (e.g. bytes).

The smallest unit of measurement used for measuring data is a bit. A single bit can have a value of either 0 or 1. It may contain a binary value (such as On/Off or True/False), but nothing more. Therefore, a byte, or eight bits, is used as the fundamental unit of measurement for data. A byte can store 28 or 256 different values, which is sufficient to represent standard ASCII characters, such as letters, numbers and symbols.

Since most files contain thousands of bytes, file sizes are often measured in kilobytes. Larger files, such as images, videos, and audio files, contain millions of bytes and therefore are measured in megabytes. Modern storage devices can store thousands of these files, which is why storage capacity is typically measured in gigabytes or even terabytes. Larger units of measurement are usually reserved for measuring the sum of multiple storage devices or the capacity of large data storage networks.

Below is a list of all the standard units of measurement used for data storage, from the smallest to the largest.

Unit	Value	Size
bit (b)	0 or 1	1/8 of a byte
byte (B)	8 bits	1 byte
kilobyte (KB)	1000^1 bytes	1,000 bytes
megabyte (MB)	1000^2 bytes	1,000,000 bytes
gigabyte (GB)	1000^3 bytes	1,000,000,000 bytes
terabyte (TB)	1000^4 bytes	1,000,000,000,000 bytes
petabyte (PB)	1000^5 bytes	1,000,000,000,000,000 bytes
exabyte (EB)	1000^6 bytes	1,000,000,000,000,000,000 bytes
zettabyte (ZB)	1000^7 bytes	1,000,000,000,000,000,000,000 bytes
yottabyte (YB)	1000^8 bytes	1,000,000,000,000,000,000,000,000 bytes

A lowercase "b" is used as an abbreviation for bits, while an uppercase "B" represents bytes. This is an important distinction, since a byte is 8x as large as a bit.

For example, 100 KB (kilobytes) = 800 Kb (kilobits).

Process to See File Sizes

File or attachment size is usually easily accessible, if not already prominent. In Windows, right-clicking on any file, folder, or drive and choosing "Properties" will show the size. In an Explorer window, we can select "Details" from the "View" menu; or in a file open or save dialogue box there is a "View" button from which we can also choose "Details". If we then click on the word "Size" at the top of the column, we can group together the largest files in a folder. In Mac OS X, we can press Command + i to show details of an individual file, or Command + Option +i to show details of all selected items in an Inspector window. The Mac equivalent of Details view is "List" view, and Command +J gives we the option to "calculate all sizes" of folders as well as files.

Most email programs such as Windows Mail or Thunderbird always show the size of attachments next to the file name. In Thunderbird (and many other programs) we can click on the columns button up the top right of a list to add a column showing the size of each item. FTP programs, used to transfer files to websites, almost all show the size of files by default, although usually in bytes, so we need to split these large numbers by eye into groups of three digits to see which are measured in B or kB and which in MB.

Filename

A filename is a text string that identifies a file. Every file stored on a computer's hard disk has a filename that helps identify the file within a given folder. Therefore, each file within a specific folder must have a different filename, while files in different folders can have the same name.

Filenames may contain letters, numbers, and other characters. Depending on the operating system, certain characters cannot be used since they conflict with operators or other syntax used by the operating system. Different operating systems also have different limits for the number of characters a filename can have. While older operating systems limited filenames to only 8 or 16 characters, newer OS's allow filenames to be as long as 256 characters. Of course, for most practical purposes, 16 characters is usually enough.

Filenames also usually include a file extension, which identifies the type of file. The file extension is also called the "filename suffix" since it is appended to the filename, following a dot or period. For example, a Microsoft Word document may be named "document1.doc." While technically the filename in the preceding example is "document1" and "doc" is the extension, it is also acceptable to refer to "document1.doc" as the filename.

We can name a file by clicking on the file's icon or filename, waiting for a second, then clicking on the filename again. As long as the file is not locked, the filename will become highlighted, and we can type a new name for the file. We can also name a file the first time we save it from a program or by selecting "Save As" from the program's File menu.

Today, almost all programs support long file names and the file name can contain every character (including letters and numbers), except those shown below.

Invalid file name characters

/ \ : * ? " < > |

File Names with Spaces

Although all operating systems today support spaces in file names, a command line we may encounter errors because the command line doesn't know where the file name starts and ends. To prevent errors with file names with spaces surround the file name with quotes when being used in a command line.

File Names with Capital Letters

File names can contain uppercase and lowercase characters. However, the operating system that uses the files may be case sensitive. For example, Microsoft Windows is not case sensitive and treats all files the same regardless if they have all lowercase characters or some uppercase characters. However, Linux and macOS are case sensitive, which means the file "readme.txt" and "README.TXT" are treated as two different files even though they have the same file name.

File Name Character Length Limit

Every operating system has a limit to how many characters can be used in a file name that is typically around 255 characters long. When determining the length of a file both the file name and the file extension are used together to get the total length. For example, the file "myfile.txt" is ten characters long. Below is a list of Microsoft Windows versions and their file name character limits.

Windows 10 - 260 character limit

Windows 8 - 260 character limit

Windows 7 - 260 character limit

Windows Vista - 260 character limit

Windows XP - 255 character limit

Windows 2000 - 254 character limit

Note: When renaming a file the full path and file name are used which means each of the directory names, separating slashes, and the file name should not exceed the above set limits (e.g., 260 characters).

Should you be using "file name" or "filename" in your writing?

Today, both "file name" and "filename" are widely used and accepted. The original form of the word was "file name" and "filename" became popular as more people and software programs began to use that version of the word. According to the Microsoft Manual of Style, a file name is "Two words both as an adjective and as a noun when referring to the name of a file. Do not hyphenate."

If we are referring to a programming term such as the FileName property or fileName variable, we should be using the same version of the word in the program in our writing.

Should "file name" or "filename" be capitalized in our writing?

No. Unless "file name" is at the beginning of a sentence, no part of the word should be capitalized in our writing.

Data File

Data files are the most common type of computer files. They may be installed with applications or created by users. Most data files are saved in a binary format, though some store data as plain text. Examples of data files include libraries, project files, and saved documents.

The Data Files category encompasses other more specific categories. File types that do not fit within these subcategories are placed in this category.

Types of Data File

There are top six types of data files used in an information system.

Work File

Any other file which is required to enable the processing of business data to be carried out is a work file (excluding files required for security or audit purposes).

The designer may or may not have to design such files himself.

Examples where he would not be involved in the design would be:

1. Work files used by system software or utilities such as sort/merge processers.

2. Work files used as intermediate or inter-process files in computer programs at a low level. The design of these files would be better left to the programming team.

If a file is needed to store Data created by one business process before being used by another business process, then the designer would have to be involved. These files are sometimes referred to as transfer files. The temporary files which hold information for printing also fall into this category. Here the designer needs to specify the record definitions required to produce the correctly formatted to output.

Master File

Master files are files of a fairly permanent nature, e.g., customer ledger, purchase ledger, inventory pay roll etc. They include some information which is continuously updated by recent transactions. For example, a sales ledger might contain the customer's names and addresses as well as their current position which is updated periodically.

The description information in a master file may include such items as product code, description, specifications etc. The normal means of updating a master file is by adding, deleting or amending records in the file.

Master files can be further subdivided into two types of files:

i. Static master file/reference files

ii. Dynamic master files/table files

(i) Static master files (or reference files)

The business entities that these files describe are at a permanent or semi-permanent nature (e.g., products, suppliers, customers, employees etc.). These are subject to occasional relation.

(ii) Dynamic master files (or table files)

The business entities these files describes are of transitory importance to the business (e.g., customer orders, work orders, job tickets, projects, price lists, wage rates) etc.

Audit File

Audit files are a particular the of transaction file. They play the same role in computerised information systems as the postings in a traditional manual ledger. They enable the auditor to check the correct functioning of the computer procedures, by storing copies of all the transactions which cause the permanent system file to be altered.

For example, in a sales ledger system, the transactions to be recorded might be:

1. Invoice number, data, cash amount for each invoice raised.

2. Date and amount of cash received.

3. Credit note number, date amount of money credit.

4. Account adjustment, amount of money, cross reference to authorisation, adjustment code.

These files will normally be serial, the records being created at the time of the master file update and accumulated in the sequence of the update, on the audit file.

Transaction File

Transaction files are files in which the data relating to business events is recorded, prior to a further stage of processing and are created from source documents used for recording events or transactions. This further processing may be the use of the transaction data to update master files, or the achieving of the transaction for audit purposes.

After the transaction file is processed, it is usually reinitialized, and further transactions are then recorded in it.

Examples of transaction files are:

1. Customer's orders for products (to update an order file)

2. Details of price changes for products (to update a product file)

3. Details of cash postings in customer accounts (to be held for audit purposes)

4. Purchase orders, job cards, invoice dispatch notes etc.

Back Up or Security File

These files are taken in order to provide back copies, in case of loss or damage to current versions, and arc copies of currently used master files kept in the computer library as a measure of security.

In practice, the designer is unlikely to be involved in the detail design of such files, as he would rely either on system security software (e.g., dump/restore utilities; the transaction logging and recovery routines in teleprocessing monitors); or in batch up date system, in holding superseded versions of master files with back copies of transaction files.

History Files

History files are often stored on magnetic tape and are kept in case past information is ever required. For example, an employee who was dismissed three years back may wish to apply for unemployment insurance. The past employee's record must be retrieved by personnel to complete the necessary paper work.

Binary and Text Files

On a computer, every file is a long string of ones and zeros. Specifically, a file is a finite-length sequence of bytes, where each byte is an integer between 0 and 255 inclusive (represented in binary as 00000000 to 11111111). Files can be broadly classified as either binary or text. These categories have different characteristics and need different tools to work with such files. Knowing the differences between binary and text files can save we time and mistakes when reading or writing data.

Here is the primary difference: Binary files have no inherent constraints (can be any sequence of bytes), and must be opened in an appropriate program that knows the specific file format (such as Media Player, Photoshop, Office, etc.). Text files must represent reasonable text (explained later), and can be edited in *any* text editor program.

Remember that all files, whether binary or text, are composed of bytes. The difference between binary and text files is in how these bytes are interpreted. Every text file is indeed a binary file, but this interpretation gives us no useful operations to work with. The reverse is not true, and treating a binary file as a text file can lead to data corruption. As a method of last resort, a hex editor can always be used to view and edit the raw bytes in any file.

File Extensions

We can usually tell if a file is binary or text based on its file extension. This is because by convention the extension reflects the file format, and it is ultimately the file format that dictates whether the file data is binary or text.

Common extensions that are binary file formats:

- Images: jpg, png, gif, bmp, tiff, psd, etc.
- Videos: mp4, mkv, avi, mov, mpg, vob, etc.
- Audio: mp3, aac, wav, flac, ogg, mka, wma, etc.
- Documents: pdf, doc, xls, ppt, docx, odt, etc.
- Archive: zip, rar, 7z, tar, iso, etc.
- Database: mdb, accde, frm, sqlite, etc.
- Executable: exe, dll, so, class, etc.

Common extensions that are text file formats:

- Web standards: html, xml, css, svg, json, etc.
- Source code: c, cpp, h, cs, js, py, java, rb, pl, php, sh, etc.
- Documents: txt, tex, markdown, asciidoc, rtf, ps, etc.
- Configuration: ini, cfg, rc, reg, etc.
- Tabular data: csv, tsv, etc.

Binary File Characteristics

For most software that people use in their daily lives, the software consumes and produces binary files. Examples of such software include Microsoft Office, Adobe Photoshop, and various audio/video/media players. A typical computer user works with mostly binary files and very few text files.

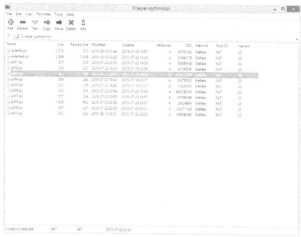

Binary file in application (good)

A binary file always needs a matching software to read or write it. For example, an MP3 file can be produced by a sound recorder or audio editor, and it can be played in a music player or audio editor. But an MP3 file cannot be played in an image viewer or a database software.

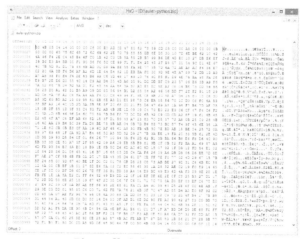

Binary file in hex editor (okay)

Some binary formats are popular enough that a wide variety of programs can produce or consume it. Image formats like JPEG are the best example – not only can they be used in image viewers and editors, they can be viewed in web browsers, audio players (for album art), and document software (such as adding a picture into a Word doc). But other binary formats, especially for niche proprietary software, might have only one program in the world that can read and write it. For example, a high-end video editing software might let we save our project to a file, but this software is the only one that can understand its own file format; the binary file will never be useful anywhere else.

Binary file in text editor (bad)

If we use a text editor to open a binary file, we will see copious amounts of garbage, seemingly random accented and Asian characters, and long lines overflowing with text – this exercise is safe but pointless. However, editing or saving a binary file in a text editor will corrupt the file, so never do this. The reason corruption happens is because applying a text mode interpretation will change certain byte sequences – such as discarding NUL bytes, converting newlines, discarding sequences that are invalid under a certain character encoding, etc. – which means that opening and saving a binary file will almost surely produce a file with different bytes.

Text File Characteristics

Text file in text editor (good)

By convention, the data in every text file obeys a number of rules:

- The text looks readable to a human or at least moderately sane. Even if it contains a heavy proportion of punctuation symbols (like HTML, RTF, and other markup formats), there is some visible structure and it's not seemingly random garbage.

- The data format is usually line-oriented. Each line could be a separate command, or a list of values could put each item on a different line, etc. The maximum number of characters in each line is usually a reasonable value like 100, not like 1000.

- Non-printable ASCII characters are discouraged or disallowed. Examples include the NUL byte (0x00), DEL byte (0x7F), and most of the range 0x01 to 0x1F (except tab, carriage return, newline, etc.). Some text editors silently convert or discard these bytes, which is why binary files should never be edited in a text editor.

- The reading of newline sequences is usually universal – namely, CR (classic Mac OS), LF (Unix), or CR+LF (Windows) all mean the same thing, which is to end the current line and start the next one. The writing of newline sequences usually normalizes to the preferred one on the current platform, regardless of which variant was read. (For example, a text file "Hello CR LF world CR Lorem LF ipsum" read in a Unix text editor would likely be written out as "Hello LF world LF Lorem LF ipsum".)

- There is some character encoding that governs how extended-ASCII bytes are handled. Byte values from 0x80 to 0xFF are not covered by the universally accepted ASCII standard, and the interpretation of these bytes depends on the choice of character encoding – such as UTF-8, ISO-8859-1, Shift JIS. Thus the interpretation of a text file depends on the character encoding used (unless the file format is known to be pure-ASCII), whereas a binary file is just a sequence of plain bytes with no inherent notion of character encoding.

- In most text file formats, some flexibility is given to whitespace characters. For example, using one space or two space might not change the meaning of a command. And in C-like programming languages, one whitespace character has the same meaning as any positive number of whitespace or newline characters (except within strings).

Observations regarding the general computing environment around text files:

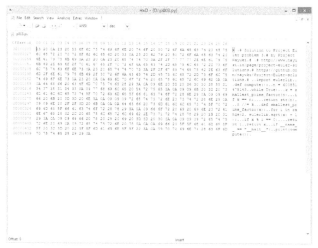

Text file in hex editor (inconvenient)

- Any text file can be viewed or edited in any text editor. The creator of a text-based file format doesn't need to know or care about what editor program a future user will use. This contrasts with binary formats, where each format is generally coupled to a specific program that can handle it.

- Software developer's work with many kinds of text files all the time – program source code, setup scripts, technical documentation, program-generated output and logs, configuration files, we name it. Much of the world of computer programming revolves around text files, since they are easy to create, edit, and consume. This contrasts with how an average computer user mainly works with binary files.

- Text files are usually viewed and edited in a monospaced font. The historical reason is that the earliest computer terminals could only display monospaced text. A modern reason is that monospaced allows an author to visually align characters in different lines for ASCII art, tabular data, etc.

- On the Unix platform, text files are so ubiquitous that they often have no file name extension at all. For example, "README" and "config" are the full names of popular files that exist in many places.

- Beyond text editors, there exist many standard Unix tools to generate, manipulate, or view textual data: ls, more, sort, grep, awk, etc.

- Version control software (Git, Mercurial, SVN, Perforce, etc.) work best with text files. For binary files they can only tell we whether a file has changed or not. For text files, they can show line-by-line differences, perform automatic merges, and do many other useful things.

Sparse File

Sparse files are a result of the way file systems allocate storage space. Sparse files appear to take up much more disk space than they actually do (use ls -s, which shows blocks used, to see if a file is sparse).

Most modern file systems support sparse files to some degree or another.

Traditional Unix file systems have thirteen disk block pointers in the inode. The first 10 are direct pointers; that is they point to actual disk blocks.

The next pointer is an indirect pointer: it points to a block that contains pointers to actual storage blocks. If the pointers are 32 bit numbers (more likely to be larger nowadays but this makes the math easy for us), there will be 128 blocks covered by the 11th pointer. The next points to double indirect blocks: blocks which themselves contain more pointers to the actual blocks. The 13th is triple indirect: pointers to blocks of pointers to blocks of pointers. This scheme lets us have very large files without very large inode records.

If a program opens a new file and seeks to a point beyond that covered by the first 10 pointers and writes data there, the OS doesn't bother to allocate data blocks that are not used, so those first 10 pointers are still empty. The same is true for some of the indirect pointers if the next seek extends beyond their reach. Database files using hash keys often create such files as a natural result of the hash key creation. The file may show it has a very large size in an ls -l listing, but it could actually be consuming only a very few disk blocks. If we read data from such a file, the OS just returns null bytes for the unallocated space, which means that naively copying it will NOT create another sparse file (although GNU cp is aware of sparse files and will preserve the sparseness).

File System

A filesystem is the methods and data structures that an operating system uses to keep track of files on a disk or partition; that is, the way the files are organized on the disk. The word is also used to refer to a partition or disk that is used to store the files or the type of the filesystem. Thus, one might say "I have two filesystems" meaning one has two partitions on which one stores files, or that one is using the "extended filesystem", meaning the type of the filesystem.

The difference between a disk or partition and the filesystem it contains is important. A few programs (including, reasonably enough, programs that create filesystems) operate directly on the raw sectors of a disk or partition; if there is an existing file system there it will be destroyed or seriously corrupted. Most programs operate on a filesystem, and therefore won't work on a partition that doesn't contain one (or that contains one of the wrong type).

Before a partition or disk can be used as a filesystem, it needs to be initialized, and the bookkeeping data structures need to be written to the disk. This process is called making a filesystem.

Example

Most UNIX filesystem types have a similar general structure, although the exact details vary quite a bit. The central concepts are superblock, inode , data block, directory block , and indirection block. The superblock contains information about the filesystem as a whole, such as its size (the exact information here depends on the filesystem). An inode contains all information about a file, except its name. The name is stored in the directory, together with the number of the inode. A directory entry consists of a filename and the number of the inode which represents the file. The inode contains the numbers of several data blocks, which are used to store the data in the file. There is space only for a few data block numbers in the inode, however, and if more are needed, more space for pointers to the data blocks is allocated dynamically. These dynamically allocated blocks are indirect blocks; the name indicates that in order to find the data block, one has to find its number in the indirect block first.

UNIX filesystems usually allow one to create a hole in a file (this is done with the lseek() system call), which means that the filesystem just pretends that at a particular place in the file there is just zero bytes, but no actual disk sectors are reserved for that place in the file (this means that the file will use a bit less disk space). This happens especially often for small binaries; Linux shared libraries, some databases, and a few other special cases. (Holes are implemented by storing a special value as the address of the data block in the indirect block or inode. This special address means that no data block is allocated for that part of the file, ergo, there is a hole in the file.)

File Fragmentation and Defragmentation

Fragmentation occurs on a hard drive, a memory module, or other media when data is not written closely enough physically on the drive. Those fragmented, individual pieces of data are referred to generally as fragments.

Defragmentation, then, is the process of un-fragmenting or piecing together, those fragmented files so they sit closer - physically - on the drive or other media, potentially speeding up the drive's ability to access the file.

File Fragments

Fragments, like we just read, are simply pieces of files that aren't placed next to each other on the drive. That might be kind of strange to think about, and nothing we would ever notice, but it's true.

For example, when we create a new Microsoft Word file, we see the whole file in one place, like on the Desktop or in our Documents folder. We can open it, edit it, remove it, rename it - whatever we want. From our perspective, this is all happening in one place, but in reality, at least *physically on the drive*, this is often not the case.

Instead, our hard drive is probably saving portions of the file in one area of the storage device while the rest of it exists somewhere else on the device, potentially far away relatively speaking, of course. When we open the file, our hard drive quickly pulls together all the pieces of the file so it can be used by the rest of our computer system.

When a drive has to read pieces of data from multiple different areas on the drive, it can not access the whole of the data as fast as it could if it had all been written together in the same area of the drive.

Fragmentation: An Analogy

As an analogy, imagine that we want to play a card game that requires an entire deck of cards. Before we can play the game, we have to retrieve the deck from wherever it might be.

If the cards are spread all over a room, the time needed to gather them together and put them in order would be much greater than if they were sitting on the table, nicely organized.

A deck of cards spread all over a room can be thought of as a fragmented deck of cards, much like the fragmented data on a hard drive that, when gathered together (defragmented), might equal a file we want to open or a process from a particular software program that needs to run.

Reasons behind Fragmentation

Fragments happen when the file system allows gaps to develop between the different pieces of a file. If we know anything about file systems in general, we may have already guessed that the file system was the culprit in this fragmentation business, but why?

Sometimes fragmentation happens because the file system reserved too much space for the file when it was first created, and therefore left open areas around it.

Previously deleted files are also another reason the file system fragments data when written. When a file is removed, its previously occupied space is now open for new files to be saved to it. As we can imagine, if that now open space isn't large enough to support the whole size of the new file, then only a part of it can be saved there. The rest must be positioned somewhere else, *hopefully*, nearby but not always.

Having some pieces of a file in one place while the others are located elsewhere is going to require the hard drive to look through the gaps or spaces occupied by other files until it can gather all the necessary pieces to bring the file together.

This method of storing data is completely normal and likely won't ever change. The alternative would be for the file system to constantly reshuffle all existing data on the drive each and every time a file is changed, which would bring the data writing process to a crawl, slowing down everything else with it.

So, while it's frustrating that fragmentation exists, which slows the computer down a little bit, we might think about it as a "necessary evil" in a sense - this small problem instead of a much larger one.

Defragmentation to the Rescue

Files on a storage device can be accessed much faster, at least on a traditional hard drive, when the pieces that make them up are close together.

Over time, as more and more fragmentation occurs, there can be a measurable, even noticeable, slowdown. We might experience it as general computer sluggishness but, assuming excessive fragmentation has occurred, much of that slowness may be due to the time it takes our hard drive to access file after file, each in any number of different physical places on the drive.

So, on occasion, defragmentation, or the act of reversing fragmentation (i.e. gathering all the pieces closer together) is a smart computer maintenance task. This is usually just referred to as defragging.

The defragging process isn't something we do manually. Like we already mentioned, our experience with our files is consistent, so there's no rearranging needed on our end. Fragmentation isn't just a disorganized collection of files and folders.

A dedicated defragging tool is what we need. Disk Defragmenter is one such defragger and is included for free in the Windows operating system. That said, there are many third-party options as well, the better of which do a considerably better job at the defragmentation.

Filesystem-level Encryption

Filesystem-level encryption tools allow computer users to encrypt individual files and directories. The technology offers several advantages over full-disk encryption, most notably the ability to prevent unauthorized users from accessing certain files on networks or shared computers without barring those users from accessing other files on the disk.

Because encryption occurs on the filesystem level, encrypted data is extremely secure when paired with an appropriate cryptographic algorithm. Most newer encryption tools use 256-bit encryption, and many use several levels of encryption and hashing to prevent unauthorized access.

There are several disadvantages to filesystem-level encryption as compared to disk-level encryption. Disk-level encryption eliminates security threats from attackers with physical access to the encrypted disk, while some filesystem-level tools do not. Users also need to manage multiple private keys for larger systems. Encryption programs typically provide tools that make access control management easier for system administrators. For the best possible security, businesses often coordinate disk-level encryption with filesystem-level encryption.

Popular filesystem-level encryption tools like Microsoft's Encrypting File System (EFS) provide excellent flexibility and reliable security. However, if we lose access to data due to a hard drive failure or other unexpected event, encryption can complicate the data recovery process. For the best chances of a successful recovery, locate a data recovery provider that has experience with folder-level encryption products.

Common causes of data loss for encrypted media include:

- Physical Hard Drive Failure
- Controller Board Damage
- Data Corruption
- Bad Sectors
- Accidental File Deletion
- Failed RAID Rebuild
- Overheating
- Fire, Smoke and Water Damage
- Accidental Repartitioning

Extent File System

An extent file system (EFS) is a method of managing files and memory on a computer hard drive or other physical storage device that uses a series of contiguous areas of memory to store information instead of using smaller, more scattered units known as blocks. Some file systems allocate the space required for files in small units known as blocks, which can lead to a single file of average length being physically scattered throughout a disk, reducing the speed and efficiency of reading from that file. In the case of an extent file system, all of the smaller blocks are bound together into a larger structure known as an extent, meaning that larger files can be stored in a single contiguous location on the physical disk, increasing the speed of the drive when reading from that file. Although many operating systems support the use of extents, the term originally was applied to the specific early extent file system of the now discontinued Unix-like operating system known as IRIX®, developed by Silicon Graphics®.

The individual bits and bytes on a physical disk, such as a hard disk or a compact disk (CD), are divided into groups by the hardware, operating system and file system. These are known as logical groupings, because they do not necessarily have physical boundaries, only those that are imposed by the system. For several file systems, the logical grouping known as blocks are used as the basic amount of space that can be allocated to store a file. A block can be set to any size but generally is very small, sometimes consisting of as little as 128 bytes of space.

An extent file system groups blocks together on a disk if they are contiguous, meaning they are all physically next to one another on a disk. This collection of blocks is known as an extent. In an extent file system, when a file is written to a physical disk, an extent is allocated instead of single blocks. The advantage of using extents instead of blocks is that large files require less overhead to create and maintain, and the risk of fragmentation is reduced greatly, though not necessarily eliminated.

File fragmentation occurs when a file requires more space than any available block or extent can provide, meaning the file must be broken up and occupy two or more physically different spaces on a disk. With small blocks, large files can occupy hundreds or thousands of blocks across an entire disk, reducing the speed at which the file can be accessed. An extent file system does allow for a large file to be broken into different extents, known as indirect extents, although the number of extents that are required usually is less than if the file were allocated using smaller blocks.

In addition to reducing the amount of overhead needed for large files, because information about only a single extent needs to be stored in the file system instead of multiple pointers to different blocks, using extents also can extend the life of some storage hardware. This can occur because contiguous files require less movement from the read head mechanism of the disk drive to access information. An extent file system also allows the creation of single files that can be terabytes or more in length, because, in some cases, an extent can theoretically occupy all available physical space without the need to create extensive tables or other overhead for management.

Flash File System

A flash file system is designed to store files on flash-based memory storage devices. Flash file systems vary in their architecture, but most of them include an application programming interface, a file system core, a block driver for sector-based file systems and a memory technology device (MTD) layer.

When stored flash is to be updated, the file system writes a new copy of the changed data to a fresh block and remaps the file pointers. The old block of data can then be erased when the flash file system has time to do so.

Advantages and Disadvantages

Flash file systems are generally used only for MTDs, which are embedded flash memories that lack a controller. An MTD provides specific information about a flash device, such as device type, buffer size, and block and partition size.

Flash file systems are designed to spread writes out as evenly as possible to increase the lifespan of a flash device. A flash file system can ensure a flash-based design uses all of the capabilities of the flash device as efficiently as possible.

A flash file system cannot be accessed by end users. It is built into the firmware and is used by the flash controller to manage program/erase cycles on the flash media. Flash file systems, such as a NAND flash file system, are generally proprietary and specific to individual controllers.

Clustered File System

A cluster file system (CFS) is a file system that may be accessed by all the members in the cluster at the same time. This implies that all the members of the cluster have the same view. Some of the popular and widely used cluster file system products for Oracle RAC include: HP Tru64 CFS, Veritas CFS, IBM GPFS, Polyserve Matrix Server, and Oracle Cluster File system. The cluster file system offers:

- Simple management.

- The use of Oracle Managed Files with RAC.

- A Single Oracle Software Installation.

- Auto-extend Enabled on Oracle Data Files.

- Uniform accessibility of Archive Logs.

- ODM compliant File systems.

Linear Tape File System

LTFS (Linear Tape File System) is a file system specification that allows Linear Tape-Open (LTO) storage technology to be indexed.

LTFS partitions LTO-5 or LTO-6 tapes into two segments called partitions. Partition 0 holds directory structures and pointers that let the tape drive quickly seek specific data from the tape; the data itself is stored in Partition 1. Applying a file system to a tape allows users to organize and search the contents of tape as they would on hard disk, improving access time for data stored on tape. LTFS makes it possible to drag and drop files to tape in the same way that files might be dragged and dropped to disk.

IBM developed the LTFS format in 2010 to address tape archive requirements. The LTO Consortium of Hewlett-Packard, IBM and Seagate (now Quantum Corp.) formally adopted the LTFS Format specification, which defines how data and metadata on tape are stored in a hierarchical directory structure.

Directory

A directory is a location for storing files on our computer. Directories are found in a hierarchical file system, such as Linux, MS-DOS, OS/2, and Unix.

In the picture to the right is an example of the tree command output that shows all the local and subdirectories (e.g., the "big" directory in the cdn directory). When looking at this overview, the C: drive is considered the current directory and root directory because there is nothing beneath it and we can't go back any further. If we are using an operating system with multiple user accounts the directory may also be referred to as a home directory.

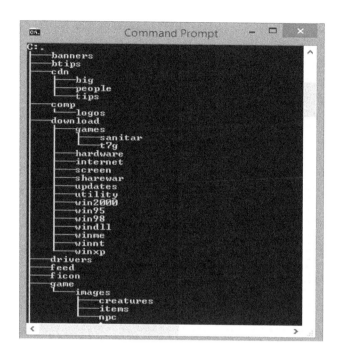

Root Directory

The root folder, also called the root directory or sometimes just the root, of any partition or folder is the "highest" directory in the hierarchy. We can also think of it in general as the start or beginning of a particular folder structure.

The root directory contains all other folders in the drive or folder, and can, of course, also contain files. We can visualize this with an upside-down tree where the roots (the root folder) are at the top and the branches (subfolders) fall below; the root is what holds together all of its lower items.

For example, the root directory of the main partition on our computer is probably C:\. The root folder of our DVD or CD drive might be D:\. The root of the Windows Registry is where hives like HKEY_CLASSES_ROOT are stored.

ROOT is also an acronym for ROOT's Object Oriented Technologies, but it has nothing to do with root folders.

Examples of Root Folders

The term root may also be relative to whatever location we're talking about.

Say, for another example, that we're working on the C:\Program Files\Adobe\ folder for whatever reason. If the software we're using or the troubleshooting guide we're reading is telling we to go to the root of the Adobe installation folder, it's talking about the "main" folder that houses all of the Adobe files related to whatever it is we're doing.

In this example, since C:\Program Files\ holds lots of folders for other programs, too, the root of the Adobe folder, specifically, would be the \Adobe\ folder. However, the root folder for all the program files on our computer would be the C:\Program Files\ folder.

This same thing applies to any other folder. Do we need to go to the root of the user folder for User1 in Windows? That's the C:\Users\Name1\ folder. This, of course, changes depending on what user we're talking about — the root folder of User2 would be C:\Users\User2\.

Accessing a Root Folder

A quick way to get to the root folder of the hard drive when we're in a Windows Command Prompt is to execute the change directory (cd) command like this:

cd \

After executing, we'll immediately be moved from the current working directory all the way up to the root folder. So, for example, if we're in the C:\Windows\System32 folder and then enter the cd command with the backslash (as shown above), we'll immediately be moved from where we're at to C:\.

Similarly, executing the cd command like this:

cd..

This will move the directory up one position, which is helpful if we need to get to the root of a folder but not the root of the entire drive. For example, executing cd.. while in the C:\Users\User1\ Downloads\ folder will change the current directory to C:\Users\User1\. Doing it again would take we to C:\Users\, and so on.

Below is an example where we start in a folder called Germany on the C:\ drive. As we can see, executing that same command in Command Prompt moves the working directory to the folder just before/above it, all the way to the root of the hard drive.

C:\AMYS-PHONE\Pictures\Germany>cd..

C:\AMYS-PHONE\Pictures>cd..

C:\AMYS-PHONE>cd..

C:\>

We may try to access a root folder only to find that we can't see it when we're browsing through Explorer. This is because some folders are hidden in Windows by default.

More About Root Folders & Directories

The term web root folder may sometimes be used to describe the directory that holds all of the files that make up a website. The same concept applies here as on our local computer — the files and folders in this root folder contain the main web page files, such as HTML files, that should be displayed when someone accesses the main URL of the website.

The term root used here shouldn't be confused with the /root folder found on some Unix operating systems, where it's instead of the home directory of a specific user account (which is sometimes called the root account). In a sense, though, since it's the main folder for that specific user, we could refer to it as the root folder.

In some operating systems, files can be stored in the root directory, like the C:/ drive in Windows, but some OSs don't support that.

The term root directory is used in the VMS operating system to define where all the user's files are stored.

Working Directory or Current Directory

Alternatively referred to as the working directory or current working directory (CWD), the current directory is the directory or folder in which you are currently working.

Windows Current Directory

While in Windows Explorer, the current working directory is shown at the top of the active window in what appears to look like an address bar. For example, if you were in the System32 folder, you would see "C:\Windows\System32" or "Computer > C:>Windows\System32" depending on your version of Windows. In this example, System32 is the current directory.

Tip: While in Windows a directory is more properly referred to as a folder and not a directory.

MS-DOS and Windows Command Line Current Directory

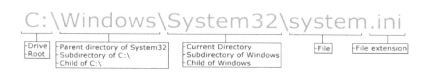

Windows Command Line Path

In the MS-DOS or Windows command line, the current working directory is displayed as the prompt. For example, if the prompt was "C:\Windows\System32>" the "System32" directory is the current directory, "Windows" is the parent directory, and "C:\" is the drive or root directory. To list the files in the current directory use the dir command, and if you want to change the current directory, use the cd command.

Tip: You can use the chdir command by itself to print the current directory in MS-DOS and the Windows command line.

Show the Current Directory in Linux and Unix

Depending on your variant of Linux or Unix and the shell you're using the Current directory may be shown as the prompt, or can be seen by using the pwd command.

Ways to List Files in the Current Directory

To list the files and directories in the current directory depends on your operating system. If you're using Microsoft Windows or MS-DOS, you can use the dir command to list the files and directories in the current directory. If you're using Linux, you can use the ls command to list the files and directories in the current directory.

Home Directory

A home directory, also called a login directory, is the directory on Unix-like operating systems that serves as the repository for a user's personal files, directories and programs. It is also the directory that a user is first in after logging into the system.

A home directory is created automatically for every ordinary user in the directory called /home. A standard subdirectory of the root directory, /home has the sole purpose of containing users' home directories. The root directory, which is designated by a forward slash (/), is the directory that contains all other directories and their subdirectories as well as all files on the system.

The name of a user's home directory is by default identical to that of the user. Thus, for example, a user with a user name of mary would typically have a home directory named mary. It would have an absolute pathname of /home/mary. An absolute pathname is the location of a directory or file relative to the root directory, and it always starts with the root directory (i.e., with a forward slash).

The only user that will by default have its home directory in a different location is the root (i.e., administrative) user, whose home directory is /root. /root is another standard subdirectory of the root directory, and it should not be confused with the root directory (although it sometimes is by new users). For security purposes, even system administrators should have ordinary accounts with home directories in /home into which they routinely log in, and they should use the root account only when absolutely necessary.

There are several easy ways for a user to return to its home directory regardless of its current directory (i.e., the directory in which it is currently working in). The simplest of these is to use the cd (i.e., change directory) command without any options or arguments (i.e., input files), i.e., by merely typing the following and then pressing the ENTER key:

cd

The tilde (the wavy horizontal line character) is used to represent users' home directories on Unix-like operating systems, including users' home directories that are used to store web pages on Unix-like web servers. Thus, a user could also return to its home directory by using the tilde as an argument to cd, i.e.,

cd ~

The absolute pathname of a user's home directory is stored in that user's $HOME environmental variable. Environmental variables are a class of variables that tell the shell (i.e., the program that provides the text-only user interface for entering commands) how to behave as a user works at the command line (i.e., all-text mode). Thus a third way for a user to return to its home directory is to use $HOME as an argument to cd, i.e.,

cd $HOME

References

- Understanding-file-sizes: greennet.org.uk, Retrieved 26 May 2018

- Information-system, management, top-6-types-of-data-files-used-in-any-information-system-mis-70373: yourarticlelibrary.com, Retrieved 21 March 2018

- What-are-binary-and-text-files: nayuki.io, Retrieved 11 April 2018

- What-is-an-extent-file-system: wisegeek.com, Retrieved 14 May 2018

- Flash-file-system: searchstorage.techtarget.com, Retrieved 25 April 2018

- What-is-a-root-folder-or-root-directory-2625989: lifewire.com, Retrieved 24 July 2018

Permissions

Index

CPSIA information can be obtained
at www.ICGtesting.com
Printed in the USA
BVHW051540060619
550362BV00002B/17/P

9 781632 409126